S0-AXO-942

Mobile App Development with HTML5

Mobile App Development with HTML5

Mark Lassoff
with Tom Stachowitz

LearnToProgram, Inc.
Vernon, Connecticut

LearnToProgram.tv, Incorporated
27 Hartford Turnpike Suite 206
Vernon, CT 06066
contact@learntoprogram.tv
(860) 840-7090

©2015 by LearnToProgram.tv, Incorporated

ISBN-13: 978-0692405055
ISBN-10: 0692405054

All rights reserved. No part of this document may be reproduced or transmitted in any form or by any means, electronic, mechanical, photocopying, recording, or otherwise, without prior written permission of LearnToProgram.tv, Incorporated.

Limit of Liability/Disclaimer of Warranty: While the publisher and author have used their best efforts in preparing this book, they make no representations or warranties with respect to the accuracy or completeness of the contents of this book and specifically disclaim any implied warranties of merchantability or fitness for a particular purpose. No warranty may be created or extended by sales representatives or written sales materials. The advice and strategies contained herein may not be suitable for your situation. You should consult with a professional where appropriate. By following the instructions contained herein, the reader willingly assumes all risks in connection with such instructions. Neither the publisher nor author shall be liable for any loss of profit or any other commercial damages, including but not limited to special, incidental, consequential, exemplary, or other damages resulting in whole or part, from the readers' use of, or reliance upon, this material.

Mark Lassoff, Author and Publisher
Tom Stachowitz, Technical Writer
Kevin Hernandez, VP/ Production
Alison Downs, Copy Editor
Alexandria O'Brien, Book Layout
Ben Oldham, Intern

Dedication:
To the internet cats of the world. We would pet you all if we could.

Courses Available from LearnToProgram, Inc.

10 Apps in 10 Weeks
3D Fundamentals with iOS
Advanced Javascript Development
AJAX Development
Android Development for Beginners
Become a Certified Web Developer (Level 1)
Become a Certified Web Developer (Level 2)
C Programming for Beginners
C++ for Beginners
Codeless Development with Adobe Muse
Construct 2 for Beginners
Creating a PHP Login Script
CSS Development (with CSS3!)
Design for Coders
Famu.os Javascript Framework
Game Development Fundamentals with Python
Game Development with Python
GitHub Fundamentals
HTML and CSS for Beginners (with HTML5)
HTML5 Mobile App Development with PhoneGap

Introduction to Web Development
iOS Development Code Camp
iOS Development for Beginners Featuring iOS6/7
Java Programming for Beginners
Javascript for Beginners
Joomla for Beginners
jQuery for Beginners
Mobile App Development with HTML5
Mobile Game Development with iOS
Node.js for Beginners
Objective C for Beginners
Photoshop for Coders
PHP & MySQL for Beginners
Programming for Absolute Beginners
Project Management with Microsoft Project
Python for Beginners
Ruby on Rails for Beginners
Swift Language Fundamentals
SQL Database for Beginners
User Experience Design

Books from LearnToProgram, Inc.

Create Your Own MP3 Player with HTML5
CSS Development (with CSS3!)
Game Development with Python
HTML and CSS for Beginners
Javascript for Beginners
PHP and MySQL for Beginners
Programming for Absolute Beginners
Python for Beginners
SQL Database for Beginners
Swift Fundamentals: The Language of iOS Development

TABLE OF CONTENTS

Chapter 1: Development Environments **13**
  1.1 Tools of the Trade 14
    Questions for Review 25
  1.2 Hello World - Your First App 26
    Questions for Review 38
  Chapter Summary 40
Chapter 2: HTML5 For Mobile **41**
  2.1 Document Structure 42
    Questions for Review 50
  2.2 Multi-Screen Applications 51
    Questions for Review 59
  2.3 Obtaining User Data 60
    Questions for Review 64
  2.4 Displaying Images 65
    Questions for Review 73
  Chapter 02 Lab Exercise 74
  Chapter Summary 76
Chapter 3: CSS3 for Mobile **77**
  3.1 Styling Text Elements 78
    Questions for Review 88
  3.2 Basic Page Layout 89
    Questions for Review 101
  3.3 Supporting Multiple Screen Sizes 102
    Questions for Review 107
  Chapter 03 Lab Exercise 108
  Chapter Summary 110
Chapter 4: Service-Oriented Architecture for Mobile **111**
  4.1 Receiving Text from the Server 112
    Questions for Review 120
  4.2 Sending Queries to the Server 121
    Questions for Review 128
  4.3 Parsing XML Data from the Server 129
    Questions for Review 139
  4.4 Parsing JSON Data from the Server 140
    Questions for Review 150

Chapter 04 Lab Exercise 151
Chapter Summary 152
Chapter 5: Storing Data **153**
5.1 Storing Data with store.js 154
Questions for Review 161
5.2 Storing Data on a Server 162
Questions for Review 168
Chapter 05 Lab Exercise 169
Chapter Summary 170
Chapter 6: Audio and Video **171**
6.1 Playing Audio and Video 172
Questions for Review 176
6.2 Controlling Media with JavaScript 177
Questions for Review 181
6.3 Building a Complete Music Player 182
Questions for Review 188
6.4 Using the PhoneGap Media Object 189
Questions for Review 198
6.5 Using the Onboard Camera 199
Questions for Review 204
Chapter 06 Lab Exercise 205
Chapter Summary 206
Chapter 7: Geolocation **207**
7.1 Intro to Geolocation 208
Questions for Review 213
7.2 Displaying a Map 214
Questions for Review 222
7.3 Working with the Compass 223
Questions for Review 227
Chapter 07 Lab Exercise 228
Chapter Summary 230
Chapter 8: Working with the Accelerometer **231**
8.1 Obtaining Accelerometer Readings 232
Questions for Review 236
8.2 Using the Accelerometer for Input 237
Questions for Review 243
Chapter 08 Lab Exercise 244

Chapter Summary 246
Chapter 9: Interfaces with jQuery Mobile **247**
9.1 jQuery Mobile Basics 248
   Questions for Review 254
9.2 jQuery Mobile Pages 255
   Questions for Review 259
9.3 jQuery Mobile Toolbars 260
   Questions for Review 265
9.4 jQuery Mobile Buttons 266
   Questions for Review 270
Chapter Summary 271
Chapter 10: Interfaces with jQuery Mobile Part II ... **273**
10.1 jQuery Mobile Forms 274
   Questions for Review 281
10.2 jQuery Mobile Listvew 282
   Questions for Review 286
10.3 jQuery Mobile Events 287
   Questions for Review 291
Chapter 10 Lab Exercise 292
Chapter Summary 294
Chapter 11: Other Important PhoneGap APIs **295**
11.1 PhoneGap File API 296
   Questions for Review 306
11.2 PhoneGap Device API 307
   Questions for Review 309
11.3 PhoneGap Contacts API 310
   Questions for Review 314
11.4 PhoneGap Notifications API 315
   Questions for Review 318
11.5 The config.xml File 319
   Questions for Review 322
Chapter Summary 323
Appendix **339**
Glossary **340**

About the Author:

Mark Lassoff

Mark Lassoff's parents frequently claim that Mark was born to be a programmer. In the mid-eighties when the neighborhood kids were outside playing kickball and throwing snowballs, Mark was hard at work on his Commodore 64 writing games in the BASIC programming language. Computers and programming continued to be a strong interest in college where Mark majored in communication and computer science. Upon completing his college career, Mark worked in the software and web development departments at several large corporations.

In 2001, on a whim, while his contemporaries were conquering the dot com world, Mark accepted a position training programmers in a technical training center in Austin, Texas. It was there that he fell in love with teaching programming.

Teaching programming has been Mark's passion for the last 10 years. Today, Mark is a top technical trainer, traveling the country providing leading courses for software and web developers. Mark's training clients include the Department of Defense, Lockheed Martin, Discover Card Services, and Kaiser Permanente. In addition to traditional classroom training, Mark releases courses on the web, which have been taken by programming students all over the world.

He lives near Hartford, Connecticut where he is in the process of redecorating his condominium.

About the Technical Writer:

Tom Stachowitz

Tom Stachowitz was born in Florida but spent his childhood in northwestern Connecticut. He had always been interested in writing and technology but didn't begin programming until high school. Tom studied Journalism at the University of Indianapolis' overseas campus in Athens, Greece and, after living in England, Greece, New York, Arizona, Colorado, Washington DC, and Virginia and then serving in the Army, he returned to Connecticut to focus on writing and technology.

In his spare time Tom enjoys hiking, games, and spending time with his beautiful wife, Krista, and their two cats.

Access the complete lab solutions for this book at:

https://learntoprogram.tv/pages/book-lab-solutions

Development Environments

CHAPTER OBJECTIVES:

- You will learn what PhoneGap is.
- You will be able to set up and install PhoneGap.
- You will create a PhoneGap template application.
- You will understand how to test PhoneGap applications on an emulator and a physical device.

1.1 Tools of the Trade

Welcome to Mobile App Development with HTML5! In this book, you will learn how to use PhoneGap to leverage your already existing HTML5, JavaScript, and CSS skills in order to create and deploy cross-platform mobile apps.

PhoneGap is a development framework that creates hybrid web/native applications for mobile devices. We call PhoneGap applications hybrid applications because they utilize web views for layouts instead of native UI frameworks, but they are packaged as apps and can access native mobile device APIs. The result is a packaged application that can be distributed to mobile devices but that has a consistent style and design across platforms.

PhoneGap was created by a startup named Nitobi in 2009 and was later purchased by Adobe. When Adobe purchased PhoneGap, PhoneGap's core—the API to map JavaScript functions to native code—was donated to the Apache Software Foundation and released as the open-source Cordova framework. Cordova is still the software that underpins PhoneGap, but Adobe has added a substantial set of features to the PhoneGap ecosystem.

PhoneGap itself is simple to download and install, and available for anyone to use, but some of the advanced features require users to log in to Adobe's site with an Adobe ID.

In this first chapter, we're going to introduce and set up the programs that you'll need to be able to use PhoneGap. You may — in fact, you probably do — already have a development environment that is effective for your working style, so don't feel obligated to use the software presented here. We will make it clear what software is absolutely required, and what software is optional. It is good to be aware of what environment we are using, however, so that as you work through the examples in the book you will understand that there may be subtle differences between what we show and what you are working on.

The primary tool that you will need in order to develop a PhoneGap application is PhoneGap itself. PhoneGap does have one prerequisite, and that is node.js. If you do not already have node.js, point the browser of your choice (although we recommend Chrome, for reasons we will detail later in this section) to *http://www. nodejs.org*.

Figure 1-1: The node.js download page.

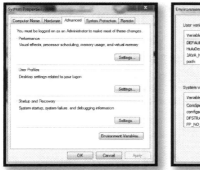

Figure 1-2: The PATH variable in Windows 7 is located in System Properties. Under the "Advanced" tab choose "Environment Variables."

Figure 1-3: Node.js is correctly installed.

Node.js is a cross-platform runtime environment that provides a framework for real-time web applications. If you already have node.js installed, skip these steps.

1 Go to *http://www.nodejs.org* to download node.js. The "Install" link will automatically begin a download of the appropriate node.js version for your operating system. This is shown in Figure 1-1.

2 Once downloaded, the install process for node.js is painless. When it is complete, ensure that the node.js directory is included in your system's PATH environment variable. This is done differently depending on the environment that you are working in. The path location in Windows 7 is shown in Figure 1-2.

3 Verify that node.js is installed by entering "npm" on your command line, as shown in Figure 1-3.

Now, with node.js installed, it's time to install PhoneGap!

Figure 1-4: The PhoneGap website.

4 Go to: *http://www.phonegap.com*. The main page is shown in figure 1-4. There are a few things to note on this page.

5 First, to get an idea of what PhoneGap can do, you can explore "Apps Created with PhoneGap," shown in figure 1-5. This may also give you ideas for future app projects.

Figure 1-5: Apps created with PhoneGap.

6 Below "Apps Create with PhoneGap" are links to documentation about the API and a selection of PhoneGap "Getting Started" guides for various platforms, shown in figure 1-6.

Figure 1-6: Documentation for PhoneGap.

7 Further down you can see the PhoneGap blog and the PhoneGap Build blog, shown in figure 1-7. These are both good sources of up-to-date information regarding PhoneGap.

Figure 1-7: The PhoneGap blog and Build blog.

Figure 1-8: The PhoneGap install page.

```
▸  npm install -g phonegap
```

Example 1-1: The command to install PhoneGap from your command line.

Figure 1-9: The PhoneGap command line tool.

8 When you're ready to install PhoneGap, click on the prominent "Install PhoneGap" link on the main page (shown in figure 1-4 on the previous page). You will be brought to the install page, shown in figure 1-8.

9 PhoneGap uses the node.js command line interface to install. Figure1-8 shows the command for a Windows 7 system, although the PhoneGap website will display the appropriate command for your operating system.

10 Example 1-1 displays the command that will install PhoneGap using node.js. After you run the command, the PhoneGap files will be downloaded from the internet. The "-g" flag installs PhoneGap globally and ensures that you can use PhoneGap from any directory.

11 After the installation process has completed, type "phonegap" into your command line to verify that it is installed, as shown in figure 1-9.

Great, PhoneGap is up and running! Now you can start writing your PhoneGap applications.

PhoneGap apps are written using HTML5, CSS, and JavaScript, so it's possible that you already have a preferred text editor that you can use. In fact, if you were so inclined, you even could create your apps using Notepad — but that's not recommended.

If you have an environment you're comfortable in then you can continue using it, but in case you're in the market for a new editor, we're going to suggest Brackets.

The installation process for Brackets is much friendlier than for node.js or PhoneGap.

Figure 1-10: The Brackets website.

⑫ Go to *http://www.brackets.io*

⑬ Select the "Download Brackets 1.0" link, shown in figure 1-10.

Figure 1-11: Download and install Brackets.

⑭ Once downloaded, follow the install instructions for your system. The Windows 7 dialog box is shown in figure 1-11.

⑮ Open Brackets, and you'll be looking at the included sample project. It should be similar to what's shown in figure 1-12.

Figure 1-12: Brackets running the sample project.

Text editors like Brackets are similar to word processors, but the key difference is that they are specifically designed to help you write code. Some of the additional features are code suggestions, custom shortcuts, and helpful visual cues.

Brackets is written in HTML, CSS, and JavaScript, so it is very easy to extend or modify. Within Brackets, under the File menu, is the Extension Manager, where you can see how many extensions are available.

Next, we will be using Chrome as our test browser for its developer features.

Figure 1-13: The Chrome download page.

16   Go to *http://www.google. com/chrome/browser*.

17   Select the "Download Chrome" button to begin the download, as shown in figure 1-13.

18   Follow the installation instructions to install Chrome. We will be using it to test our app. Also, although we won't be using them here, Brackets has features that link directly to Chrome.

One excellent feature of Chrome for mobile web app developers is the ability to simulate how an app will appear on certain devices within the browser.

19 Open up Chrome and navigate to the Chrome homepage.

20 On Windows or Linux, use the keyboard shortcut Ctrl + Shift + I, and on Mac use the keyboard shortcut Cmd + Opt + I. Windows or Linux computers can also just press the F12 key.

21 You will now be looking at the Developer Tools provided by Chrome, as shown in figure 1-14. There are a number of very useful tools here, but at the moment we are interested in one tool in particular.

22 On the left hand side of the menu bar that appeared there is a small icon that looks like a smartphone. ⬜ Click on it to launch "Device Mode." You will see the mobile version of the page represented in a simulated device screen, as shown in figure 1-15.

Figure 1-14: The Chrome Developer Tools.

Figure 1-15: The Chrome page viewed in the browser's "Device Mode."

Figure 1-16: The drop-down menu to select a device to simulate.

Figure 1-17: The Chrome page viewed on a simulated Kindle Fire HDX.

23 The drop-down menus above the simulated device screen, shown in figure 1-16, allow you to see how your app or webpage will look on different devices.

24 Select a different device—we have chosen the Amazon Kindle Fire HDX—and see how the webpage is rendered, demonstrated in figure 1-17.

There are a huge number of mobile devices available with a wide variety of screen sizes and resolutions, and you need to make sure that your app looks the way you intend on the devices that you plan on targeting.

The Chrome "Device Mode" does not replace actual, on-device testing, of course, and it should not be confused with a software emulator, but it is a good way to get a general idea of how your PhoneGap application will look.

The tools that you've downloaded so far, node.js, PhoneGap, Brackets, and Chrome, are the general requirements for developing PhoneGap applications. PhoneGap is intended to make cross-platform application development simpler, faster, and easier, but PhoneGap does not include the tools required to actually build an app for a particular mobile platform.

Adobe does offer a tool, Adobe PhoneGap Build, that will compile your PhoneGap application for iOS, Android, or Windows Phone 8, however, you need to have an Adobe ID in order to use Adobe PhoneGap Build. PhoneGap Build is a cloud-based service that builds your project from either assets that you upload or a Git or SVN repository. Adobe PhoneGap Build offers a free service, but there is an important limitation: the free PhoneGap Build only offers users a single private app, whereas paid subscribers can have up to 25 private apps. All users have unlimited collaborators and open source apps. You can find PhoneGap Build at *http://build. phonegap.com*.

Private apps are applications that are hosted on a private GitHub repository or that are uploaded to PhoneGap Build as a .zip file. No one else can view your private applications. Open source apps, on the other hand, are built from a publicly accessible GitHub repository.

Whether or not you decide to use Adobe PhoneGap Build, you will still need the appropriate authentications from Google or Apple in order to build an app that can be sold on their respective marketplaces.

At the moment there are three major smartphone marketplaces: the Apple App Store, the Google Play Store, and the Amazon Appstore for Android. Each market has different requirements for application developers.

To develop an iPhone application, you need to be registered as an Apple Developer, which costs $99 annually, and you need to be using a Mac with the Xcode software. You can create an iPhone app with PhoneGap Build if you do not have a Mac, but you will still need an iPhone developer certificate.

To develop an Android application, you need the Android SDK from Google and the latest version of the Java SDK. In order to build an Android app, either locally or using PhoneGap build, you will need to sign the app with a private key that you generate locally. Creating, building, and distributing an Android application is free, but if you want to distribute an application through the Google Play Store, you'll need to pay a one-time $25 developer fee.

The Amazon Appstore for Android requires that Android applications be signed using a private key, but does not have any distribution fee. Once you sign up with Amazon, an Android application developed and built either locally or using PhoneGap can be freely distributed at the Amazon Appstore for Android.

There are other platforms and marketplaces where you might want to distribute your application. PhoneGap applications can be built for the Windows Phone App+Games Store. Developers for Microsoft's platform need a Microsoft Developer Account that costs $19 for individuals or $99 for companies.

Figure 1-18: The Google Play Store

Figure 1-20: The Microsoft App+Games Store

Figure 1-19: The Apple App Store

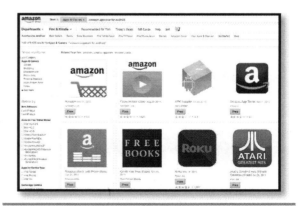

Figure 1-21: The Amazon Appstore for Android

Your PhoneGap development environment, Brackets or otherwise, is separate from the build and test environment that you will have to set up to actually run your apps on a mobile device. If you elect not to use the Adobe PhoneGap Build service to build your projects, you will have to set up an appropriate environment on your computer.

To build an application for iPhone you need to be using a Mac with the Xcode software installed. When you test a PhoneGap iPhone app on a Mac, the Xcode software provides the APIs to build the application and also features iPhone simulators that can simulate an iPhone on your Mac desktop without having an actual device.

Building an Android app can be done on a Mac, Windows, or Linux machine. You will need to download the Java Developer's Kit from Oracle and the Android SDK from Google in order to build and test applications. The Android SDK is available as a stand-alone download or as a part of either the Eclipse IDE or Google's Android Studio. Setting up the Android SDK is not always the most painless procedure, but there are extensive guides available from Google and elsewhere. It's important to remember to download and install the Java Developer's Kit first, and then install the Android SDK.

Amazon's Fire devices are built on a modified version of the Android operating system called Amazon Fire OS. There are certain modifications and optimizations to Amazon's Fire OS that allow applications targeting that platform to perform better than they would on Android. In order to target Fire OS you have to first download and install the Java Developer's Kit and the Android SDK, and then install the Amazon WebView SDK from the Amazon Developer Portal.

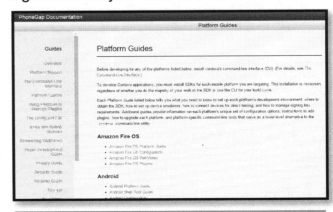

The PhoneGap website has a set of getting started guides that will guide you through the specific requirements of each platform, and walk you through the particular set up processes.

In the next section, we'll use PhoneGap to create and test a basic "Hello World" app.

Figure 1-22: The PhoneGap getting started guides for various platforms.

WHAT HAVE YOU LEARNED?

Questions for Review

1 What is PhoneGap?

a. A program that creates mobile applications.

b. That little space between the edge of your phone's screen and the edge of the phone itself.

c. A library that lets developers create native apps with HTML5, CSS, and JavaScript.

d. A term to refer to the differences in usage patterns for mobile devices between countries.

2 Which of the following is a requirement in order to use PhoneGap?

a. A Linux computer.

b. Extensive experience with the C++ programming language.

c. node.js.

d. Angular.js.

3 PhoneGap contains all of the software required to build an Android .apk file.

a. True.

b. False.

4 Which of the following is a benefit of using Chrome for app development?

a. Chrome includes a built-in mobile device emulator.

b. Chrome "Device Mode" allows you to see how an app might look on a certain device.

c. Chrome has a built-in compiler for your PhoneGap app.

d. There is no benefit to using Chrome for app development.

1.2 Hello World - Your First App

In this section we will create that old standby, the "Hello World" application. We will also create the basic template that we will use throughout this book as the starting point for our PhoneGap projects.

Now that PhoneGap is installed, you might be ready to fire it up and start developing! Don't spend too much time searching for a PhoneGap icon, though, because PhoneGap is a command line tool. Development will be done with a text editor, such as Brackets, and much of the testing will be done using Chrome. PhoneGap will be employed to create projects and build them for testing and distribution.

Let's begin by creating our first PhoneGap project. In this book we will be developing on a Windows 7 platform, so screenshots of the command line will reflect that. Where necessary, we will note differences between commands for different operating systems.

---

1 First, create the folder that will house your PhoneGap projects. We have chosen C:\ phonegapApps, but you may choose whatever is convenient.

```
›   phonegap create HelloWorld
```

Example 1-2: The PhoneGap command to create a project.

2 Open the command line and navigate to your PhoneGap project folder. Once there, use the **phonegap create** command to create a project named HelloWorld, as shown in example 1-2 and figure 1-23.

Figure 1-23: The command line output on Windows 7

Figure 1-24: The PhoneGap template running in an Android emulator.

Figure 1-25: The HelloWorld app shown in Brackets.

3 PhoneGap will have created everything that you need for a basic application. If you choose to, you can run the application on any platform that is set up for development with the command **phonegap run** followed by a platform name, such as "**phonegap run android**". Figure 1-24 demonstrates the PhoneGap example running in an Android emulator.

4 If you are using Brackets, choose "File" and "Open Folder" to select the folder where you created HelloWorld. If you are using another editor, then navigate to the HelloWorld folder and examine the contents of the default PhoneGap template. The directory, opened in Brackets, is shown in figure 1-25.

Because PhoneGap applications are web apps running in a web view on a mobile device, the application directories will seem familiar if you have ever designed a website. The "www/" folder holds the actual application code.

Open the "www/" folder in HelloWorld. You'll find folders for CSS, JavaScript, and resources, as well as a "www/spec" folder. There is also an index.html (which you can open in any web browser), an icon image file, and a spec.html file. We do not need many of these files, so we can start to clear them out.

5   First, remove the existing index.css file from the "www/css" folder and the existing index.js from the "www/js" folder.

6   We will not need the spec.html file or the "www/spec" folder, so they can be safely deleted. Also, the logo.png file in the "www/img" folder and the icon.png file in the main root folder can be removed.

7   Now we're ready to create our template. Open index.html. If you're using Brackets, your window should look like figure 1-26.

8   Before we add our code, we'll remove what we don't need. First, remove the reference to the stylesheet, shown in example 1-3.

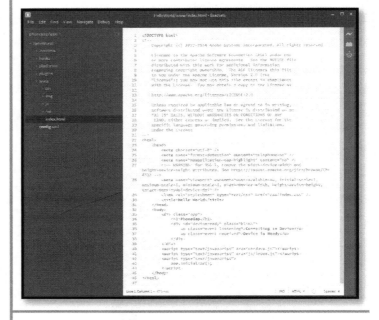

Figure 1-26: The Brackets environment with index.html open and ready for editing.

```
<link rel="stylesheet" type="text/css"
href="css/index.css" />
```

Example 1-3: We no longer need the reference to the stylesheet, so delete this line of code from index.html.

```
▸  <div class="app">
▸     <h1>PhoneGap</h1>
▸     <div id="deviceready"
   class="blink">
▸      <p class="event
   listening">Connecting to Device</p>
▸      <p class="event received">Device
   is Ready</p>
▸     </div>
▸  </div>
```

Example 1-4: Remove this **<div>** from the index.html file.

```
▸  <script type="text/javascript"
   src="js/index.js"></script>
▸  <script type="text/javascript">
▸     app.initialize();
▸  </script>
```

Example 1-5: We do not need either of these **<script>** tags.

```
▸  <head>
▸     <script type="text/javascript"
   src="cordova.js"></script>
▸  ...
▸  </head>
```

Example 1-6: The **<script>** tag we need to keep, moved into the **<head>** of the document.

9 Next, remove the **<div>** that contains the *app* class, shown in example 1-4.

10 Below the **<div>** you've just removed are three **<script>** tags. The tag containing a reference to index.js is no longer needed because we've just deleted index.js, and the script that runs the **app.initialize()** method is also no longer needed. Those two lines are shown in example 1-5.

11 The third **<script>** tag is needed, but for the sake of organization we're going to move it from the **<body>** of the document to the **<head>**, as in example 1-6.

The **<script>** tag that we kept includes the Cordova library and is required for PhoneGap. PhoneGap is, as you recall from section one, based on Cordova.

Now we'll take a look at what's left in the index.html file.

12 First, look at the **<meta>** tag with the attribute *name="viewport"*, shown in example 1-7. The viewport is the element that contains the **<html>** tags. The viewport meta tag defines attributes for the top level element and determines how your app will be displayed to a user. In this case, we are saying that the application will use the screen dimensions of the user's device with no scaling, magnification, or stretching, and with a pixel density set by the device.

Applications developed with PhoneGap will likely be running on a wide variety of devices, so it's important to note that there is a variety of potential screen sizes, aspect ratios, and pixel densities. The specific requirements of an application will determine how the viewport is set up.

13 Below the viewport meta tag, add a link to the jQuery mobile CDN, as shown in example 1-8.

```
<meta name="viewport" content="user-
scalable=no, initial-scale=1,
maximum-scale=1, minimum-scale=1,
width=device-width, height=device-
height, target-densitydpi=device-dpi"
/>
```

Example 1-7: The viewport meta tag in the index.html file.

```
<link rel="stylesheet" href="http://
code.jquery.com/mobile/1.4.3/jquery.
mobile-1.4.3.min.css" />
<script src="http://code.jquery.com/
jquery-1.11.1.min.js"></script>
<script src="http://code.jquery.com/
mobile/1.4.3/jquery.mobile-1.4.3.min.
js"></script>
```

Example 1-8: Link to the jQuery mobile CDN.

If you are already a web developer then you are likely familiar with jQuery. jQuery is a JavaScript library used by over 60% of the top 10,000 websites that simplifies client-side HTML scripting. We will be using the jQuery Mobile extension of jQuery.

We are linking to the Content Delivery Network, or CDN, version of the library instead of downloading a local version. We can instead download the jQuery files, place them within our project, and link directly to them. That is needed for apps that can function offline, but at the moment we will use the CDN versions.

```
<body>
    <button>Hi There</button>
</body>
```

Example 1-9: A simple button.

Figure 1-27: The standard html button (top) compared to the jQuery Mobile button (bottom).

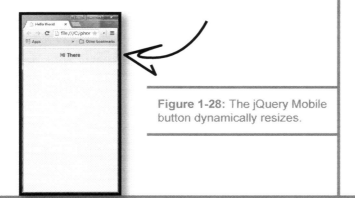

Figure 1-28: The jQuery Mobile button dynamically resizes.

We're going to make a simple button to demonstrate why jQuery Mobile can be so useful when building apps.

14 In the **<body>** of your document, add a **<button>** tag with some text, as shown in example 1-9.

15 Load the index.html page in your browser. You will see a large button that spans the entire page. Figure 1-27 compares the jQuery Mobile button to the standard HTML button.

16 Shrink the browser window with the jQuery Mobile button. It will resize, as shown in figure 1-28, making it ideal for phone apps.

Our basic template is almost complete! There is one small addition before it is finished. You may have noticed that the edges of the button are flush with the edge of the browser window. We do not want our app elements to be exactly flush with the edge of the mobile screen, so we will use CSS to create a small margin between the edges of our application and the edge of window.

```
<style>
    #container
    {
     margin: 3px;
    }
</style>
```

Example 1-10: A small margin styled for the "container" id.

17   In the **<head>** add a **<style>** tag that styles an element with the **id** *container* as having a margin of 3 pixels, as shown in example 1-10.

18   In the **<body>**, surround your **<button>** with a **<div>** that has the **id** of *container*. This is shown in example 1-11.

```
<body>
    <div id="container">
     <button>Hi There</button>
    </div>
</body>
```

Example 1-11: Using a container around the jQuery button.

19   Figure 1-29 demonstrates the difference between the jQuery button with and without using the *container* **<div>**.

Figure 1-29: Comparing the jQuery button with and without using a CSS margin.

Below is the finished empty template including the "Hi There" button. This is the code that will be modified to create our example application as this section continues.

```html
<html>
    <head>
        <script type="text/javascript" src="cordova.js"></script>
        <meta charset="utf-8" />
        <meta name="format-detection" content="telephone=no" />
        <meta name="msapplication-tap-highlight" content="no" />
        <!-- WARNING: for iOS 7, remove the width=device-width and
height=device-height attributes. See https://issues.apache.org/jira/browse/
CB-4323 -->
        <meta name="viewport" content="user-scalable=no, initial-scale=1,
maximum-scale=1, minimum-scale=1, width=device-width, height=device-height,
target-densitydpi=device-dpi" />
        <link rel="stylesheet" href="http://code.jquery.com/mobile/1.4.3/
jquery.mobile-1.4.3.min.css" />
        <script src="http://code.jquery.com/jquery-1.11.1.min.js"></script>
        <script src="http://code.jquery.com/mobile/1.4.3/jquery.mobile-
1.4.3.min.js"></script>
        <title>Hello World</title>
        <style>
            #container
            {
                margin: 3px;
            }
        </style>
    </head>
    <body>
        <div id="container">
            <button>Hi There</button>
        </div>
    </body>
</html>
```

Example 1-12: The complete template index.html file.

```
▸  <div id="container">
▸      <div id="result"></div>
▸      <button>Hi There</button>
▸  </div>
```

Example 1-13: The "result" <div>.

Now we are going to add interactivity to this template.

20 Before the **<button>**, create a **<div>** with the **id** *result*, as shown in example 1-13. This is where the output of the application will be displayed.

21 Modify the **<button>** so that it reads "Press Me!" and give it the **id** *btnPress*, as shown in example 1-14.

22 Save the file and open it in Chrome. Using the developer tools, emulate how the same application will look based on the screen sizes of different devices. In figure 1-30 we demonstrate an Amazon Fire HD 7, a Google Nexus 5, and an Apple iPhone 5.

```
▸  <div id="container">
▸      <div id="result"></div>
▸      <button id="btnPress">Press Me!</
   button>
▸  </div>
```

Example 1-14: The modified <button>.

Figure 1-30: Using Chrome to test the webpage on different devices. An Amazon Fire HD 7, top, a Google Nexus 5, bottom right, and an Apple iPhone 5, bottom left.

```
<script>
   window.onload = function()
   {
    document.
getElementById('btnPress').
addEventListener('click', greeting,
false);
   }
</script>
```

Example 1-15: Set the event listener of "btnPress" to call a function named *greeting()*.

```
<script>
   window.onload = function()
   {
    document.
getElementById('btnPress').
addEventListener('click', greeting,
false);
   }

   function greeting()
   {
    document.getElementById('result').
innerHTML = "<h1>Hello! Welcome to
Mobile Development!</h1>";
   }
</script>
```

Example 1-16: The complete **<script>**, with the *greeting()* function.

Next we will use JavaScript to add some interactivity to this first application.

23 After the **<style>** tag you created earlier, add a **<script>** tag and set **window. onload** to an anonymous function. Within that function, add an Event Listener to the *btnPress* HTML element. Have that listener call the *greeting()* function when it registers an event, and set its final attribute (it is the **useCapture** attribute, but we are not concerned with that right now) to *"false*, as shown in example 1-15.

24 Now create the *greeting()* function immediately below the preceding code. It will replace the **innerHTML** attribute of the *result* element with the phrase "Hello! Welcome to Mobile Development!" Format the phrase using **<h1>** tags. The complete content of the **<script>** tag is shown in example 1-16.

Take a moment to test this in your browser and you will see that the message,"Hello! Welcome to Mobile Development!" displays after you click on the "Press Me!" button. You can use the Chrome developer tools to verify that this simple app displays appropriately in a variety of device form factors, but you are still looking at a website and not at a mobile app.

PhoneGap will take this simple webpage and convert it into an application that can be run on your mobile device.

If you have installed the Android SDK and have set up an Android Virtual Device, or AVD, according to the instructions from Google, you can use PhoneGap to test the app on an emulated Android device.

Note that the Android emulator is notoriously slow, especially the first time it is run. Even though this program is simple, expect it to take a while to load. Perhaps you may want to make a pot of coffee.

25 At the command prompt, navigate to the root directory of your project and type "**phonegap run android**." PhoneGap will compile your program into a .apk file, load the default AVD from the AVD Manager, and then display your application in the AVD, as seen in figure 1-31.

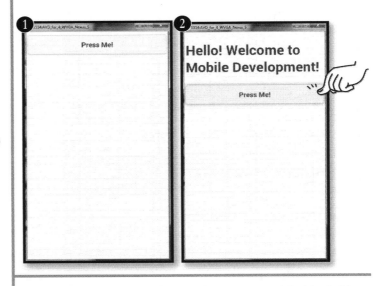

Figure 1-31: The application running on an emulated Android device.

Running software virtual devices of hardware is possible for iOS and Android devices. In order to set up an emulator for Android or a simulator for iOS, you'll need to follow the instructions available at their respective websites. For Android, that site is *http://developer.android.com/*, and for iOS that site is *http://developer.apple.com*. Once you are able to run a virtual mobile device of your chosen platform, PhoneGap will launch that virtual device when you invoke the "phonegap run" command for the specified mobile platform. We used "phonegap run android" in our example, but "phonegap run ios" would also work if an iOS simulator is available.

Congratulations, you've used PhoneGap to create a simple application built with HTML, JavaScript, and CSS! As you can see, using those standard technologies, and the infrastructure that supports them, along with PhoneGap makes it quick and easy to create applications for mobile devices.

Now that you have a working application, you probably want to test it on a real device. Using emulated or simulated devices is a very effective way to test a mobile application on a variety of devices — especially useful when considering the variety of Android devices available — but it does not replace testing on a real, physical device. In order to test your application on a physical device, the device needs to be set up for development. How that is done will vary across operating systems and platforms, although the developer sites, *http://developer.android.com* and *http://developer.apple.com*, have instructions for setting devices up for testing. Note that because Android development can be done across development environments, you will have to follow different steps if you are developing on Windows, OSX, or Linux.

Once a physical device is prepared for testing, PhoneGap will push the built application to the connected device using the same "phonegap run" command. If you intend to test on an iPhone, for example, you would connect the iPhone to your Mac and use "phonegap run ios". PhoneGap will build and run your application on the connected iPhone. If no physical device is present, then PhoneGap will instead launch and run the application on an available virtual device. If, for example, you have an iPhone connected to your development computer and an Android emulator set up, "phonegap run ios" will launch the application on the connected device, and "phonegap run android" will launch the same application on an emulated Android device.

Questions for Review

1 After installation, where can you find the PhoneGap application icon?

   a. Its location varies according to development platform.

   b. On the desktop.

   c. In the user's home directory.

   d. There is no icon, PhoneGap is a command line tool.

2 When creating a new PhoneGap project, which of the following are created for you?

   a. An index.html file.

   b. An index.css file.

   c. An index.js file.

   d. All of the above.

3 What is the proper command to run a PhoneGap application on an Android emulator?

   a. phonegap run android.

   b. phonegap run android emulator.

   c. phonegap install android.

   d. phonegap install android emulator

4 What is the proper command to install and run a PhoneGap application on a connected iPhone?

   a. phonegap build install iphone.

   b. phonegap run iphone.

   c. phonegap run ios.

   d. phonegap install ios.

CHAPTER 01 LAB EXERCISE

In this exercise you will become more familiar with the PhoneGap website and the resources available to PhoneGap developers online.

1 Navigate to *http://www.phonegap.com* and then find the documentation page, shown below.

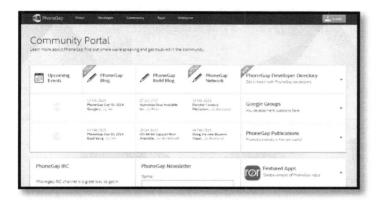

2 Once there, find the Google Groups page for PhoneGap developers and view a few of the topics.

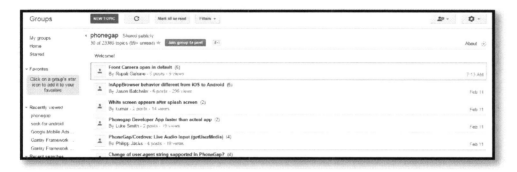

Development is no longer an isolated activity. There are innumerable resources available to application makers via the PhoneGap website and through a normal Internet search. Taking the time to become familiar with them will pay dividends down the road.

Chapter Summary

In this chapter we have introduced PhoneGap, demonstrated the basics of PhoneGap development, and set up a development environment to use when creating PhoneGap applications. We have also discussed building and deploying applications on virtual devices, emulators for Android and simulators for iOS, as well as building and installing applications on connected physical devices.

We also took a look at some of the distribution options that are available for mobile application developers. Later in this book, we will take a look more in-depth look at distribution. When we do so, we will be focusing on the Amazon Appstore for Android instead of the Google Play Store, the Apple App Store, or the Microsoft App+Games Store. The reason for this is because the Amazon Appstore for Android is both a free avenue for distribution and a distribution option with a very large audience.

In chapter two we will look into using HTML5 for mobile development.

HTML5 For Mobile

CHAPTER OBJECTIVES:

- You will learn how a PhoneGap project is structured.
- You will understand how to create multiple content pages.
- You will work with HTML5 form elements for user input.
- You will learn how to display images in PhoneGap.

2.1 Document Structure

Now that we have a development environment ready and we understand how to create and test a simple application with PhoneGap, we are going to look into the structure of a PhoneGap application. In this section we will create another simple test app and explore its file structure in order to understand how PhoneGap applications are organized.

HTML5 development for mobile devices is very similar to traditional HTML5 development, however, there are certain special circumstances that you will have to take into consideration while you're creating your application. The most efficient way to use PhoneGap is to reuse as much code as possible across a variety of platforms and form factors. This means that when you're developing you have to plan for a variety of screen resolutions, sizes, pixel densities, and layouts. As you'll see, PhoneGap makes this relatively painless.

The first thing that we will do in this section is to create a new PhoneGap application. Using the syntax that you learned in the previous chapter, "phonegap create," create an application simply titled, Structure.

```
C:\phonegapApps>phonegap create Structure
```

Example 2-1: Create a new PhoneGap app named Structure.

1 Enter the command to create a PhoneGap application named Structure using the command "phonegap create Structure."

2 Navigate to the folder containing Structure, shown in figure 2-1. We will begin exploring this folder to show exactly how a PhoneGap application is organized.

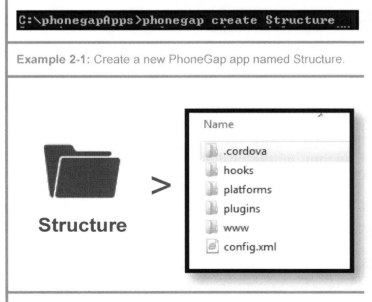

Structure

Name
.cordova
hooks
platforms
plugins
www
config.xml

Figure 2-1: The root directory structure of Structure.

As we did with the sample app in chapter one, remove all of the unneeded content from Structure. If you don't recall, you will delete the default index.cs from the "/www/css" folder, the default index.js from the "/www/js" folder, logo.jpg from the "/www/img" folder, the entire "www/spec" folder, and the spec.html and icon.png files from the "/www" folder. If you choose, this can all be done from the Brackets editor.

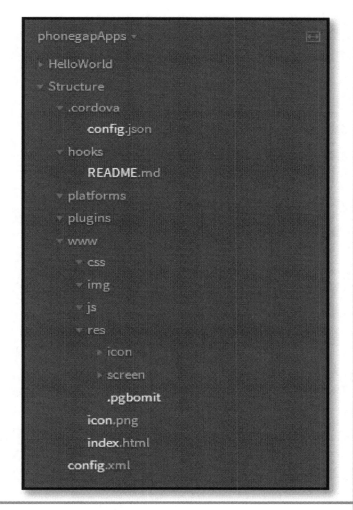

Figure 2-2: The structure of Structure displayed in the Brackets editor.

3 First is the "/.cordova" folder. We will talk about this folder later.

4 The next folder is the "/hooks" folder. This folder currently contains only a Readme.md file. Hooks are scripts that PhoneGap runs at specified points in the application build process. We are not concerned with hooks right now.

5 Next is the "/platforms" folder. Currently, this folder is empty. As you create builds of your application for different platforms, this folder will be populated with the required data for that platform.

6 Next is the "/plugins" folder. Plug-ins are add-on code that allows your application to interface with native device components, such as the camera or the accelerometer. Currently, this directory is also empty.

7 The final file in the root folder is config.xml. This file specifies application preferences, paths to required files, and application descriptions, among other things. When you are ready to deploy your application to an app store you will need to spend time ensuring that the config.xml file is correct.

8 The "/www" folder is where you will place your application code. PhoneGap apps are webapps, so the structure of the "/www" folder, shown in figure 2-3, reflects common website organization. There is a "/www/js" folder for JavaScript, a "/www/css" folder for CSS, and an "www/img" folder for images.

9 The "/www/res" folder stores resources related to your application. Note that by default it is populated with templates for the icon and splash screen sizes of various platforms. These can be used to create the icons and splash screens for your applications.

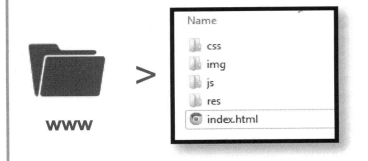

Figure 2-3: The contents of the "/www" folder.

Figure 2-4: The contents of the resources folder.

Template index.html Structure

```
▸  <html>
▸      <head>
▸          <script type="text/javascript"
   src="cordova.js"></script>
▸          <meta charset="utf-8" />
▸          <meta name="format-detection"
   content="telephone=no" />
▸          <meta name="msapplication-tap-
   highlight" content="no" />
▸          <!-- WARNING: for iOS 7,
   remove the width=device-width and
   height=device-height attributes. See
   https://issues.apache.org/jira/browse/
   CB-4323 -->
▸          <meta name="viewport"
   content="user-scalable=no, initial-
   scale=1, maximum-scale=1, minimum-
   scale=1, width=device-width,
   height=device-height, target-
   densitydpi=device-dpi" />
▸          <link rel="stylesheet"
   href="http://code.jquery.com/
   mobile/1.4.3/jquery.mobile-1.4.3.min.
   css" />
▸          <script src="http://code.
   jquery.com/jquery-1.11.1.min.js"></
   script>
▸          <script src="http://code.
   jquery.com/mobile/1.4.3/jquery.mobile-
   1.4.3.min.js"></script>
▸          <title>Hello World</title>
▸      </head>
▸      <body>
▸          <div id="container">
▸          </div>
▸      </body>
▸  </html>
```

Example 2-2: Our empty template index.html file.

10 Lastly, there is an index. html file. The default index. html file is designed for the PhoneGap example application. Modify it so that it matches our template from chapter one, shown again in example 2-2.

11 Astute readers probably noticed that we have removed the **<style>** tags from our template, but we retain the reference to the *container* **id** that we had styled. Don't worry, we are going to resolve this shortly.

```
<link href="css/mainAppStyles.css"
    type="text/css" rel="stylesheet" />
```

Example 2-3: Link to the mainAppStyles.css stylesheet from index.html.

12 In the index.html **<head>** add a link to mainAppStyles. css in the "/www/css" folder, as shown in example 2-3.

13 Create a new file in the "/www/css" folder and immediately save it as mainAppStyles. css, shown in figure 2-5.

14 In mainAppStyles. css, style the *container* **id** as having a margin of 5 pixels, as in example 2-4.

15 In index.html, in the *container* **<div>**, add a heading element with the text "Testing App Structure," as in example 2-5. This text will verify that the CSS style is applying properly.

Now your CSS file has been created and your index.html correctly links to it. The *container* **<div>** element will now function as it did in the template from chapter one.

Figure 2-5: Create a new file and save it as mainAppStyles in the "/www/css" directory.

```
#container {
    margin: 5px;
}
```

Example 2-4: Style the *container* element to have a margin of 5 pixels.

```
<div id="container">
    <h1>Testing App Structure</h1>
</div>
```

Example 2-5: Simple text to verify our layout.

```
<script type="text/javascript"
src="js/main.js"></script>
```

Example 2-6: Link to main.js from index.html.

Figure 2-6: Create a new file and save it as main.js in the "/www/js" directory.

```
window.onload=function()
{
    alert("Application Running!");
}
```

Figure 2-7: Run some simple JavaScript to verify that the file is linked correctly.

We will create and link our JavaScript file in the same way that we created and linked our CSS file.

16 In the index.html **<head>**, add a link to main.js in the "/www/js" folder, as shown in example 2-6.

17 Create a new file in the "/www/js" folder and immediately save it as main.js, as shown in figure 2-6.

18 In main.js, write some simple JavaScript to **alert()** the user that the application is running once the window loads, as shown in example 2-7.

Figure 2-8: The test app running on a Chrome desktop browser.

19 Navigate to the index.html file on your computer and run it in Chrome. You should see an alert window popping up over your test text, as shown in figure 2-8.

20 Switch Chrome to developer mode and test the layout of your app in a mobile form factor. In figure 2-9, we have tested it on a virtual Kindle Fire HDX 7" screen.

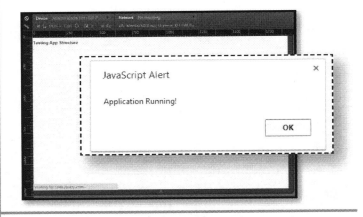

Figure 2-9: The test app on a desktop browser emulating a Kindle Fire HDX 7" screen.

It's important to note that when you use Chrome to test the application in a given form factor, you are not seeing the selected platform's platform-specific elements. The **alert()** method is a good example of this. The Chrome browser handles an **alert()** differently than a mobile device. For comparison, figure 2-10 shows the app running on an actual Kindle Fire HDX 7". Note the differences.

Figure 2-10: The test app running on an actual Kindle Fire HDX 7".

```
C:\phonegapApps\Structure>phonegap build android
[phonegap] executing 'cordova build android'...
[phonegap] completed 'cordova build android'
```

Example 2-7: Building the app for an Android device.

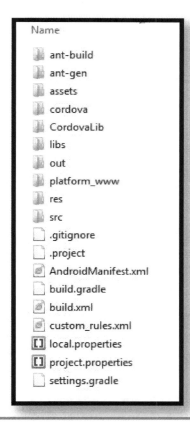

Figure 2-11: The contents of "/platforms/android" after building the application for Android devices.

21 Now that this simple application is complete, we are going to build it for an Android device. At the command prompt in the root directory of your project, enter "phonegap build android," as shown in example 2-7.

22 Navigate to the "/platforms" folder of your project and inspect it again. You will see that where before it was empty, now it has a "/platforms/android" directory. If you open that directory, you will see all of the files needed to create Structure as an Android application, as shown in figure 2-11.

If you're developing on a Mac you can target your build to a iOS instead of Android. Once PhoneGap builds the application for iOS, you'll see another directory in the "/platforms" folder.

Now that we have an understanding of the structure of PhoneGap projects, we can move forward and begin developing actual PhoneGap applications.

In the next section we will learn how to create applications that allow the user to navigate between multiple screens, with different information on each.

Questions for Review

1 PhoneGap applications do not have a specific file structure.

    a. True.

    b. False.

2 What is the purpose of the "/platforms" folder in a PhoneGap application project?

    a. It is used to contain the logic and graphics for game elements that a player can jump onto when creating platform games.

    b. It contains templates for the code required to write a PhoneGap application for various mobile devices.

    c. It contains the code required to build a PhoneGap application for a specific platform.

    d. It serves no purpose.

3 Why do PhoneGap projects have a "/www/res" folder?

    a. To contain project resources.

    b. To contain old versions of the project that can be resurrected.

    c. To hold changes that have been rescinded.

    d. PhoneGap projects do not have a "/www/res" folder.

4 What is the purpose of the "/www/plugins" folder?

    a. To contain add-on code for the PhoneGap project.

    b. To store user-created content for the app.

    c. To allow PhoneGap to add plugins to your app when necessary.

    d. There is no "/www/plugins" folder.

2.2 Multi-Screen Applications

Now that we understand how a PhoneGap application is laid out, we are going to look into methods of navigating through an application. PhoneGap applications are based on web technologies, but some web design standards may not always be applicable to PhoneGap apps. In the same vein, standard application design practices may not always be the best choice because the underlying technology that powers PhoneGap is based on creating content for the web.

Your application is most likely going to need to display different information to the user depending on different circumstances. The traditional web method of doing this is through various pages connected with hyperlinks and supported by JavaScript to create a more dynamic experience. Another method, the single-page app method, is to create one application screen that has its content changed depending on what the user needs to see. PhoneGap can be designed to support either technique. In this section, we will create an application that navigates between multiple pages by displaying distinct files, and then we will modify the application to navigate between multiple pages by presenting different content within a single file.

First, create a new PhoneGap application named Screens ("phonegap create Screens") and prepare the application according to our established template. Note that in this application we will use the linked mainAppStyles.css file, but not the index.js file.

Figure 2-12: The files we need for the Screens app project.

1 First we are going to create an application that uses two distinct HTML files and switches between them, so copy all of the content from index.html into a new, second file called secondPage.html, as shown in figure 2-12.

```
<body>
    <div id="container">
            <button id="btnMove">Go to
End</button>
    </div>
</body>
```

Example 2-8: The <body> of index.html.

Traditionally, links between pages in HTML are created using the **<a>** tag, however we are going to use buttons instead. The reason is that **<a>** tags can be hard for mobile users to work with, while big, clear buttons are very mobile friendly.

2 First, create a button in index.html with the **id** *btnMove* and the text "Go to End," as shown in example 2-8. Note that the button is within the **<div>** with **id** *container*. Recall that this **<div>** will contain our entire app.

3 Verify the layout with Chrome's screen emulator, as shown in figure 2-13.

4 In the file secondPage. html, add similar code to what you entered in step 2, only instead of text that says "Go to End" have the text say "Go to Beginning." The code is shown in example 2-9. Verify the layout before you continue.

Figure 2-13: Testing the index.html page with a simulated iPhone5 screen.

```
<button id="btnMove">Go to Beginning</
button>
```

Example 2-9: The *btnMove* <div> from secondPage.html

```
<script type="application/javascript">
window.onload = function() {
    document.getElementById("btnMove").
    addEventListener("click", change,
    false);
}
```

Example 2-10: Attach an event listener to *btnMove*.

```
function change() {
    window.location = "secondPage.
html";
}
</script>
```

Example 2-11: Have the *change()* function load secondPage.html.

```
<script type="application/javascript">
window.onload = function() {
    document.getElementById("btnMove").
addEventListener("click", change,
false);
    }

function change() {
    window.location = "index.html";
}
</script>
```

Example 2-12: The JavaScript for secondPage.html sends the user back to index.html.

Now you have the two pages that the app will navigate between. To actually implement the navigation, we are going to use JavaScript. If you were making a production app, then in this situation you would place your JavaScript in a separate file that your HTML would link to, but for the sake of the example we will place the code in **<script>** tags in the **<head>** of the HTML pages.

5 Attach a "click" event listener to the *btnMove* element when the page loads, as demonstrated in example 2-10. This event listener will call the *change()* function that we will create.

6 Below the code you entered in step 5, create the *change()* function. In the body of the function, set the **window.location** attribute to "secondPage.html." This is shown in example 2-11.

7 On secondPage.html, recreate the same JavaScript you wrote in steps 5 and 6, but set the attribute of **window. location** in the *change()* function to "index.html." This is shown in example 2-10.

8 Load up index.html in Chrome and emulate a smartphone screen. Use the buttons to navigate between the two pages and verify that everything works correctly, as shown in figure 2-14.

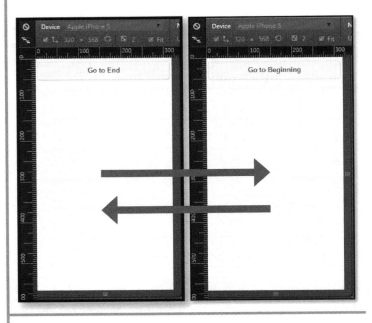

Figure 2-14: The navigation buttons will now switch between the two pages.

This first technique uses distinct pages with specified content to handle navigation through the app. As you can tell by navigating between the two pages, it's simple to move back and forth. You could extend this as much as you need by adding additional pages with the appropriate button links. To make things more manageable, you could create a button class and have your JavaScript use that class to attach event listeners. Each button's unique id attribute could be its target page, and the *change()* function could use that id to load the appropriate page.

Another technique for managing user navigation through your app is to dynamically modify the content of a single page instead of creating multiple pages. If you are accustomed to traditional web development, then this might seem a little counter-intuitive, but the idea is simple. The "page" that a user is viewing does not need to be a separate file because it is defined by the content itself, not the source of that content. Looking at it that way, a "page" can be changed without loading a new file, but by instead displaying new content in an already loaded file.

```
<div id="container">
   <!-- <button id="btnMove">Go to
End</button> -->
   <div id="title"></div>
   <div id="content"></div>
   <div id="control"></div>
</div>
```

Example 2-13: The framework for navigation with a single-page app.

```
<div id="control">
   <button id="btnOne">Story One</button>
   <button id="btnTwo">Story Two</button>
</div>
```

Example 2-14: The buttons within the *control* <div>.

Figure 2-15: How the buttons in *content* look at the moment.

The **<div>** HTML element defines a logical or thematic division in a webpage. We will use different **<div>** elements to determine where we want to place content, and then populate them with the appropriate data.

We will modify index.html to demonstrate creating a single-page app that dynamically changes its content.

9 First, comment out the JavaScript used so far in this section and comment out the *btnMove* button.

10 Within the *container* **<div>** create three additional **<div>** elements, *title*, *content*, and *control*. This is shown in example 2-13.

11 The *control* **<div>** will contain the buttons that we will use to navigate the app. Within *control*, create two buttons, one with the id *btnOne* and the other with the id *btnTwo*. The text for the buttons should read "Story One" and "Story Two," respectively. Check the code shown in example 2-14. Figure 2-15 shows how index.html should look now.

```
▶  var storyOne = "<p>Lorem ipsum dolor
   sit amet, consectetur adipiscing elit.
   ... interdum sed arcu non, posuere
   suscipit elit.</p>";
▶  var storyTwo = "<p>Donec id ornare
   enim. Maecenas libero lectus, bibendum
   ... cursus tristique, gravida sed
   ante.</p>";
```

Example 2-15: Dynamic content to be loaded into our app page.

12 The content of the *title* and *content* **<div>** elements will be dynamic, so we won't add it to the HTML. Instead, as shown in example 2-15, create JavaScript variables to contain the appropriate text. We will use "Lorem Ipsum" placeholder text generated by *http://www. lipsum.com*, but any placeholder text will do. Note the **<p>** tags in the text. We will change the **innerHTML** attribute of the **<div>** elements, so the data that we use can be any valid HTML.

```
▶  window.onload = function() {
▶     document.getElementById("btnOne").
   addEventListener("click",
   postStoryOne, false);
▶     document.getElementById("btnTwo").
   addEventListener("click",
   postStoryTwo, false);
▶  }
```

Example 2-16: Adding event listeners to *btnOne* and *btnTwo*.

13 Use JavaScript to add "click" event listeners to both *btnOne* and *btnTwo*. Have the event listeners run *postStoryOne()* for *btnOne* and *postStoryTwo()* for *btnTwo*. This is shown in example 2-16.

14 Create the *postStoryOne()* and *postStoryTwo()* functions. These functions will get the *content* and *title* **<div>** elements and replace their **innerHTML** attributes with either *storyOne* or *storyTwo* and an appropriate title, as shown in example 2-17.

```
▶  function postStoryOne() {
▶     document.getElementById("content").
   innerHTML = storyOne;
▶     document.getElementById("title").
   innerHTML = "<h1>Story One!</h1>";
▶  }
▶
▶  function postStoryTwo() {
▶     document.getElementById("content").
   innerHTML = storyTwo;
▶     document.getElementById("title").
   innerHTML = "<h1>Story Two!</h1>";
▶  }
```

Example 2-17: *postStoryOne()* and *postStoryTwo()* change the content of the *content* and *title* **<div>** elements.

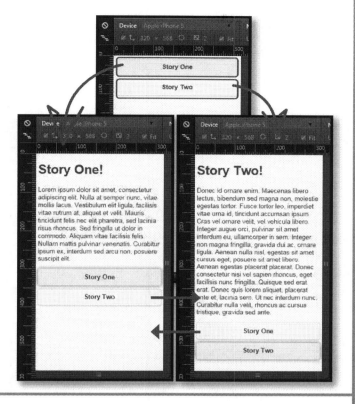

Figure 2-16: From the start, you can navigate between the two stories with ease.

15 Now load index.html in Chrome and verify that everything works. You'll be able to navigate between the two stories easily by clicking on the buttons, as shown in figure 2-16.

The data for *storyOne* and *storyTwo* could come from a variety of sources. Envisioning this as a simple news reader app, the actual content that populates the pages could come from a database, a webservice, an RSS feed, or any other source that can output compatible data.

16 Before we move on, there is something to note about usability. In this example, once either Story One or Story Two is loaded, we no longer need to have a button to navigate to that story. In the *postStoryOne()* and *postStoryTwo()* functions, use JavaScript to display only the needed buttons for each story. *postStoryOne()* is shown in example 2-18. The code for *postStoryTwo()* is nearly identical.

```
function postStoryOne() {
    document.getElementById("content").
innerHTML = storyOne;
    document.getElementById("title").
innerHTML = "<h1>Story One!</h1>";
    document.getElementById("btnOne").
style.display = "none";
    document.getElementById("btnTwo").
style.display = "block";
}
```

Example 2-18: *postStoryOne()* updated to only show the *btnTwo* navigation button.

The two techniques that we've explored in this section—creating multiple pages of content and using JavaScript to dynamically alter the content of a single page—are both useful and valid methods of creating an engaging and dynamic application for your audience. The circumstances will often dictate which approach works best, and oftentimes combinations of the two methods will give you the best results.

When considering how you intend to implement navigation in your application, it is important to understand that the user's experience of a page is defined by the content that they are viewing, not the organizational structure that underpins it. From a user's perspective, a series of pages that consist entirely of one HTML file with dynamic content is exactly the same as those same pages structured as a series of HTML files that are loaded individually.

In the next section, we are going to look at how to get information from a user and use it in our application.

Questions for Review

1 Within an application, what does "navigation" mean?

    a. Using a device's GPS to determine how to get to a location.

    b. Moving through content pages within an app.

    c. Moving from an application to a different application.

    d. Going to different webpages within an application.

2 What is a reasonable method of displaying different content in an application?

    a. Release multiple apps, each with a page of content.

    b. Have the app launch a web browser that loads the content.

    c. Create an app that loads multiple files, each of which has different content.

    d. Fit all of your content into a single page.

3 How can a single HTML page display multiple content pages?

    a. Using JavaScript to dynamically load content.

    b. A single HTML page cannot display multiple content pages.

    c. Using embedded videos of other content pages that a user can play.

    d. By breaking up the page with the <nextpage /> tag.

4 Using JavaScript to dynamically load content is always the best way to create multiple content pages for an app.

    a. True.

    b. False.

2.3 Obtaining User Data

One of the most important benefits of the modern mobile ecosystem is that phones are almost always connected to some data network, whether it's home Wi-Fi or a cellular network. It is very likely that your mobile app will take advantage of this and use user input and information in order to provide a better experience.

When designing user input and form elements with HTML5 for mobile devices, there are some important things to keep in mind. Think, for a moment, about an annoying mobile application. You may well be thinking about an app that has a particularly frustrating set of input fields that were clearly designed by someone who was not thinking about the particulars of mobile input. Luckily, HTML5 features some additions to the standard form inputs that make life much easier.

In this section we will demonstrate a very simple form that has input fields for a name, an email address, and a phone number. We will not do anything with this information yet - in fact, we will not even validate that the information is formatted correctly - but we will demonstrate some of the useful additions to HTML5.

Start off with a new PhoneGap project named Form. As with the previous section, remove all of the superfluous template data that the project will not require. You should only have the index.html file and the mainAppStyles.css file.

①   First, we are going to use the **<form>** tag to delineate a user input form. When we begin to handle the data, we will use JavaScript rather than the form functions built into HTML5, but it is still useful to use the tag for clearer structure. As usual, we will place the **<form>** in our *container* **<div>**, as in example 2-19.

```
<div id="container">
    <form>
    </form>
</div>
```

Example 2-19: Create a **<form>** within the *container* **<div>** in index.html.

```
▸  <label for="name">Name</label>
▸  <input type=text id="name" />
```

Example 2-20: The "Name" input element and label.

```
▸  <label for="email">Email</label>
▸  <input type=email id="email" />
```

Example 2-21: The "Email" input element and label.

```
▸  <label for="phone">Phone</label>
▸  <input type=tel id="phone" />
```

Example 2-22: The "Phone" input element and label.

```
▸  <div id="container">
▸     <form>
▸             <label for="name">Name</
   label>
▸             <input type=text id="name"
   />
▸             <label for="email">Email</
   label>
▸             <input type=email id="email"
   />
▸             <label for="phone">Phone</
   label>
▸             <input type=tel id="phone"
   />
▸     </form>
▸  </div>
```

Example 2-23: The complete form.

The following steps should all be entered as part of the **<form>** element that was just created.

2 We will begin with a simple textbox for a user to enter their name. The standard "text" input type is fine for this field, so create a **<label>** and an **<input>** that accepts the user's name. This is shown in example 2-20.

3 Next, we will create a field for an email address. We could use a regular "text" field, but when developing for mobile, there is a better option. There are special characters that are required for email addresses but are not normally displayed on a default mobile keyboard—namely, the "@" sign. Create a **<label>** for email and an **<input>,** but instead of "text" type, set it as an HTML5 "email" type, as shown in example 2-21.

4 Finally, create a field for a phone number. Again, a "text" input field could have been used, but HTML5 has a "tel" input type that will display a number pad instead of a keyboard, making phone number input simpler. Create a **<label>** and **<input>** for a telephone number, as in example 2-22.

5 In Chrome, you can effectively test the layout of the input form elements but you cannot test how the mobile keyboard will react to HTML5 input types. To do that, you need to test the application on either a device emulator or an actual device.

6 The left image in figure 2-17 demonstrates the app running with no keyboard, and the right image demonstrates the standard keyboard. Note the word suggestion bar above the keys and the "," character to the left of the space bar.

7 The left image in figure 2-18 demonstrates the keyboard presented from the "email" input type. Note that the word suggestion bar is gone because it is not needed for email addresses, and the "," character to the left of the space bar has been replaced with the more useful "@" symbol.

8 The right image in figure 2-18 is a standard phone keypad, used when a "tel" input type is selected.

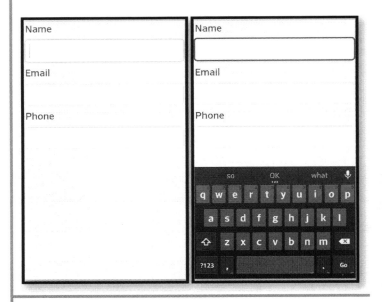

Figure 2-17: The application running on an Android device, left, and the standard input keyboard, right.

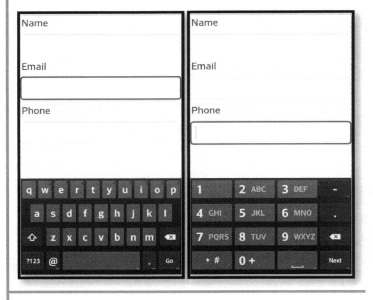

Figure 2-18: The email input keyboard, left, and the phone input keypad, right.

If we were to look at a form with the "email" or "tel" input types on a standard web browser then they would appear as standard text fields, but on a mobile device, these small but vital changes can make a huge difference when it comes to usability.

User input is important in any application, but for mobile applications, even small inconveniences are magnified substantially. When creating a desktop application, you can assume that a user has access to a full keyboard and a mouse—tools that have been explicitly designed for data entry. Mobile phones were not designed for data entry and are usually limited to software keyboards. Although some devices do ship with hardware keyboards and some users do use external keyboards, you cannot assume that those options will be available. When creating a mobile application, the only safe assumption to make about your users is that they will only have access to their device's built-in software keyboard.

Keeping the limited input methods in mind while you're designing an application and working to minimize frustration for your users can be the difference between an app that someone uses every day and an app that is tried once and then deleted. Even an application that has more advanced features may be a less attractive option for users if input and interaction are too challenging. Understanding your users and their hardware also shows them that you care about their experience and creates a connection between the user and the developer. When designing for a device that is as personal as a mobile phone or tablet, that sense of connection can be vital.

In the next section, we will look into integrating images into your PhoneGap applications and ensuring that they are displayed appropriately.

Questions for Review

1 New HTML5 input types can help ameliorate mobile input problems.

   a. True

   b. False

2 Which of the following is an effective input type for emails on mobile devices?

   a. email.

   b. mail.

   c. e-mail.

   d. e_mail.

3 When using the tel input type, which of the following will appear for the user?

   a. A list of their contacts.

   b. A keyboard with the top row replaced by numbers.

   c. A number pad for phone number entry.

   d. Nothing, tel is an invalid input type.

4 When testing emulated layouts in Chrome, it is important to remember which of the following?

   a. Chrome cannot emulate the device's keyboard.

   b. Chrome cannot display input email and tel input fields.

   c. Chrome will autofill email and tel input fields.

   d. Chrome should not be used for layout testing.

2.4 Displaying Images

In 1992, Tim Berners-Lee asked *Les Horribles Cernettes*, an all-female parody rock group comprised of members of CERN (The European Organization for Nuclear Research), for a few scanned photos to publish on a new information system he had just invented. Those pictures became the first images posted on the web. Today, pictures and images are a huge part of what makes the internet the dominant communications platform in history.

Using images in PhoneGap is syntactically no different from displaying images on a website, but there are additional considerations that need to be taken into account. As with implementing mobile input, with mobile images you cannot make the same sort of assumptions that were safe when designing for the desktop. In a desktop environment you can assume that the user has a reasonably large screen with a relatively high resolution, however, in a mobile environment that may not always be the case. You need to plan for different screen sizes and design an application that will look good whether it is displayed on an iPhone 5 or a Kindle Fire HDX 7.

To demonstrate this, we'll use two different versions of the same image. Create a new PhoneGap project named Images and prepare it according to the templates that we have been using. As with the previous section, we will not be using JavaScript but we will be using CSS, so ensure that your mainAppStyles.css file is linking correctly. Once your project is ready, find the image file to use.

1 For demonstration purposes, we will be using a freely available image from Wikimedia Commons. The file is located at *http://commons. wikimedia.org/wiki/File:TACA_ airplanes_SJO_04_2005.jpg*.

Figure 2-19: The image from Wikimedia Commons we will use for demonstration purposes.

2 We will use two versions of this file, the original size which has a resolution of 1973 by 905, and a smaller file, with a resolution of 640 by 294. Download those two files and rename them to "Airplanes.jpg" for the large file and "Airplanes_640.jpg" for the small file.

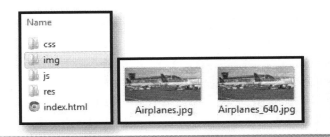

Figure 2-20: Copy the image files into the "/www/img" folder.

```
<div id="container">
    <img src="img/Airplanes_640.jpg" />
</div>
```

Example 2-24: The <img> tag is placed within the *container* <div>.

3 Copy the two files into your project's "/www/img" folder. When you build the application, these files will be included, so as you develop you can safely reference them as you would any other resource.

4 In your project's index. html file, display the small image at the top of the application using the **<img>** tags, as shown in example 2-24.

5 In Chrome, open the developer view and emulate an iPhone 5 screen, as shown in figure 2-21. You'll notice that the entire image is not displayed when the phone is in portrait orientation.

Figure 2-21: The image does not fit on an iPhone5 screen.

Figure 2-22: The iPhone 5's emulated landscape mode.

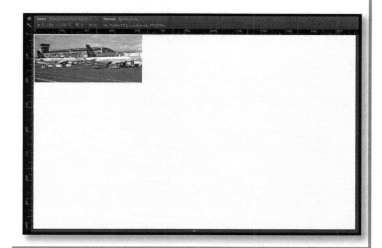

Figure 2-23: The same image on an emulated Kindle Fire HDX 7 screen.

```
►   <img src="img/Airplanes_640.jpg"
    id="airplane"/>
```

Example 2-25: The <img> tag with the *airplane* id.

6 Within the developer tools, you can change the orientation of the screen you are emulating by clicking on the "Swap Dimensions" button, highlighted in figure 2-22. Use that button to view the iPhone 5's emulated landscape orientation. Now you can see more of the image.

7 Using this same image, emulate a screen with a higher resolution, like a Kindle Fire HDX 7, as shown in figure 2-23. Note that the image only takes up a small amount of space in the upper left-hand corner of the screen.

8 Using CSS, the layout problem from step 7 can be resolved. Give the **<img>** tag an **id**, *airplane*, as in example 2-25.

9 Open up mainAppStyles. css from the "/www/css" folder.

10   Use the *airplane* **id** selector and set the width of the image to 100%, as shown in example 2-26.

```
 #airplane {
     width:100%;
 }
```

Example 2-26: The CSS code for the *airplane* image.

11   Reload the image on the emulated Kindle Fire HDX 7 screen and see how it looks. Notice that it is pixelated and blurry. This is because the smaller image is being stretched to fit the resolution of the Kindle Fire HDX 7.

If you already have experience working with images, then this is no surprise to you. There is only so much data in an image, and despite what CSI might suggest no amount of enhancing will make a low resolution image clear.

Figure 2-24: The image stretched to fit the Kindle Fire screen.

Traditional web developers are probably accustomed to finding the appropriate compromise between image quality and file size, but with a PhoneGap application you don't have the same concerns. Although you are developing with web technologies, all of the image resources will be stored local to your application so you won't have bandwidth concerns.

Figure 2-25: Detail of the image. Note how blurry it appears.

```
► <img src="img/Airplanes.jpg"
    id="airplane"/>
```

Example 2-27: Loading the high-resolution image.

Figure 2-26: Top, the low resolution image on Kindle Fire HDX 7, and bottom is the high resolution image.

12 In index.html, modify the **<img>** tag so that the **src** attribute points to the larger image, airplanes.jpg, as shown in example 2-27.

13 Refresh your emulated Kindle Fire HDX 7 screen and note the immediate difference. Figure 2-26 demonstrates this.

On the emulated iPhone 5 screen, either the large or the small image file will result in the same view for the user when the **<img>** element's width is set to 100%. The relatively low resolution of that iPhone screen means that displaying the low resolution image scaled to fit the screen's available pixels results in no loss of image data. If, on the other hand, you were to use the large image *without* setting the **<img>** element's width to 100%, then you would have a new problem — the view would only show a small portion of the full image.

```
#airplane {
    /* width: 100%; */
}
```

Example 2-28: Comment out the **width** attribute.

14 To demonstrate the view of an image that is substantially larger than the available screen resolution, comment out the **width** attribute from the *airplane* CSS selector in mainAppStyles.css, as shown in example 2-28.

15 In Chrome, view the page with the full resolution image on an emulated iPhone 5 screen, as shown in figure 2-27. You'll notice that only a portion of the image is being shown.

Figure 2-27: iPhone 5 screen displaying the full Airplanes.jpg file.

16 Remove the comments to re-enable the **width** attribute in the *airplane* CSS selector. Save the mainAppStyles.css file and reload the emulated iPhone 5 screen in Chrome. Note how even the large image appropriately fits in the lower-resolution view.

Figure 2-28: iPhone 5 screen displaying the full Airplanes.jpg file with the **width** attribute set to 100%.

```
▸   <img src="img/Airplanes_640.jpg"
      id="airplane"/>
```

Example 2-29: Set the *airplane* **<img>** element to use the smaller version of the image.

```
▸   #airplane {
▸       width: 100%;
▸       max-width: 640px;
▸   }
```

Example 2-30: Set both the **width** attribute and the **max-width** attribute.

Example 2-31: On the top is the emulated iPhone 5 screen, with the image filling all available width, and on the bottom is the emulated Kindle Fire HDX 7, with the image having a maximum width of 640 pixels.

You now have a large image that fits appropriately on either high or low resolution devices. Although bandwidth is not a concern, you may not want every image to be excessively large.

17 Change the **src** attribute of the *airplane* **<img>** element from Airplanes.jpg back to Airplanes_640.jpg, as in example 2-29.

18 In mainAppStyles.css, verify that the **with** attribute is set to 100%, and then add a **max-width** attribute that is set to the value in pixels of the width of the Airplanes_640.jpg file, as shown in example 2-30.

The **max-width** attribute defines how wide an image is permitted to be and will override the **width** attribute. Therefore, even if a screen has over 640 pixels of available width in a view, the *airplane* **<img>** element will only ever be a maximum of 640 pixels wide. If a screen has less than 640 pixels available, however, the **width** attribute will be valid and the *airplane* **<img>** element will have a width of 100%.

For anyone who has done web development work, much of the information in this section will likely have been a refresher, however, seeing image styles applied to mobile devices clarifies some important points about mobile development and development with PhoneGap.

Most importantly, layout and image use in a mobile environment has to take into consideration the vast array of possible screen sizes and resolutions. PhoneGap offers tools to handle various sizes, resolutions, and pixel densities, but it is ultimately up to the developer to understand the problem.

Questions for Review

1 Which tag is used for images in HTML5 with PhoneGap?

   a. <image />

   b. <img />

   c. <picture />

   d.

2 Standard CSS image styles do not work with PhoneGap.

   a. True.

   b. False.

3 What is one way to ensure that an image fits the space available in a view?

   a. Set the max-width to 0.

   b. Set the max-width to -1.

   c. Set the width to 100%.

   d. Set the width to "max."

4 What does the max-width attribute do?

   a. Determines the minimum width of an element.

   b. Sets the width of an element.

   c. Nothing, it is not a valid CSS style attribute.

   d. Determines the maximum width of an element.

CHAPTER 02 LAB EXERCISE

When you create a new PhoneGap project using the command line, PhoneGap is creating a specific directory structure and populating it with the required files. Now that you have a template, you can just make a copy of the template directory to create a new, valid PhoneGap project.

1 Create a new PhoneGap project from your template by copying the template directory and renaming the copied version.

2 In your new project, use what you have learned in this chapter to create an application that allows a user to navigate between a multi-page article, an image, and a form.

3 For an additional challenge, use a small image file as a thumbnail of a large image file. Have the large image load when the thumbnail is touched, and revert back to the thumbnail when the full image is touched.

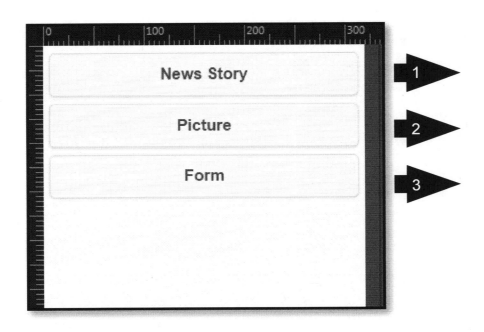

②

①

Story 1

Lorem ipsum dolor sit amet, adipiscing elit. Integer rutrum dapibus. Morbi blandit sit am ultrices. Donec tincidunt auct dapibus tellus rhoncus nec. P elementum vulputate massa Phasellus eget justo pellente ornare congue vel quis quam eget fringilla orci. Curabitur porttitor malesuada tortor, ac dignissim quam iaculis vel. Etiam aliquam elit nec rutrum porta. Nullam venenatis auctor diam, vel consectetur eros eleifend mollis. Nunc vel magna vitae nibh fringilla molestie tempus vel ipsum.

Mauris posuere odio vel lectus dictum, ac luctus odio porttitor. Nunc molestie neque quam, ac accumsan velit sollicitudin mollis. Etiam nec pretium purus, a interdum erat. Quisque neque sem, pellentesque ac ligula nec, ultricies vehicula velit. Curabitur nec ante risus. Mauris tempus convallis mauris at euismod. Aenean et laoreet purus.

③

Name

Phone Number

Email

Chapter Summary

In this chapter we introduced using HTML5 for mobile devices with PhoneGap and we created some very simple example applications. We learned about the document structure of PhoneGap projects, and we also established a solid template to use going forward with our PhoneGap projects.

Later in the chapter we explored some of the techniques that we can use to change standard HTML5 elements into mobile-friendly elements, and we gained an understanding of how important it is to focus on the idiosyncrasies of mobile devices.

In the next chapter, we will look at using CSS3 with for mobile devices with PhoneGap, learn how to style text elements, and gain an understanding of basic page layout. We will also delve into the issue of multiple mobile screen sizes and resolutions, and learn how to use PhoneGap and CSS3 to support different devices while maintaining a consistent look and feel.

Chapter 03

CSS3 for Mobile

CHAPTER OBJECTIVES:

- You will learn how to style text elements with CSS3.
- You will understand using CSS3 for page layout.
- You will learn how to use CSS3 to support multiple screen sizes.

3.1 Styling Text Elements

In this book we have been using Cascading Style Sheets, or CSS, to apply formatting to some aspects of our applications. CSS is a style sheet language used to describe the look and formatting of webpages. It was first proposed in 1994, but didn't see wide adoption until 2000. The most current version of CSS is CSS3.

The purpose of a style sheet language is to separate content from presentation. Ideally, the content contained in HTML files will be structured using tags that are purely semantic, with all of the styling done in separate CSS. Controlling presentation in this manner makes optimizing content for different devices a matter of changing the CSS rather than modifying the structure of the content.

CSS uses selectors to determine which DOM element a given set of rules applies to, and a simple syntax that uses English keywords within a declaration block to specify style properties. If you don't have much experience with CSS, this section will give you a very brief introduction to how it is used by showing you how to format and modify text. If you have used CSS, then this will be a good refresher before moving on to PhoneGap-specific topics.

For this section there is no need to create a full PhoneGap project. All you need is a basic HTML file with some sample text.

1 In Brackets or your text editor of choice, create a new file and name it css_test. html. In the file, build a bare HTML framework based on our template, as shown in example 3-1. Note that our *container* style is contained in an inline **<style>** element rather than an external file, as we had been doing.

```html
<html>
    <head>
        <title>CSS Test</title>
        <style>
            #container {
                margin: 5px;
            }
        </style>
    </head>
    <body>
        <div id="container">
        </div>
    </body>
</html>
```

Example 3-1: A bar HTML file.

```
<div id="container">
    <h1>Lorem ipsum dolor sit amet,
consectetur adipiscing</h1>
    <p>Lorem ipsum ... malesuada fames
ac turpis egestas.</p>
    <p>Suspendisse pellentesque nulla
... eu vel mi.</p>
    <p>Cras ultricies purus vitae
cursus efficitur ... vehicula
porttitor.</p>
</div>
```

Example 3-2: Placeholder content in the **<body>** of css_test. html.

Figure 3-1: The default style of css_test.html displayed on an emulated iPhone 5.

2   In order to test text layout, we will need some sample text. We used *http://www.lipsum. com* to generate example text, and put it into the *container* **<div>** of css_test.html, as shown in example 3-2. Note that we placed a small amount of text, representing a headline, in **<h1>** tags, and the body of the document in **<p>** tags.

3   In Chrome, load the css_ test.html file and emulate the page on an iPhone 5, as shown in figure 3-1. Every browser implements a default style for page elements so your browser is displaying the default styles for the **<h1>** and **<p>** tags.

In this section we are going to be modifying the style of **<h1>** elements so we will use the **h1** selector in CSS. We can select DOM elements in a variety of ways, not just by tag name. For example, the *container* style we have been using selects based on a DOM id attribute. We can also select by class name, DOM hierarchy location, and other element attributes.

4 In the css_test.html **<style>** element, add a selector for **<h1>** elements and an empty declaration block, as shown in example 3-3.

```
<style>
   #container {
        margin: 5px;
   }
   h1 {
   }
</style>
```

Example 3-3: Use the **h1** selector in the **<style>** element of css_test.html.

5 Within the declaration block, we are first going to change the style of the font to a sans-serif style. Set the **font-family** attribute as shown in example 3-4. Save the HTML file and refresh the page in Chrome. You should see the heading style change, as shown in figure 3-2.

```
h1 {
   font-family: Arial, Helvetica,
sans-serif;
}
```

Example 3-4: Setting the font for **<h1>** elements in CSS.

The **font-family** attribute will change the font that text is displayed in. We have set the attribute using three comma-separated values. When an **<h1>** element is displayed, first the Arial font will be used. If that font is not available, then the Helvetica font will be used. If *that* font is not available, then the system default sans-serif font will be used. If there is no system default sans-serif font, then the default system font will be used.

Setting fonts in this way helps to ensure that our text will display how we intend it to on a broad range of devices.

Figure 3-2: Changing the **<h1>** font-family attribute changes the style of the heading.

```
▶  h1 {
▶     font-family: Arial, Helvetica,
    sans-serif;
▶     font-size: 1em;
▶  }
```

Example 3-5: Setting the size of **<h1>** elements to one em.

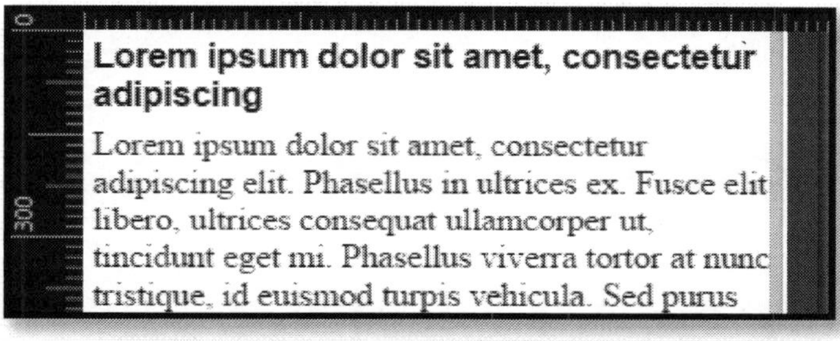

Figure 3-3: Heading elements sized to one em.

```
▶  h1 {
▶     font-family: Arial, Helvetica,
    sans-serif;
▶     font-size: 4em;
▶  }
```

Example 3-6: Setting the size of **<h1>** elements to four em.

Figure 3-4: Heading elements sized to four em.

Now that we have changed the heading font, we are going to change the heading size. Text size in HTML can be controlled by setting explicit pixel values, keyword values, or "em" values. In CSS, one em is the height of the current font and may vary depending on a number of factors. Valid keywords are xx-small, x-small, small, medium, large, x-large, and xx-large. The default setting is medium.

The key distinction between setting font sizes in pixels or keywords versus em values is that em values will always be relative, and pixel or keyword values are absolute. Em values are often preferred because circumstances that will break layouts based on absolute values can be managed by layouts based on em values.

6 Example 3-5 sets the size of the heading to one em, or the standard font size, and the results are shown in figure 3-3.

7 Example 3-6 sets the size of the heading to four em, four times the font size, and the results are shown in figure 3-4.

8 Choose a size that you consider appropriate for the heading, as we have in example 3-7. Note that em values do not have to be whole numbers.

```
h1 {
    font-family: Arial, Helvetica,
sans-serif;
    font-size: 3.75em;
}
```

Example 3-7: Set the em size of the font to an appropriate value.

9 Once you have a good font size, check the layout in other devices. In figure 3-5 we have used a first generation Kindle Fire.

For any element, the value of one em will be the value of the font size of its parent element, not the default browser font size. If no font size has been declared by a parent element, then one em is set to the browser default, which is usually 16 pixels.

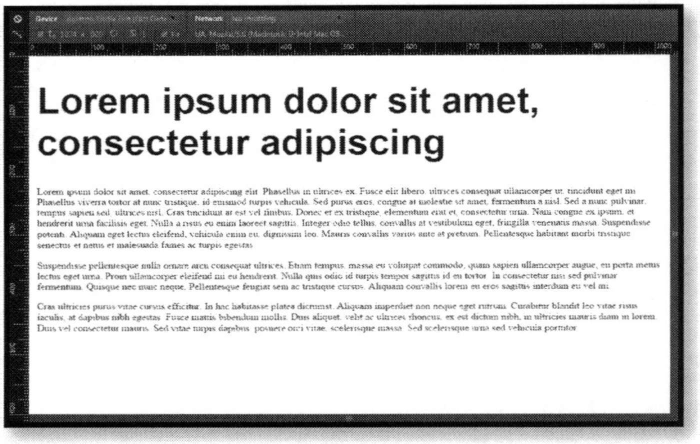

Figure 3-5: Checking the font sizes on a first generation Kindle Fire emulated screen.

10 HTML has tags for italics and bold face, but they have been deprecated because those attributes can be managed per selector with CSS. Modify the heading to be in italics by adding the **font-style** attribute and setting it to "italic," as shown in example 3-8.

```
h1 {
    font-family: Arial, Helvetica,
sans-serif;
    font-size: 3.75em;
    font-style: italic;
}
```

Example 3-8: Using CSS to italicize the heading.

Figure 3-6: Using the **font-style** attribute to italicize the heading.

```
▸   h1 {
▸       font-family: Arial, Helvetica,
    sans-serif;
▸       font-size: 3.75em;
▸       font-style: italic;
▸       font-weight: normal;
▸   }
```

Example 3-9: Use the "font-weight" attribute to set - or, in this case, remove boldface.

Figure 3-7: Now the heading does not have a boldface style applied to it.

11 The heading is now italicized, as shown in figure 3-6.

12 The CSS attribute for bold is called **font-weight**. The **<h1>** element is bold by default, but bold can be removed by setting the **font-weight** attribute to normal, like in example 3-9.

13 Figure 3-7 shows how the heading should look now.

Applying a font weight can be done using the normal and bold keywords, but it can also be achieved with the relative bolder and lighter keywords. Using bolder and lighter sets the font-weight to either bolder or lighter than its parent elements.

For more granular control, font-weight can be set as values of 100 to 900 in steps of 100, however, support for this is not consistent across browsers or platforms.

14 We want our headline to be bold, but not italicized, so remove the **font-style** and **font-weight** attributes. We do not have to set the font's weight because the **<h1>** element is bold by default.

15 Some headlines use a technique where all letters are capitalized, but letters that should be capitalized are rendered in a larger size. In CSS you can achieve this effect using the **font-variant** attribute. Set it according to example 3-10. Your example should match figure 3-8.

16 Using the small caps style accentuates the distance between the lines of the headline. Small details like that can effect the readability of a page. Using CSS, modify the **line-height** attribute to reduce the distance between lines within **<h1>** elements. Using a number for the line height computes a value by multiplying the number with the element's font size, and is the preferred method of setting line height. Enter the code from example 3-11.

```
h1 {
    font-family: Arial, Helvetica,
sans-serif;
    font-size: 3.75em;
    font-variant: small-caps;
}
```

Example 3-10: Set **font-variant** to small caps.

Figure 3-8: The small caps style applied to the headline.

```
h1 {
    font-family: Arial, Helvetica,
sans-serif;
    font-size: 3.75em;
    font-variant: small-caps;
    line-height: 0.8;
}
```

Example 3-11: Setting the spacing between the lines of **<h1>** elements with the **line-height** attribute.

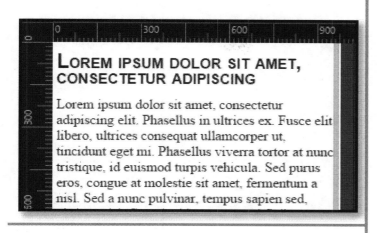

17 We chose to set the line height to 0.8, however, feel free to experiment and find a spacing that you like. It is possible to reduce line height so much that lines overlap. Our results are shown in figure 3-9.

Figure 3-9: The slightly condensed line height applied to the header.

Now our headline has a specified font family, size, font variant, and line height. The final attribute we will look at is its color. Colors in CSS are represented with either a red, green, and blue (RGB) value or with a hue, saturation, and lightness (HSL) value. Either method can also include an alpha value for transparency, and if an alpha is included, the color representation would be referred to as either an RGBA or an HSLA color.

RGB values without transparencies are the most supported color values and can be represented either using a comma-separated list of decimal values, or a hex triplet. A comma-separated list of color RGB values is a set of three decimal values ranging from 0, representing no color, to 255, representing full color. In CSS, RGB values are formatted like so: rgb(RRR, GGG, BBB).

A hex triplet is a set of RGB values represented as hexadecimal numbers ranging from 00 to FF. Hexadecimal numbering is based off of 16 rather than 10 and uses letters to represent values higher than 9. The decimal value of 10 is equal to the hexadecimal value A, decimal 11 is hexadecimal B, and so on, until hexadecimal F. Hex triplets range between 00 and FF because hexadecimal 00 is equal to decimal 0, and hexadecimal FF is equal to decimal 255. In CSS, hex triplets are formatted like so: #RRGGBB.

A color represented in CSS as either "rgb(255, 0, 150)" or "#FF0096" would render identically for the user.

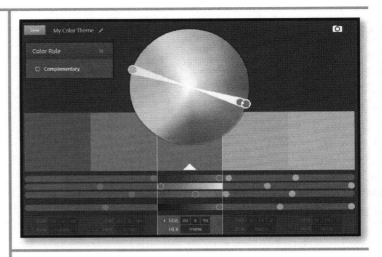

Figure 3-10: Adobe's color website.

18 Proper use of color is vital for application development. There are a number of tools available to determine appropriate colors and find their color values. Figure 3-10 shows one such tool, from *http://color.adobe.com*.

19 In the rules for your **<h1>** CSS selector, add a color attribute and set it to an RGB value, as shown in example 3-12.

```
h1 {
    font-family: Arial, Helvetica,
sans-serif;
    font-size: 3.75em;
    font-variant: small-caps;
    line-height: 0.8;
    color: rgb(255, 0, 150);
}
```

Example 3-12: Setting the color using RGB values.

Note that changing the color of the text within an element in CSS is done using the **color** attribute, however other attributes that we have used that effect the text have been prepended by "font-."

20 Change the value of the **color** attribute to a hex triplet. In our example case the corresponding hex value would be "#FF0096." Verify that the page displays properly.

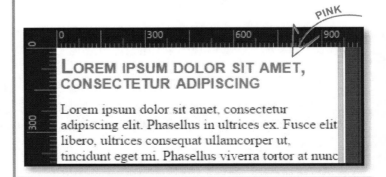

Example 3-13: Changing the color of the heading text.

If you worked through this section using Brackets or another text editor with code suggestions, then you probably noticed a number of attributes suggested as you entered the example CSS. CSS is an expansive style sheet language that can be used to affect nearly any aspect of the layout of a webpage or application. We have covered only the basics of formatting text, however as we continue to explore PhoneGap applications we will utilize much more of the power of CSS.

The basic principle to keep in mind is that CSS uses selectors to determine which DOM elements are going to be affected by specified rules. In the next section, we will use more CSS attributes to set the layout of a basic page.

Questions for Review

1 Which of the following is CSS used for?

a. Determining the content of a page.

b. Determining the presentation of a page.

c. Creating the interactive elements of a page.

d. Handling user interactions on a page.

2 What does the "font-family" attribute determine?

a. The font that an element is rendered in.

b. The size of a font that an element is rendered in.

c. It sets the default system font for a page.

d. Nothing, "font-family" does not exist.

3 What is the purpose of the "font-color" attribute?

a. It determines the color of text rendered in a certain font.

b. It sets the color of all text within an element.

c. It sets the color of all text within a document.

d. Nothing, "font-color" does not exist.

4 All HTML elements have default styles that cannot be overridden with CSS.

a. True.

b. False.

3.2 Basic Page Layout

Now that we have an understanding of text formatting with CSS, we will look into page layout. As with the previous section, if your exposure to CSS has been limited then this section will cover some layout basics, and if you are experienced with CSS then this section will act as a good refresher.

Elements in CSS are laid out according to the box model. From innermost element out, the box model consists of an element's content, its padding, its border, and its margin. The content is the actual HTML content that an element contains. The padding is the space between the content and the border. The border defines the edge of an element and can be styled. The margin is the space between an element's border and the edge of its parent element.

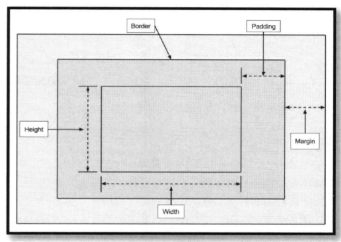

*see appendix for larger image version

The easiest way to understand the box model is to experiment with it, so create a new PhoneGap project, Layout, with the standard template.

① Create the Layout project and set up the project according to the templates that we have been using, with one addition. In the **<head>** of the index.html file, add a link to the Yahoo CSS style reset sheet, as shown in example 3-14. This style sheet will set all of the styles of every HTML element to a basic, identical style that you can build from.

```
▸   <link rel="stylesheet" href="http://
    yui.yahooapis.com/3.5.0/build/
    cssreset/cssreset-min.css" />
```

Example 3-14: The Yahoo CSS style reset sheet.

2 In the body of the HTML, create a **<div>** element with the id *test* and populate it with an **<h1>** heading and some example body text in a **<p>** tag, as shown in example 3-15. Note that comments have been added following the closing **<div>** tags to specify which tag is being closed. This is good practice and is helpful when working with multiple **<div>** elements.

```
<body>
    <div id="container">
    <div id="test">
            <h1>Sed odio leo, faucibus
    at</h1>
            <p>Lorem ipsum dolor ...
    feugiat commodo.</p>
    </div> <!-- test -->
    </div> <!-- container -->
    </body>
```

Example 3-15: The basic outline of the **<body>** of index.html.

Figure 3-11: The reset stylesheet makes all elements look identical.

3 When you view this page in a browser you will see that the reset stylesheet has made the headings identical to the rest of the body text, as shown in figure 3-11. We have a completely blank slate to work from. This allows us to be confident that the only styling applied to elements is the styling that we choose to apply.

```
h1 {
    font-size: 2em;
    font-weight: bold;
}
```

Example 3-16: Setting some styles for **<h1>** elements.

4 In your mainAppStyles.css file, select **<h1>** elements and, using what you have learned in the previous section, set the style appropriately for a heading. We have chosen to increase their size and font weight, as shown in example 3-16 and figure 3-12.

Figure 3-12: Now the **<h1>** element looks like a heading.

```
#test {
    background-color: red;
    color: white;
}
```

Example 3-17: Set the background of *test* to red and the color of its text to white.

Figure 3-13: It is now easy to see the content of *test*.

```
#container {
    margin: 0px;
}
#test {
    background-color: red;
    color: white;
}
```

Example 3-18: The current mainAppStyles.css file.

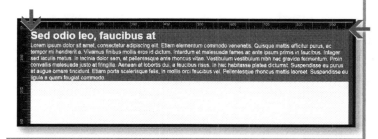

Figure 3-14: The *test* <div>, without any containing margin.

5 To display the box model we need to be able to see the elements that we are working with. For that, we will change the background of the content of *test*. Use the CSS from example 3-17 in your mainAppStyles.css file to change the background of *test* to red and the text color to white.

6 In this section, we have been using an emulated Google Nexus 7. The result of our styled div is shown in figure 3-13.

7 Note that there is a gap between the edge of *test* and the edge of the screen. This is because our template creates a small margin for our *container* <div>. For the sake of this demonstration, set that margin to 0 pixels. Your mainAppStyles. css *container* and *test* selectors should look like example 3-18, and your emulated screen should match figure 3-14.

The red part of *test* is its content. By default, a **<div>** will have a width equal to that of its parent element and a height large enough to include all of the content.

Figure 3-15: Both elements have an equal width when no width has been explicitly set.

The size of content in the box model can be controlled. Using the **width** attribute, content width can be set to either a precise pixel value or a relative value based on the size of the parent element.

8 Create a *test2* **<div>** below *test* and populate it with a heading and content using the **<h1>** and **<p>** tags. Style it identically to *test*, but make the background blue instead of red. When you view the page, both elements will have an equal width, as shown in figure 3-15.

```
#test {
    background-color: red;
    color: white;
    width: 50%;
}
#test2 {
    background-color: blue;
    color: white;
    width: 483px;
}
```

Example 3-19: Set a relative width for *test* and an absolute width for *test2*.

9 In the stylesheet, add a relative width of 50% to *test*, and a fixed width of 483 pixels, or half of the horizontal resolution of a Nexus 7, to *test2*, as shown in example 3-19.

10 Change the size of the emulated screen and note how the elements react, as shown in figure 3-16.

Figure 3-16: Changing the screen size affects relative and absolute positioned elements differently.

WIDTH 600PX

Figure 3-17: The two <div> elements, both 600 pixels wide.

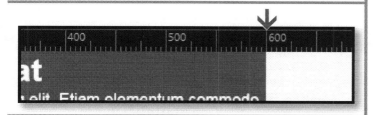

Figure 3-18: Chrome shows you the exact size in pixels.

```
#test {
    background-color: red;
    color: white;
    width: 600px;
    padding: 25px;
}
```

Example 3-20: Adding padding to *test*.

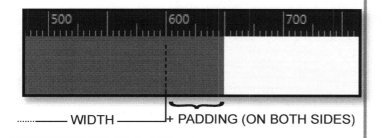

WIDTH ········+ PADDING (ON BOTH SIDES)

Figure 3-19: With padding, *test* takes up 650 pixels in width.

11 It's important to remember that the width attribute sets the width of the content, not the width of the entire element. To demonstrate this, set the widths of both *test* and *test2* to 400 pixels and view them in an emulated Nexus 7, as shown in figure 3-17. You'll note that they are both identically sized and that the ruler at the top of the Chrome emulation window shows that they are both 600 pixels wide, as in figure 3-18.

12 In the style rules for *test*, add a padding value of 25 pixels, as shown in example 3-20. Ensure that *test2* does not have any padding.

13 When you refresh the page, you can see that *test* is substantially wider than *test2*. Check the width on the ruler, as shown in figure 3-20. The width of the element went from 600 pixels exactly to 650 pixels. This is because the padding attribute added 25 pixels between the edge of the content and the edge of the <div> element. The 25 pixels on the left side and 25 pixels on the right make up the additional 50 pixel width.

14 Padding is the distance between content and the edges of its container element. Next, we will add a border. In mainAppStyles.css for *test* create a border attribute that has the value, "25px solid black," as in example 3-21.

```
#test {
    background-color: red;
    color: white;
    width: 600px;
    padding: 25px;
    border: 25px solid black;
}
```

Example 3-21: Adding a border to *test*.

15 The result, seen in figure 3-20, is a thick black, border around the content and its padding. Note also how the border affected the width of the entire element, shown in figure 3-21. The *test* **<div>** is now 700 pixels wide. This is because the border that was added has a width of 25 pixels on every side, and, like with padding, the 25 pixels on the left and the 25 pixels on the right together add 50 pixels to the width of the element.

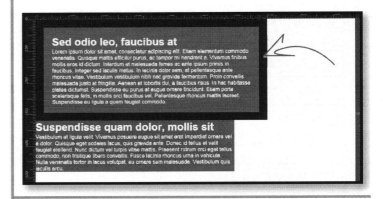

Figure 3-20: The border attribute adds, styles, and sizes a border around content and content padding.

The three values that were used to generate the border represent its width, its style, and its color. Borders can be given a radius with the **border-radius** attribute to create rounded buttons.

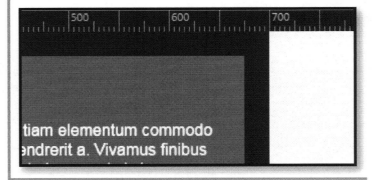

Figure 3-21: The addition of the border increased the element's size to 700 pixels.

```
▸  #test {
▸      background-color: red;
▸      color: white;
▸      width: 600px;
▸      padding: 25px;
▸      border: 25px solid black;
▸      margin: 25px;
▸      margin-top: 0px;
▸  }
```

Example 3-22: Adding margins to *test*.

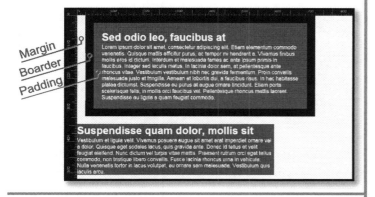

Figure 3-22: The margin attribute adds space between the end of an element and the inside edge of its parent.

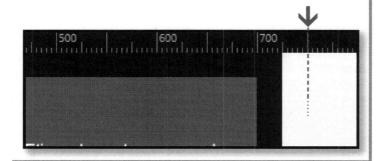

Figure 3-23: With a margin, the visible portion of *test* extends to 725 pixels, although it occupies an additional 25 pixels that are not visible.

16   The final element of the box model is the margin setting. We have already used margins with the *container* **<div>**, and so it is probably clear how they work. Just to demonstrate, though, add a 25 pixel margin to *test*, as in example 3-22. Note that we have set **margin-top** to 0 pixels. This will keep *test* flush with the top of the screen, making it easier to see its width.

17   Test the page in the emulator and you can see that every side of *test* which has a margin applied is 25 pixels away from the next layout element. Although it is not visible, *test* extends an additional 25 pixels out on the right making the complete width of the element 750 pixels. The **width** attribute, however, is still set to the absolute value of 600 pixels, just like *test2*.

The padding, border, and margin of each side of an element can be set independently, as we did with **margin-top** in step 16.

Understanding the box model is key to being able to effectively layout page elements. The most important aspect of the box model to remember is that the actual size of an element is the combination of the content, padding, borders, and margins.

When placing these elements on a page, the browser will always attempt to lay elements out vertically. Often this is not the layout that you want. In order to ensure that elements are laid out appropriately, CSS allows you to override the default action.

18 First, set both *test* and *test2* to a less garish style and re-enable the *container* margin from our template, as shown in example 3-23.

In order to override the default layout, CSS has a **float** attribute. Float places an element on either the right or left side of its parent element, and has the remaining elements flow around it. Any elements in the document before the floated element will not be affected.

Multiple floated elements in a row will display next to each other if there is room in their parent element. Elements floated on the left and right side of their parent element will also be displayed next to each other if there is room. Figure 3-24 shows how elements float.

```css
#container {
    margin: 5px;
}
#test {
    padding: 3px;
}
#test2 {
    padding: 3px;
}
```

Example 3-23: The test <div> elements, reset.

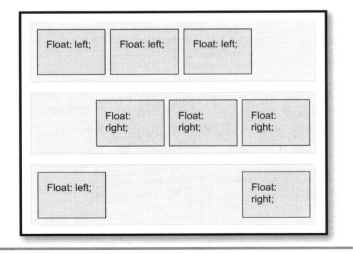

Figure 3-24: Examples of how elements float.

```
#test {
    padding: 3px;
    float: left;
}
#test2 {
    padding: 3px;
    float: left;
}
```

Example 3-24: Floating the test **<div>** elements.

```
#test {
    padding: 3px;
    float: left;
    width: 48%;
    border: 1px solid black;
}
#test2 {
    padding: 3px;
    float: left;
    width: 48%;
    border: 1px solid black;
}
```

Example 3-25: Creating columns of content.

Figure 3-25: The test <div> elements as floated columns.

In order to show how elements float, we'll make a multi-column layout. A multi-column layout references traditional newspapers by presenting multiple pieces of content on one page. This type of layout is most effective on large screen devices, such as tablets.

19 Set the two test **<div>** elements to float on the left, as in example 3-24. When you view this in your browser, you'll notice that nothing appears to have changed. This is because the elements are floating to the left, but they are both the default width, 100% of their parent element.

20 Set the width of the two test **<div>** elements to 48%, and add a thin border to better visualize their locations, as in example 3-25.

21 Examine how the content looks in Chrome on an emulated tablet screen, as shown in figure 3-25. You'll notice that the left edge of *test2* is flush with the right edge of *test*. This is because both elements are floated left and neither have margins.

```
#test2 {
    padding: 3px;
    float: right;
    width: 48%;
    border: 1px solid black;
}
```

Example 3-26: Float *test2* to the right.

22 While this works and creates a multi-column layout, having both columns aligned to the left looks awkward. Fix this by floating *test2* to the right, as shown in example 3-26. Check your result against figure 3-26. This gives each element a little more space and improves readability. Also, now that you are comfortable with the location of the content elements, you can remove the borders from *test* and *test2*. Your currently styled page should match figure 3-27.

Figure 3-26: The two column layout with borders.

Finally, we will examine how the **clear** attribute works by adding a footer that contains copyright information. The clear attribute in CSS specifies a side of an element on which floating elements are not allowed.

Figure 3-27: The two column layout without borders.

23 Add a **<footer>** element to your index.html, below the *test2* **<div>**, as shown in example 3-27.

```
<footer>
    Copyright 2015 | LearnToProgram
Media
</footer>
```

Example 3-27: Add a footer with copyright information.

```
footer {
    font-size: 0.75em;
    background-color: black;
    color: white;
}
```

Example 3-28: The footer styling.

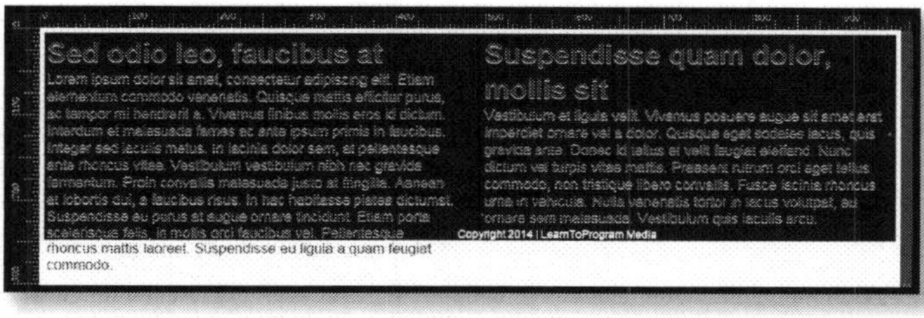

Figure 3-28: Without using the clear attribute, the footer renders incorrectly.

```
footer {
    font-size: 0.75em;
    background-color: black;
    color: white;
    clear: both;
}
```

Example 3-29: The corrected footer styling.

Figure 3-29: The correctly rendered footer.

24 Using CSS, style the footer with a black background, white text, and a slightly smaller font size, as in example 3-28. The width will default to 100% of the width of the parent element. Your result will look something like figure 3-28. Unfortunately, that result is not ideal.

The problem is that the footer text is flowing around elements that have been floated, but because the footer itself has not been floated, its default size extends from the start of its parent element, *container*, to the end of its text. In order to display it properly, we will use the **clear** attribute to ensure that the footer does not render next to any floating elements.

25 Use the **clear** attribute to have the footer clear both *test* and *test2*, as shown in example 3-29. Figure 3-29 shows how the page should look now.

With the footer displaying correctly, it's time to check the layout in a different emulated device, such as the Samsung Galaxy S4 (shown in figure 3-30) or another smartphone. Note that the content does not look very appealing in the default portrait layout.

Figure 3-30: This layout does not look good on a phone.

The final figure of this section, figure 3-30, demonstrates how important it is to understand the devices that you're developing for. Creating a workable layout for tablet devices can very easily result in a nearly unreadable layout on a smaller screen device.

Using the box model effectively and understanding how to float and clear elements in CSS are very important for laying out a webpage and a PhoneGap-powered application. As we continue to develop applications using PhoneGap you will get more practice using these CSS techniques to create tailored experiences for a variety of devices.

In the next section, we are going to be looking at using CSS to support multiple mobile device screen sizes.

Questions for Review

1 The CSS box model includes which elements?

   a. Content, border, padding, and margin.

   b. Border, padding, margin, and structure.

   c. Content and border.

   d. Margins, padding, and float.

2 What does the width attribute determine?

   a. The width of an entire element, including all parts of the box model.

   b. The width of the content, padding, and border.

   c. The width of the content and padding.

   d. Only the width of the content.

3 Given an element with a set width of 500 pixels, how wide would it be with a 10 pixel border and 10 pixel padding?

   a. 520 pixels.

   b. 540 pixels.

   c. 500 pixels.

   d. 530 pixels.

4 Where will an element with "float: left" and "clear: right" display in relation to a following element with "float: right?"

   a. On the same line as the following element, on the far left of the page.

   b. On the preceding line of the following element, on the far right of the page.

   c. On the preceding line of the following element, on the far left of the page.

   d. On the line following the following element, on the far left of the page.

3.3 Supporting Multiple Screen Sizes

While working through the previous section, we developed a simple two column layout for our content which worked well in a tablet view. We used that layout to understand how the CSS box model works and how to use the float and clear attributes to break the default vertical layout. Once we finished our layout, we changed our emulator view from a tablet with a large screen to a phone with a small screen and found out that all of our work had resulted in a page that worked on tablets but that was a mess on phones.

In this section we will use the media query to ensure that our example code displays appropriately across devices with screens of all sizes. A media query allows us to write different CSS rules for different media types and screen sizes.

In order to more clearly demonstrate how effective media queries can be, we will first modify our example code and then use media queries to tailor its layout for specific devices. In this example, we will use an image from Wikimedia Commons, found at the following location: *http://commons.wikimedia.org/wiki/File:AC_Cobra_-_Oldtimertreffen_Wengerter_(14483248359).jpg*. You can use this image, or find an image of your own. We moved the image into our "/www/img" folder and renamed it "AC_Cobra.jpg."

1 First, rename the **<div>** elements from *test* and *test2* to *nav* and *content* in order to better reflect what we are demonstrating.

2 Remove the content from *nav* and replace it with a heading, the image you intend to use, and a few placeholder navigation buttons, as shown in example 3-30.

```
<div id="nav">
    <h1>Navigation</h1>
    <img src="img/AC_Cobra.jpg" />
    <button>Page 1</button>
    <button>Page 2</button>
    <button>Page 3</button>
    <button>Page 4</button>
</div> <!-- nav -->
```

Example 3-30: The *test* **<div>** modified into a simple navigation menu template with a header and an image.

```
<div id="content">
    <h1>Suspendisse quam dolor, mollis
sit</h1>
    <p>Vestibulum et ligula ... iaculis
arcu.</p>
    <p>Nunc lobortis lacus id mauris
pulvinar, ... magna, sit amet vehicula
neque lobortis nec.</p>
    <p>Curabitur pulvinar pulvinar
euismod.... nunc vitae, porttitor
viverra quam.</p>
</div> <!-- content -->
```

Example 3-31: The *test2* **<div>** modified into a content template with additional lipsum text.

③ Add some additional text to *content*, as shown in example 3-31.

④ In the CSS we need to update the selectors from *test* and *test2* to *nav* and *content*, and we also need to update their rules to better accommodate the page style we are targeting. In this case, we will decrease the width of the navigation menu and float it to the left, and we will reset the content to the default page flow. We've also added a slight margin around the navigation menu and set any **<img>** elements within *nav* to scale to the size of *nav*. This is all shown in example 3-32.

```
#nav {
    padding: 3px;
    float: left;
    width: 25%;
    margin: 1em;
}
#nav img {
    width: 100%;
}
#content {
    padding: 3px;
}
```

Example 3-32: The updated CSS for our navigation page template.

5 Loading your webpage in the same Google Nexus 7 emulator used in the previous section should give the result shown in figure 3-31.

6 If you load this same page into the iPhone 4 emulator, as we did at the close of the previous section, you will see a clear problem, shown in figure 3-32. The *nav* **<div>** element is narrow, the buttons are unreadable, and the image is tiny. The *content* **<div>** element is reasonably well laid out, though.

Figure 3-31: Thew new layout in an emulated Google Nexus 7.

7 To fix this, create a media query in mainAppStyles.css. Enter the code shown in example 3-33 to create an outline for a media query.

Figure 3-32: In an emulated iPhone 4, the layout has substantial usability issues.

The media query that we created will affect all media types with a maximum width of 649 pixels and a minimum width of 300 pixels. Those values reflect a reasonable horizontal resolution that we could expect from a standard smartphone. If we expected the size to be less than 300 pixels, we would likely add another media query.

```
@media all and (max-width: 649px) and
(min-width: 300px) {
}
```

Example 3-33: An outline for a media query that will optimize the CSS for lower resolution screens.

```
@media all and (max-width: 649px) and
(min-width: 300px) {
    #nav, #content {
        float: none;
        width: 100%;
        margin: 0px;
        padding: 0px;
    }
    #nav img {
        display: none;
    }
}
```

Example 3-34: The complete media query.

Figure 3-33: The simplified page running on a simulated iPhone 4 screen.

Now, what rules would we want to set or override if a device running this application has a horizontal resolution between 300 and 649 pixels?

8 First, we will select the *nav* and *content* elements.

9 We want everything to display vertically, so we set the **float** attributes to *none*.

10 We also want every element to use the full available width, so we will set the width to 100%.

11 We have set a margin and padding for *nav* and a padding for *content*, so we will reset those to zero.

12 A large image on a small screen can dominate the display, so we will select any images within *nav* and set them to no longer display.

Example 3-34 shows how the media query should look, and figure 3-33 demonstrates the results running on an iPhone 4 screen.

13 Now, whether you load your app in a phone or a tablet, the layout will be readable and intuitive for your users, as shown in figure 3-34.

Media queries can be leveraged to account for a variety of situations. You can specify CSS based not just on screen width, but on aspect ratio, available colors, screen DPI, device orientation, and more.

It's also possible to use media queries within HTML links to CSS resource files. In this way, you can have completely different CSS files for different devices, making it easier to develop and organize your code.

Figure 3-34: The same page rendered on an iPhone 4 (top) and a Nexus 7 (bottom).

In this section we covered using CSS media queries to ensure that the layout of your application is appropriate for the user's device. Media queries are a powerful tool that allow you to ensure that all of your users have a tailored experience when they are working with your application.

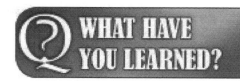

Questions for Review

1 What is a media query?

a. A phone call from your local newspaper looking for information.

b. A method of determining properties of the display device so that a page's CSS can be customized.

c. A way to check on the status of any media that a page is playing.

d. None of the above.

2 What problem does a media query solve?

a. Many possible display sizes and resolutions.

b. Unknown media sources in embedded video players.

c. Unknown font availability on the end user's device.

d. All of the above.

3 Media queries can only check for one attribute.

a. True.

b. False.

4 Media queries can be used to link different CSS files depending on device specifications.

a. True.

b. False.

CHAPTER 03 LAB EXERCISE

CSS is a very powerful tool. Separating your content from its styling allows you to quickly and easily change how your information is displayed. In this exercise, you will edit the mainAppStyles.css file from the final example project. All of the changes should be made in CSS only - there is no need to touch the HTML file.

1. Modify the heading of the content **<div>** so that it has a more unique style. Change its color, modify its font variant, and center the heading above the content text.

2. Change the content text itself. At the moment it is difficult to read, so improve readability by increasing the space between lines and by adding a clear separation between paragraphs.

3. Give the image a colored border with slightly rounded edges to differentiate it from the page slightly.

4. For further challenge, find out how to use CSS to ensure that the image *with* a border still fits precisely into its parent element.

5. For an even greater challenge, use CSS pseudo-selectors to color each button in the navigation **<div>** differently.

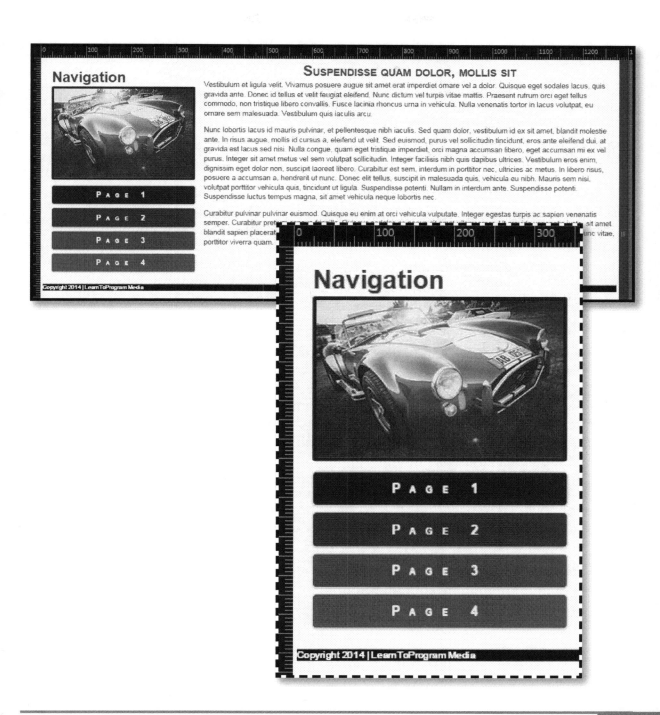

Chapter Summary

In this chapter we covered CSS basics. We learned how to modify the style, size, and color of fonts. We understood how the CSS box model works and then applied that knowledge to demonstrate exactly how content, padding, borders, and margins are rendered by the browser. We also used the float and clear attributes to break out of the default vertical page layout in order to align elements horizontally. Finally, we used media queries to optimize a page for displays with specific resolutions and we learned that media queries can be used for much more precise layout specification.

The intent of this chapter was to get readers who have only had a minimal exposure to CSS up to speed for the examples that will be used throughout the rest of this book. Hopefully it also acted as a good refresher for those with an already strong knowledge of CSS. CSS provides extensive layout possibilities for desktop and mobile webpages, mobile applications, and print layouts, among other things. Experimenting with CSS and exploring the resources that are available online will help you develop more interesting and dynamic content as you learn more about creating mobile applications.

In the next chapter, we will begin creating PhoneGap applications. First, we will learn about using a service oriented architecture for mobile devices, beginning with receiving text from a remote server. We will move on to sending queries back to the server, and finally we will learn how to parse the XML or JSON data received in response to our queries.

Service-Oriented Architecture for Mobile

CHAPTER OBJECTIVES:

- You will understand how to communicate with a server.

- You will learn how to use AJAX with PhoneGap applications.

- You will parse XML data received from a server.

- You will parse JSON data received from a server.

4.1 Receiving Text from the Server

The example applications that we've created so far have been very basic and have not needed to communicate with a server in order to function. All of the information existed locally. Many applications that you might be interested in creating, though, will need to retrieve data from another source in order to function.

Service-oriented architecture is structuring an application around communicating with a service to retrieve data, and then processing that data before generating a display that is presented to the end user. This is most common for applications that need access to the most current version of a rapidly changing data set. For example, a weather application is only useful if the weather information is up-to-date and tracks weather changes, a stock market tracking application needs to stay abreast of a dynamic market, and an application delivering sports scores needs to ensure that score changes are updated quickly.

It's important to note, however, that relying on a server as an integral part of your application experience also means that your application requires an internet connection.

To demonstrate a service-oriented PhoneGap application, we will create a Chuck Norris joke generator that is based on a freely available API from *http://www.icndb. com/api/*. It will connect to a service, fetch a random Chuck Norris joke, and display it.

1 First, create a new PhoneGap project named JokeGen. Modify the default project according to the template that we have been using, and be sure to include a reference to the main.js JavaScript file in the header, as in example 4-1.

```
<script src="js/main.js"></script>
```

Example 4-1: Ensure that "/js/main.js" is referenced by index. html.

```
▸   <div id="container">
▸   <h1>Chuck Norris Joke Generator</h1>
▸   <button id="btnGetJoke">Get Joke</
    button>
▸   <p>Press the button to retrieve a
    Chuck Norris joke.</p>
▸   <div id="joke">A joke about Chuck
    Norris? You're very brave.</div>
▸   </div> <!-- container -->
```

Example 4-2: The body of the index.html file.

Figure 4-1: The application running on an emulated iPhone 4 screen.

```
▸   var xmlhttp;
```

Example 4-3: Begin the main.js JavaScript file by creating a variable for the **XMLHttpRequest** object.

2   The application will have a name, "Chuck Norris Joke Generator," a button to generate jokes, a simple set of instructions, and a **<div>** for results. Create this within the *container* **<div>** in the **<body>** of the HTML, as shown in example 4-2.

3   Test your code in an emulator. An emulated iPhone 4 screen is shown in figure 4-1, to verify that the layout works.

Now that we have a working layout, open the main.js file. Our application will be powered by JavaScript and will use AJAX to retrieve the data as a JSON object from the server.

4   Start by creating a variable for the **XMLHttpRequest** object, as shown in example 4-3.

5 When PhoneGap registers that the device is ready and the application is loaded, run a function to initialize the AJAX request, as shown in example 4-4.

```
  var xmlhttp;

  window.onload = function () {
      document.
  addEventListener("deviceready", init,
  false);
  };
```

Example 4-4: When the application loads and the device is ready, call the *init()* function.

6 Create the initialization function, *init()*, below **window. onload**. The *init()* function will add a click event listener to the *btnGetJoke* button that will run a *getJoke()* function, initialize *xmlhttp* as an **XMLHttpRequest** object, and finally will run the *receiveJoke()* function when the ready state of *xmlhttp* changes. This is shown in example 4-5.

```
  function init() {
      document.
  getElementById('btnGetJoke').
  addEventListener('click', getJoke,
  false);
      xmlhttp = new XMLHttpRequest();
      xmlhttp.onreadystatechange =
  receiveJoke;
  }
```

Example 4-5: Within *init()*, attach a click event listener to the *btnGetJoke* element, and then prepare the **XMLHttpRequest** object.

7 The *getJoke()* function will use the **XMLHttpRequest** object, *xmlhttp*, to communicate with a remote server, as shown in example 4-6. The GET method is used to communicate with the Chuck Norris Joke API, specifically with the random joke generator.

```
  function getJoke() {
      xmlhttp.open('GET', 'http://api.
  icndb.com/jokes/random/', true);
      xmlhttp.send();
  }
```

Example 4-6: To receive a joke, use *getJoke()* to begin communicating with the server.

When we send the request to the Chuck Norris Joke API via an XML http request, the ready state of the **XMLHttpRequest** object changes. In step 6, we set *xmlhttp.onreadystatechange* to the function *receiveJoke()*, so whenever the ready state of *xmlhttp* changes, *receiveJoke()* is executed.

When we create the *receiveJoke()* function, it will parse the data received from the Internet Chuck Norris Database. In order to parse that data, we first need to determine whether or not the data is valid. To make that determination, we use the **readyState** and **status** of the **XMLHttpRequest** object.

The **readyState** value reflects the status of the client side of the communication. The ready state can have five values: "0" for "request not initialized," "1" for "server connection established," "2" for "request received," "3" for "processing request," and "4" for "request finished and response is ready." We will only ever want to parse returned data—also know as response data—after it is ready, so we check for the fourth ready state.

The **status** refers to the status of the server and can be any standard HTTP status code. The most widely known status code is "404", for "page not found." The most common status code, and the status code that we are looking for, is "200," the code for "OK." There are a number of other status codes that reflect the current status of the server.

It is important to check the status of both the client and the server before processing the response. For example, the server could respond with an error message instead of the data you anticipate, and the client would still consider the request to be finished and the response to be ready.

```
▸   function receiveJoke() {
▸       if (xmlhttp.readyState==4 &&
    xmlhttp.status==200) {
▸       }
▸   }
```

Example 4-7: In *receiveJoke()* we check the **readyState** and **status** of *xmlhttp*.

8 Below *getJoke()*, create *receiveJoke()*. In the *receiveJoke()* function, create a conditional to test if *xmlhttp.readyState* is 4 and *xmlhttp.status* is 200, as shown in example 4-7.

9   Once we are certain that the request completed successfully and the server returned the correct information, we can parse the data. We know from the Chuck Norris Internet Database that their API returns a Chuck Norris joke as a JSON element. We could parse the JSON ourselves, but jQuery can easily do that for us. Using **parseJSON()** from jQuery, create a variable *json* that will store the parsed data. Finally, set the inner HTML of the *joke* **<div>** to the value of the joke stored in *json*. This is shown in example 4-8.

10   Now, when you run the application in your device emulator on Chrome you'll see that when you click on "Get Joke" you're rewarded with absolutely nothing. For some reason, nothing happens when you try to retrieve a joke. The problem with testing the application on Chrome before pushing it to a mobile device is that the application uses PhoneGap-specific functions.

```
function receiveJoke() {
    if (xmlhttp.readyState==4 &&
xmlhttp.status==200) {
        var json = jQuery.
parseJSON(xmlhttp.responseText);
        document.
getElementById('joke').innerHTML =
json.value.joke;
    }
}
```

Example 4-8: The *receiveJoke()* function parses a JSON element and sets the value of the *joke* **<div>**.

```
▸   window.onload = function () {
▸       document.
    addEventListener("deviceready", init,
    false);
▸       init();
▸   };
```

Example 4-9: Explicitly call *init()* to test the app in Chrome.

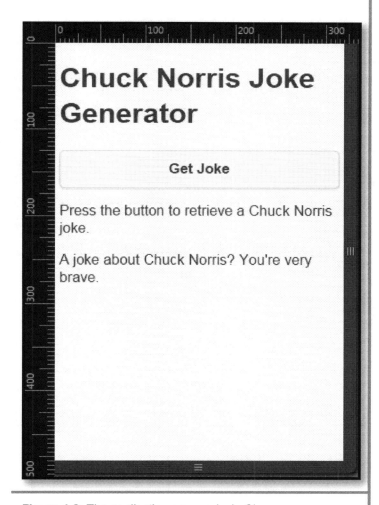

Figure 4-2: The application now works in Chrome.

Look back at **window.onload**. The *init()* function is called when the document's event listener registers the "deviceready" event. However, "deviceready" is a PhoneGap exclusive event that will never occur in Chrome. Therefore, *init()* will never be called and our program will not run.

11 In order to test the application with Chrome, we need to ensure that *init()* is called whether or not the application is running on a mobile device. The simplest way to do this is to add *init()* to **window.onload**, as shown in example 4-9.

12 Now when you load the Joke Generator in Chrome and press the "Get Joke" button, you will get a fresh Chuck Norris joke from the Internet Chuck Norris Database.

With the application working properly in Chrome, you can make any changes that you need to layout and styling while also being able to test the basic functionality. When you are ready to deploy the application on to a physical device, though, you should remove the additional *init()* function call from **window.onload**. Verify that it works on your testing device.

That data that we received from the Internet Chuck Norris Database was in JSON format. JSON stands for JavaScript Object Notation, and is a standard data interchange format that is intended to be both human readable and easy for machines to parse or generate. JSON is used very frequently in developing web applications, and if you are unfamiliar with it a brief but clear overview can be found online at *http://www.json.org*.

From the Internet Chuck Norris Database, we received a JSON file similar to the following:

```
{ "type": "success", "value": { "id": 268, "joke": "Time waits for no man.
Unless that man is Chuck Norris." } }
```

We could parse this data ourselves but we instead chose to use the jQuery JSON parser. To access the joke's text in our code, we assigned the parsed JSON to a variable named *json* and then used the following code:

```
json.value.joke
```

Comparing the preceding code to the JSON output from the Internet Chuck Norris Database, we can see how simple it is to use dot notation to access relevant data. For example, if we were interested in the joke's id number instead of its text, we would use:

```
json.value.id
```

At this point, you have a simple—hopefully entertaining—service-oriented mobile application. Wherever you go you can use your phone to see a random Chuck Norris joke provided by a remote server, the Internet Chuck Norris Database. When they update their jokes, you'll immediately have access to the new data without having to update your application.

This application demonstrates creating a service-oriented mobile application, however, the application itself could work just as well without needing to communicate with a server. The dataset of Chuck Norris jokes could be stored locally because it isn't very large, and the jokes are probably not going to be updated very frequently. It's worth considering those two conditions when determining how to architect your application.

In our example, we needed only a small piece of data—one single joke—from a small data set. The available jokes number in the hundreds, but even if there were thousands of Chuck Norris jokes, the database would still be small. If, on the other hand, we were displaying a random image from a database of hundreds of Chuck Norris images, the database would be so large that we would not want it included with the application. Pulling an image from a remote server as needed would be a better option.

Our example application pulls joke data from a data set that is not expected to change. Even if the dataset does change, those changes will be of trivial importance to most users. If the data instead needed to be up-to-date, like the weather, or needed to reflect changes immediately, like price fluctuations, then pulling it from a remote database would be required.

There are many other things to consider when designing service-oriented applications, including data speeds, data availability, data usage, security, and privacy. These potential concerns shouldn't put you off of creating feature rich, service-oriented applications, though. As we will see throughout this book, the availability of data connections on mobile devices and the ease of communication with remote servers allow us to create some truly interesting and useful applications.

In the next section, we will modify our Chuck Norris Joke Generator to send parameterized queries to the server, allowing us to request more specific data from the remote computer.

Questions for Review

1 What is service-oriented architecture?

    a. Designing an application that interacts with a server to retrieve data that is displayed to the user.

    b. Creating an application that works as a service rather than as a stand-alone program.

    c. Designing buildings that are intended to be used by the service industry.

    d. Creating server-side applications that push data to clients.

2 Which of the following ready state and status combinations means that your XMLHttpRequest is ready to process?

    a. readyState == 4 && status == 404

    b. readyState == 3 && status == 404

    c. readyState == 3 && status == 200

    d. readyState == 4 && status == 200

3 Why is JSON useful?

    a. It establishes communication between a client and a server.

    b. It provides a known, consistent format for data transfer.

    c. It is delicious and pairs well with Merlot.

    d. It is not useful.

4 When Chuck Norris does a push-up, he is actually pushing the Earth down.

    a. True.

    b. True.

4.2 Sending Queries to the Server

In the previous section, we created a Chuck Norris joke generator that displayed a random Chuck Norris joke returned from the Internet Chuck Norris Database. The application communicated with the database server using a freely available API. In this section, we will use another feature of the Internet Chuck Norris Database to generate a Chuck Norris joke with the name "Chuck Norris" replaced by another name.

In order to do this, we will communicate with a server using a parameterized query. A parameterized query is an AJAX request, like the GET request from the previous section, that includes parameters in order to obtain a more specific response. We will use parameters to pass a new first and last name to the server and then receive a customized joke. Parameterized queries are very useful, for example, a ZIP code could be passed to a weather application to get data for a specific location.

When using APIs to communicate with remote servers, it's important to understand what data the API is expecting and how it expects that data to be formatted. The first step to creating our updated joke generator is to examine the API documentation from the Internet Chuck Norris Database.

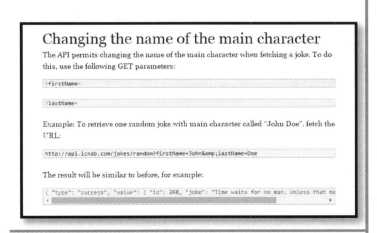

1 Go to *http://www.icndb. com/api/* to get to the Internet Chuck Norris Database API reference page. Scroll down until you see a section headed, "Changing the name of the main character," as shown in figure 4-3.

Figure 4-3: The API reference from the Internet Chuck Norris Joke Database.

2 The API reference informs us that the GET parameters "?firstName" and "?lastName" will allow us to change the name from "Chuck Norris" to whatever we choose. Those parameters are appended to the API's URL. They can be used individually, to change either the first name or the last name, or combined to change both the first name and the last name. Possible combinations are shown in example 4-10.

3 The API can be tested in your browser by navigating to the appropriate URL. The resulting JSON will be displayed in the browser window, as shown in figure 4-4.

Our code from the previous section uses that same API URL, without the parameters, to get a random Chuck Norris joke. If we were to modify the URL to include the parameters shown in example 4-10, then all of our Chuck Norris jokes would be John Doe jokes. To personalize the jokes, we will use user input with HTML and JavaScript to build the URL that queries the API.

```
►  http://api.icndb.com/jokes/
   random?firstName=John
►
►  http://api.icndb.com/jokes/
   random?lastName=Doe
►
►  http://api.icndb.com/jokes/
   random?firstName=John&lastName=Doe
```

Example 4-10: Possible modifications to a Chuck Norris joke. The first example will change the name to "John Norris," the second will change the name to "Chuck Doe," and the third will change the name to "John Doe."

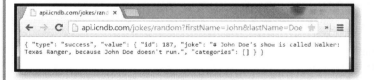

Figure 4-4: Replacing "Chuck Norris" with "John Doe."

```
function getJoke() {
    xmlhttp.open('GET',
'http://api.icndb.com/jokes/
random/?firstName=John&lastName=Doe',
true);
    xmlhttp.send();
}
```

Example 4-11: Changing main.js to request a "John Doe" joke instead of a "Chuck Norris" joke.

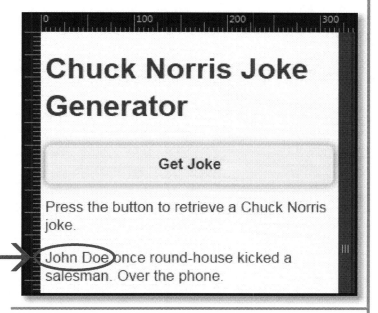

Example 4-12: Using the modified joke generator results in a different response from the API.

④ The code in this section will build on the application that we created in the previous section, so open up the Chuck Norris Joke Generator from section one.

⑤ First, modify the URL in main.js to request a John Doe joke instead of a Chuck Norris joke. Verifying that this works will ensure that you have a baseline functionality before doing more modifications. Example 4-11 shows the code and figure 4-12 shows example output.

The next step is to modify our HTML to include text input boxes. The user will enter text data into those boxes and we will use that data to build the URL.

In its current state, *xmlhttp. open()* includes the entire API target URL as a parameter, but it can just as easily take a string variable. Using JavaScript we will build that string variable from user-supplied data and then pass the string variable to *xmlhttp.open()* as a parameter.

6 Open the index.html file. First, add two text input boxes. We chose to put them below the app heading, but above the "Get Joke" button. People will read your page from top to bottom, so by placing the input boxes above the button that performs an action dependent on those input boxes, you can be more confident that a user will have already entered the required data. Example 4-13 shows the HTML code.

7 For the sake of consistency, some of the wording in the application should be changed. It is no longer strictly a Chuck Norris Joke Generator, now it is just a Joke Generator. A few changes result in application text that is more relevant.

The HTML for our updated Joke Generator is now complete. Return to main.js to make the appropriate changes to the remaining JavaScript code.

```html
<h1>Chuck Norris Joke Generator</h1>
<label for="firstName">First Name:</label>
<input id="firstName" type=text />
<label for="lastName">Last Name:</label>
<input id="lastName" />
<button id="btnGetJoke">Get Joke</button>
```

Example 4-13: The HTML in index.html creates text input boxes with the **ids** *firstName* and *lastName*.

```html
<div id="container">
    <h1>Joke Generator</h1>
    <label for="firstName">First Name:</label>
    <input id="firstName" type=text />
    <label for="lastName">Last Name:</label>
    <input id="lastName" />
    <button id="btnGetJoke">Get Joke</button>
    <p>Press the button to retrieve a joke.</p>
    <div id="joke">Here be the comedy!</div>
</div> <!-- container -->
```

Example 4-14: Modifying the verbiage in the HTML to be more appropriate.

▸ **8** Within the *getJoke()* function we will use the values entered into the *firstName* and *lastName* input boxes. Store the data from those DOM elements in string variables, as shown in example 4-15.

```
▸ var firstName = document.
  getElementById("firstName").value;
▸ var lastName = document.
  getElementById("lastName").value;
```

Example 4-15: Set up string variables for the values entered into the *firstName* and *lastName* text boxes.

9 The API target URL will be constructed as a string variable. The initial part of the URL will not change, so create a *jokeURL* string variable with the value "http://api.icndb.com/jokes/random/?firstName=" as shown in example 4-16.

```
▸ var jokeURL = 'http://api.icndb.com/
  jokes/random/?firstName=';
```

Example 4-16: Create a string variable to hold the API URL.

10 Build the *jokeURL* string by sequentially appending the appropriate data, as shown in example 4-17. The first operation returns *jokeURL* with the *firstName* parameter added, the second operation returns *jokeURL* with the *lastName* API syntax added, and the final operation returns the complete *jokeURL* with the *lastName* parameter added.

```
▸ jokeURL += firstName;
▸ jokeURL += '&lastName=';
▸ jokeURL += lastName;
```

Example 4-17: Using the known API syntax and the *firstName* and *lastName* string variables, generate the complete API URL.

11 Finally, pass *jokeURL* to *xmlhttp.open()* as the URL parameter, shown in example 4-17.

```
▸ xmlhttp.open('GET', jokeURL, true);
```

Example 4-18: Replace the hard-coded URL with the *jokeURL* string variable.

You do not need to modify any other aspect of the main.js file. The returned JSON data will be parsed and displayed in the same manner as before.

12 Once main.js is ready, test the new Joke Generator application. You should see that you can enter any name and return a random Chuck Norris joke, with Chuck Norris' name replaced!

This app requires user text input. Although you can test the basic functionality using Chrome's screen emulator, in order to test a mobile keyboard overlay you need to use either an actual device or a full device emulator. We have used a Google Nexus 7 in our tests.

It is important to consider how much of the screen will be obstructed by a mobile device's keyboard overlay. Figure 4-5 shows the app running on a Nexus 7. In this example, users can still clearly see the text input boxes and the labels that describe the input boxes, however, the "Get Joke" button is partially obscured by the keyboard.

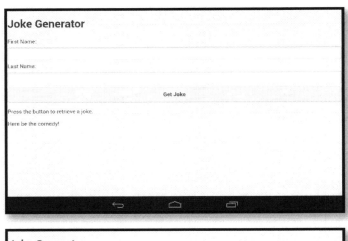

Figure 4-5: The application running on a Google Nexus 7.

Our Joke Generator application demonstrates the basic functionality of the major components of many mobile applications. The user requires certain data, a joke, that is determined by specific parameters, the first and last name. To get that data the user enters input into the *firstName* and *lastName* input boxes, and then requests a response by pressing the "Get Joke" button. The application then uses that data to communicate with a server—the Internet Chuck Norris Database—using a specific method—the API. That server takes the data and returns a response—the joke JSON—that the application parses and displays to the user.

You could replace the joke with movie times, the first and last names with movie theater locations and movie titles, the Internet Chuck Norris Database API with a movie time API, and "Get Joke" with "Get Movie Times" and create an application that returns when a movie is playing at a certain theater. Or you could replace the joke with a list of flight numbers, the first and last names with an airport code and a time range, the joke API with a flight information API, and "Get Joke" with "Get Flights" to create an application that returns a list of flights arriving at a certain airport at a certain time. Service-oriented architecture on mobile devices can give your users quick access to the information that they need, when they need it.

In the next section, we will learn how to parse XML data from a server by creating a simple (but useful) weather application.

Questions for Review

1 Using parameterized queries allows your application to do which of the following?

    a. Give the API provider user metrics.

    b. Request specific data from the server.

    c. Both A and B.

    d. None of the above.

2 What is the first place to look when determining how to use an API?

    a. Google.

    b. Stack Exchange.

    c. The API documentation.

    d. Bing.

3 The GET method of communication cannot use a string variable for its URL parameter.

    a. True.

    b. False.

4 When designing for mobile, what should you take into consideration?

    a. How much text you require a user to enter.

    b. What is obscured by the on-screen keyboard.

    c. How your layout appears across multiple devices.

    d. All of the above.

4.3 Parsing XML Data from the Server

In this chapter we have been communicating with a server that responds with data in the JSON format. We have parsed that data using the method available with jQuery. JSON is a widely used format, but it is not the only way that you will receive information from a server.

The method of communication that we have been using is called AJAX. AJAX stands for Asynchronous JavaScript and XML, and it is a set of web development techniques to create asynchronous web applications. XML, or Extensible Markup Language, is a simple and widely used method for encoding documents or other data.

XML documents are comprised of markup and content. Markup elements are the structural elements that define the document, and content is everything else. The XML tag, just like the HTML tag, defines a logical element within the document. Also like HTML tags, XML tags can have attributes.

As with the JSON joke data we received in the previous sections, XML data that is returned from an AJAX request will need to be parsed and then displayed for the user. In this section, we will create a simple application that will get the current weather in a specific ZIP code. The data will be returned to us as XML that we will parse using JavaScript.

1 Before we begin, look at the API that we will be using. It is available from *http://wiki.cdyne.com/index.php/CDYNE_Weather*, as shown in figure 4-6. Take a moment to read the description. We will be using the method that provides a city's current weather.

Figure 4-6: The CDYNE weather APIs wiki page.

2   Clicking on the link to "Testing URL" on the weather APIs wiki page brings up a list of the available operations, shown in figure 4-7. Select the "GetCityWeatherByZIP" option.

3   You will now see a list of valid parameters that you can test. In this case, there is only the ZIP parameter, shown in figure 4-8. If you scroll down, you will see request and response examples for the different communication methods. We will be using the HTTP GET request. The page shows a sample HTTP GET request, shown in example 4-19.

The data following "GET" is the address path to the API on the host, and the data following "Host:" is the host's web address. The API target URL would then be "http://wsf.cdyne.com/WeatherWS/Weather.asmx/GetCityWeatherByZIP?Zip=" The "string" text in the example is where you would insert the "ZIP" parameter value.

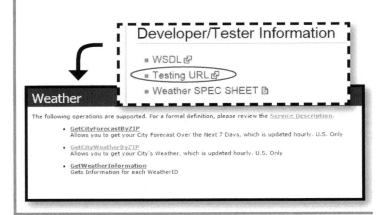

Figure 4-7: The Weather API list of available operations.

Weather

Click here for a complete list of operations.

GetCityWeatherByZIP

Allows you to get your City's Weather, which is updated hourly. U.S. Only

Test

To test the operation using the HTTP POST protocol, click the 'Invoke' button.

Parameter	Value
ZIP:	

    Invoke

Figure 4-8: The list of API parameters.

```
▸  GET /WeatherWS/Weather.asmx/
   GetCityWeatherByZIP?ZIP=string
   HTTP/1.1
▸  Host: wsf.cdyne.com
```

Example 4-19: The GetCityWeatherByZIP example GET request data.

```
This XML file does not appear to have any style information associated with it. The document
tree is shown below.

▼<WeatherReturn xmlns:xsi="http://www.w3.org/2001/XMLSchema-instance"
  xmlns:xsd="http://www.w3.org/2001/XMLSchema" xmlns="http://ws.cdyne.com/WeatherWS/">
    <Success>true</Success>
    <ResponseText>City Found</ResponseText>
    <State>CT</State>
    <City>Manchester</City>
    <WeatherStationCity>Hartford</WeatherStationCity>
    <WeatherID>14</WeatherID>
    <Description>Cloudy</Description>
    <Temperature>61</Temperature>
    <RelativeHumidity>81</RelativeHumidity>
    <Wind>N8</Wind>
    <Pressure>30.00S</Pressure>
    <Visibility/>
    <WindChill/>
    <Remarks/>
</WeatherReturn>
```

Figure 4-9: An example of the XML result from a GET request to the GetCityWeatherByZIP API.

4 Input a ZIP code into the ZIP parameter input box on the GetCityWeatherByZIP test page. The resulting page, shown in figure 4-9, is the XML that we will be parsing in our weather application. The markup tags will be the same, however the content values will vary depending on the ZIP code entered.

The XML data that you're looking at will form the basis of our application. When we read that data from the XML file, it will be according to the tag names. XML tag names, like HTML tag names, are not exclusive. Selecting elements by tag names will therefore result in arrays of elements. In the case of the weather data, each tag name happens to be unique and so, as you will see when we create the JavaScript code later, we can access the first member of the resulting arrays and be confident that we are accessing the appropriate data. It is important to note that this will not always be the case when you work with XML files.

Create a new PhoneGap application according to the template that we have been using, ensuring that the main.js file is correctly linked. If you have not already done so, it will save you time to create a bare-bones template project that you can copy and rename as needed. Give the new project an appropriate name — we have chosen to simply call it "WeatherApp."

Before we go further, it is important to note that in order to properly test this application you must run it either on a device or on a full emulator. The basic HTML layout can be tested in the Chrome emulator, as we have been doing, but the API requests must be made from a built PhoneGap application in order to function.

We will be testing this application on a Google Nexus 7 device, however, any functioning device or fully emulated device will work.

5 Open the index.html file and create a heading, "Get the Weather," a label and input box for the ZIP code, a "Get Weather Conditions" button, and an empty **<div>** element to store the result. This code is shown in example 4-21.

6 A very important note in this code is that the input type is set to "number," and not "text." With the number input type, a mobile device will launch a number pad for user input instead of a full keyboard. Usability details like this can have a substantial impact on user experience.

7 Open main.js. As with the Joke Generator, create a global variable named *xmlhttp* and have an *init()* function that is called when the device is ready. As you may recall, we know that the device is ready when the "deviceready" PhoneGap event occurs. Example 4-22 shows what the beginning of main.js should look like.

```
<div id="container">
<h1>Get The Weather</h1>
<label for="zip">ZIP Code:</label>
<input type="number" id="zip" />
<button id="btnGetForecast">Get
Weather Conditions</button>
<div id="result"></div>
</div> <!-- container -->
```

Example 4-20: The index.html code to create the user interface.

```
var xmlhttp;

window.onload = function () {
    document.
addEventListener("deviceready", init,
false);
};

function init() {

}
```

Example 4-21: The initial main.js.

8   Much of the code in this application will be familiar to you from the Joke Generator application, with only some details changed. The *init()* function needs to first add an event listener to the "Get Weather Conditions" button, and then initialize *xmlhttp* as an XMLHttpRequest object. For this project, the function called when the button is pressed will be named *getData*, and the function called when *xmlhttp* has a ready state change will be named *processResult()*. The code is shown in example 4-23.

```
function init() {
    document.
getElementById('btnGetForecast').
addEventListener('click', getData,
false);
    xmlhttp = new XMLHttpRequest();
    xmlhttp.onreadystatechange =
processResult;
}
```

Example 4-22: The *init()* function.

```
function getData() {
    var zip = document.
getElementById('zip').value;
    var url = 'http://wsf.cdyne.
com/WeatherWS/Weather.asmx/
GetCityWeatherByZIP?ZIP=';
    url += zip;
    xmlhttp.open('GET', url, true);
    xmlhttp.send();
}
```

Example 4-23: The *getData()* function.

9   Next, create the *getData()* function. This function will, again, be structured very similarly to the Joke Generator's *getJoke()* function. First, the ZIP code from the *zip* input box is stored into a variable. Next, the APIs GET request URL is stored into the *url* variable. Then, *zip* is appended to *url* to create the complete target URL. Finally, the AJAX GET request is built and sent to the API.

Next, we will parse the XML.

First, look at the XML returned from a request with the ZIP parameter "06040:"

```
<WeatherReturn xmlns:xsi="http://www.w3.org/2001/XMLSchema-instance"
xmlns:xsd="http://www.w3.org/2001/XMLSchema" xmlns="http://ws.cdyne.com/
WeatherWS/">
    <Success>true</Success>
    <ResponseText>City Found</ResponseText>
    <State>CT</State>
    <City>Manchester</City>
    <WeatherStationCity>Hartford</WeatherStationCity>
    <WeatherID>14</WeatherID>
    <Description>Cloudy</Description>
    <Temperature>61</Temperature>
    <RelativeHumidity>81</RelativeHumidity>
    <Wind>N8</Wind>
    <Pressure>30.00S</Pressure>
    <Visibility/>
    <WindChill/>
    <Remarks/>
</WeatherReturn>
```

This file contains all of the information that we are interested in but we need to know how to access it. The parent node of the XML file is <WeatherReturn> There are a number of child node elements, starting with <Success> and ending with <Remarks />. With the exception of <Visibility/>, <WindChill/>, and <Remarks/>, each of those elements has a single child node. It is the data contained in those child nodes, or their node value, that we are interested in.

When we access the response data it will be stored as a document element with a DOM that we can navigate. The document will be built from the parent node of the file. Thus, to access any particular piece of data we will first access the XML document, then the first element in the appropriate tag array, then that element's first child node, and finally that child node's value. Remember that tag names are not unique, so when navigating a DOM by tag values we are always working with arrays of elements.

If we stored the returned XML document element in the variable *theXML*, to access the wind value we would use the following code:

```
theXML.getElementsByTagName('Wind')[0].firstChild.nodeValue
```

The preceding code uses standard JavaScript DOM navigation syntax to obtain an array of elements with the tag name "Wind," then the first element of that zero-indexed array, then that element's first child node—a text node—and then the value of that child node, which is the text "N8." We will use this syntax in our code to access the data we intend to output to the user. To create that output, we will store the data that we access in string variables, and then we will use those string variables to create HTML. That HTML will be set as the inner HTML of the *result* <div> that we created in index.html.

```
function processResult() {
    if (xmlhttp.readyState==4 &&
xmlhttp.status==200) {
    }
}
```

Example 4-24: The *processResult()* function has a conditional that ensures that the client's ready state is four and the server's status is 200.

```
var city;
var state;
var temperature;
var relativeHumidity;
var description;
var wind;

var output = "Weather For: ";
```

Example 4-25: We will use string variables to store the XML response data, and then we will use those strings to build the output HTML.

10 In main.js, create the *processResult()* function. This function is processing the result of an AJAX request, so first we need to ensure that the request completed correctly. Verify the ready state and status, as shown in example 4-25.

11 Before we parse the XML, we will create the HTML output. Within the ready state and status conditional, create variables to hold the data we intend to collect: *city*, *state*, *temperature*, *relativeHumidity*, *description*, and *wind*. Also create a variable to hold the eventual output, *output*. This is shown in example 4-26.

12 Use those variables to build the HTML code that will be inserted into index.html. Once *output* is complete, get the *result* div and insert *output* as the **innerHTML** of *result*. This is shown in example 4-27.

13 Install and run the app on your test device now to verify the HTML layout. The variables that were used were never defined, so they will output as "undefined" in your HTML. That's fine for this app, but if you were creating a more precisely laid out application you could instead use appropriate test values. Figure 4-10 shows the current output on our test Nexus 7 device.

14 Now that the output layout works properly, we can begin to parse the XML. First, create a variable named *theXML* and set it to a document element of the XML response text, shown in example 4-28. As we mentioned earlier, this will create a document object model based on the root XML node that can then be navigated through using JavaScript.

```
var output = "Weather For: ";
output += city + ", " + state;
output += "<br />Temperature: " +
temperature;
output += "<br />Humidity: " +
relativeHumidity;
output += "<br />Description: " +
description;
output += "<br />Wind: " + wind;

document.getElementById("result").
innerHTML = output;
```

Example 4-26: Create the HTML that will display the output.

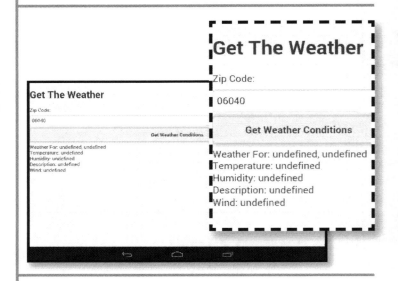

Figure 4-10: Verify that the output is formatted correctly.

```
var theXML = xmlhttp.responseXML.
documentElement;
```

Example 4-27: Set *theXML* as a document element from the response XML.

```
▸ var city = theXML.
  getElementsByTagName('City')[0].
  firstChild.nodeValue;
▸ var state = theXML.
  getElementsByTagName('State')[0].
  firstChild.nodeValue;
▸ var temperature = theXML.
  getElementsByTagName('Temperature')[0].
  firstChild.nodeValue;
▸ var relativeHumidity = theXML.
  getElementsByTagName('RelativeHumidity')
  [0].firstChild.nodeValue;
▸ var description = theXML.
  getElementsByTagName('Description')[0].
  firstChild.nodeValue;
▸ var wind = theXML.
  getElementsByTagName('Wind')[0].
  firstChild.nodeValue;
```

Example 4-28: Set the string variables to the appropriate XML data node values.

15 Now we can get elements from the *theXML* DOM as we would from the HTML DOM. Using the syntax we looked at earlier, update your JavaScript to set the values of the *city*, *state*, *temperature*, *relativeHumidity*, *description*, and *wind* variables to the appropriate node values from *theXML*, as shown in example 4-29.

16 We have already created and tested the HTML output, so run the program on your testing device. Input a few ZIP codes and verify that the application is correctly retrieving weather data from the remote server, as shown in figure 4-11.

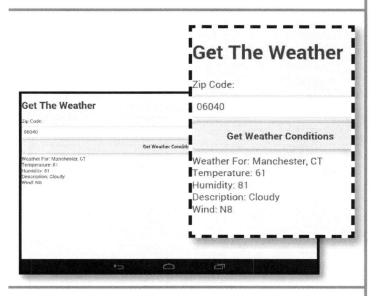

Figure 4-11: Now when we run the application it gives us the weather from the chosen ZIP code!

Congratulations, you've created an application that uses AJAX to retrieve XML data, and then you've parsed that XML data to display relevant information to the user!

As convenient as structured response data is, you can't always expect the servers your applications communicate with to send you easy-to-use information. XML is a broadly used standard, so being able to understand XML data and write JavaScript that correctly parses it will allow your applications to communicate with a wide variety of data sources. This will, in turn, increase the value of your application for your users.

In the next section we will take another look at JSON and parse JSON data for use in an application that retrieves airport travel data.

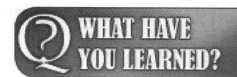

Questions for Review

1 What does XML stand for?

  a. Extraneous Markup Language.

  b. Extended Markup Language.

  c. Extensible Markup Language.

  d. Extended Marking Language.

2 What is AJAX used for?

  a. Communication between multiple client browsers over the internet.

  b. Communication between HTML and a server.

  c. Cleaning tough stains.

  d. Asynchronous communication between a browser and a server.

3 When XML response text is received, what is a method for parsing data from it?

  a. Convert the text to a string variable and use pattern matching to find specific information.

  b. Set the text to a document element and navigate its DOM using JavaScript.

  c. Either A or B.

  d. None of the above.

4 Very few people use XML anymore.

  a. True.

  b. False.

4.4 Parsing JSON Data from the Server

So far in this chapter we have used an individual JSON element that was returned from a server, and then we parsed a more complex XML document that contained multiple tags. In this section we will again work with JSON data, however, that data will contain multiple elements, each with key/value pairs of information that we want to display.

As we mentioned in section 4.1, JSON stands for JavaScript Object Notation. It is a popular, lightweight method of transferring data, based on key/value pairs, that is often used as an alternative to XML. JSON was originally developed for use with JavaScript, but it is actually language-independent. When developing service-oriented applications, you will need to parse the data that you receive from a server, so the decision whether to use JSON or XML will depend on your data source.

In the previous sections we dealt with a single data element that needed to be displayed. In this section, we will display information from multiple data elements. To do that, we will use arrays and loops to extract and display the relevant information. Our example application will communicate with the Southeastern Pennsylvania Transportation Authority and display upcoming train departures from the Philadelphia International Airport.

Before we create our app, we will look at our data source.

① First, view the data that we will be parsing. It can be found at *http://www3.septa.org/hackathon/ Arrivals/90404/10/*. Navigate to that website in your browser. You should see something similar to the screenshot in figure 4-12.

Figure 4-12: The JSON data we will parse.

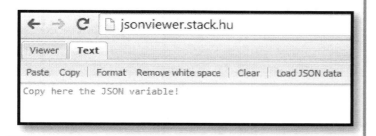

Figure 4-13: The JSON viewer tool.

Figure 4-14: Once loaded into the tool, the raw JSON is presented in a human-readable format.

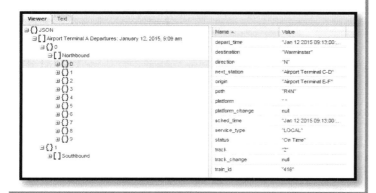

Figure 4-15: Navigating through the JSON is simple, and we are able to locate the information that we are interested in.

2 If you look at that jumble of text you'll notice that it shares many of the structural elements of the Chuck Norris joke JSON from section one, however, it is much more dense and complicated. Determining how to loop through this data from the raw information would be a challenge, but luckily there are tools to help. Copy the raw JSON to your clipboard and navigate to *http://jsonviewer.stack.hu/*, as shown in figure 4-13.

3 There are two tabs at the top of the page, "Viewer" and "Text." Ensure that "Text" is selected (it should be by default) and paste the raw JSON data into the textbox that says "Copy here the JSON variable." Once it's been pasted, navigate to the "Viewer" tab. You should see a menu tree as shown in figure 4-14.

4 Now, the JSON data is displayed in an easy to understand and navigate format! Expand the "Airport" item until you can select element "0" under "Northbound," as in figure 4-15.

Name ▲	Value
depart_time	"Jan 12 2015 12:43:00:...
destination	"West Trenton"
direction	"N"
next_station	null
origin	null
path	"R4/3N"
platform	" "
platform_change	null
sched_time	"Jan 12 2015 12:43:00:...
service_type	"LOCAL"
status	"On Time"
track	"2"
track_change	null
train_id	"4354"

Figure 4-16: The data for an individual train.

Once you're looking at the formatted JSON data, it's much easier to engineer our JavaScript to parse and display it appropriately. We will only concern ourselves with the variables *train_id*, *depart_time*, *destination*, *service_type*, and *status*. Figure 4-16 shows the returned data for an individual train.

5 Looking at this data's context in the visualized JSON, shown in figure 4-17, allows us to determine the variables we will need to define in our JavaScript code. The parent JSON element contains an array for the Airport Terminal. That array has two members, the elements "0" and "1." Each of those elements has an array as its single member, "Northbound" for "0" and "Southbound" for "1." Those arrays have ten members, each of which represents a train. The list of key/value pairs shown in figure 4-16 is the content of one of those train elements.

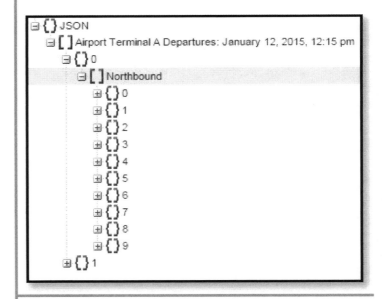

Figure 4-17: The location of train data within the JSON.

When we display the train data to the end user, we will organize it according to the direction of the trains, northbound or southbound. In order to display the individual train data we will use a table. Each train's data will be presented as a row on the table, so our goal will be to create the outline of a northbound train table, loop through every element in the JSON's *Northbound* array, create a table row for each element, and then close the table. Below that, similar code will create a second table for southbound trains.

As we have done in the previous application examples, we will first create the HTML and then the JavaScript. Create a new project based on the established template and name it "AirportInfo." We will need to edit index.html, main.js, and mainAppStyles.css, so ensure that all of those files are either open or readily accessible.

As with the previous example, this application will only work properly when it is run from either an actual mobile device, or a full emulator. It will not function properly if run from Chrome's built-in mobile screen emulator.

```html
<h2>SEPTA Airport Station</h2>
<button id="btnGetSchedule">Get Train
Schedule</button>
<div>Press the button to retrieve the
current train schedule.</div>
<div id="schedule"></div>
```

Example 4-29: The contents of our index.html.

6 First, in index.html's **<body>** element, create a heading, "SEPTA Airport Station," then a button to get the train schedule, brief instructions, and finally create an empty div with the id *schedule* as a target for our dynamically generated HTML. This code is shown in example 4-30.

7 Next, in mainAppStyles. css, add two simple tag styles for *odd* and *even*, as in example 4-31. We will use these styles when creating the result tables.

```css
.odd {
    background-color: #244fa1;
    color: white;
}
.even {
    background-color: #f1442a;
    color: white;
}
```

Example 4-30: An *odd* and *even* style for the tables.

8 You can test the layout in Chrome to ensure that the heading is a good size and that the elements are positioned as you like them. Once you are ready, open main.js. We will use jQuery to handle the AJAX in this example, so we do not need to create an *xmlhttp* variable. We will test for device readiness and create an *init()* function, as we have been doing. This is shown in example 4-32.

9 Touching *btnGetSchedule* calls *getSchedule()*, so we will create that now. This is where we will create the AJAX request using jQuery. Example 4-33 demonstrates this, with a successful AJAX response resulting in calling the *parseJSON()* function. Notice that we pass the result of the AJAX to *parseJSON()*. Once this is complete, more jQuery ensures that the content of the *schedule* **<div>** is empty.

The *parseJSON()* function will do the heavy lifting. In the function, we will organize the response JSON and then loop through all of the train data in order to build our response HTML.

```
window.onload = function () {
    document.
addEventListener("deviceready", init,
false);
};

function init() {
    document.
getElementById('btnGetSchedule').
addEventListener('click', getSchedule,
false);
}
```

Example 4-31: When the window loads, verify that the device is ready and then launch the *init()* function. Within *init()*, create an event listener for our button.

```
function getSchedule() {
    $.ajax({url:"http://www3.septa.
org/hackathon/Arrivals/90404/10/",
            success: function(result){
                parseJSON(result);
            }});
    $("#schedule").html("");
}
```

Example 4-32: The AJAX GET request simplifies the traditional JavaScript AJAX syntax.

```
function parseJSON(result) {
    var output = "<h3>Northbound</
h3>";
    output += "<table>";
    output += "<tr
class='odd'><th>Train #</th><th>Time</
th><th>Destination</th><th>Service</
th><th>Status</th></tr>"
```

Example 4-33: The *parseJSON()* function begins by setting up our HTML output.

```
var data = jQuery.parseJSON(result);
var arr = data[Object.keys(data)];
var northbound = arr[0].Northbound;
```

Example 4-34: Setting up the returned JSON data for use within the *parseJSON()* function.

```
for(var x = 0; x < northbound.length;
x++)
    {
    }
```

Example 4-35: A loop skeleton that will iterate through all of the elements in *northbound*. Each element contains key/value pairs of information about a specific train.

10 Create the *parseJSON()* function. It will take one argument—*result*—which is the response JSON from the AJAX request. In the function first create an *output* variable and populated it with the header for the northbound train table, and the beginning HTML for that table. This is shown in example 4-34. Notice how we have labeled the columns. This will be the order of the data when we build each row.

11 Next, we will create some variables. Our first variable, *data*, will hold the result of jQuery's **parseJSON()**. This will return the JavaScript value of a JSON string. Next, we assign *arr* to be an array of the elements within *data*. Finally, we know from our JSON visualizer that the first element in *arr* will contain a key, *Northbound*, with a value of an array of train elements, so we set the value of *northbound* to that array. This is shown in example 4-35.

12 Now *northbound* contains all of the northbound train elements. Begin looping through them as shown in example 4-36.

13 The loop from step 12 will loop through every element in *northbound*. The body of that loop, shown in example 4-37, will build one row of the output table. First, an if/else conditional uses the modulus operator to determine if a given row is even or odd, and styles it accordingly. After that, we simply set variables for each value we are interested in using to the element's key/value pairs. Refer to the JSON visualizer to determine the appropriate keys. Once that is done, we complete the table row HTML.

You've probably noticed that we used a substring of the time value returned from the JSON. This is because the JSON time value includes much more data than we need.

14 Outside of the loop, end the initial table by appending a closing **<table>** tag to *output*, as shown in example 4-38.

Much of the remaining code simply repeats what was done above, for northbound train data, with southbound train data.

```
if((x%2 == 0))
{
    output += "<tr class='even'>";
} else
{
    output += "<tr class='odd'>";
}
var trainID = northbound[x].train_id;
var destination = northbound[x].
destination;
var service = northbound[x].service_
type;
var status = northbound[x].status;
var time = northbound[x].depart_time;
time = time.substring(11, 17);
output += "<td>" + trainID + "</
td><td>" + time + "</td><td>" +
destination + "</td>";
output += "<td>" + service + "</
td><td>" + status + "</td>";
output += "</tr>";
```

Example 4-36: Within the loop from step 12 and code example4-36, build each row for the northbound train table.

```
output += "</table>";
```

Example 4-37: Outside of the loop, end the table.

```
▶  var southbound = arr[1].Southbound;
▶  output += "<h3>Southbound</h3>";
▶  output += "<table>";
▶  output += "<tr class='odd'><th>Train
   #</th><th>Time</th><th>Destination</
   th><th>Service</th><th>Status</th></
   tr>"
▶
▶  for(var x = 0; x < southbound.length;
   x++)
▶  {
▶      if((x%2 == 0))
▶      {
▶              output += "<tr
   class='even'>";
▶      } else
▶      {
▶              output += "<tr
   class='odd'>";
▶      }
▶      var trainID = southbound[x].train_
   id;
▶      var destinatoin = southbound[x].
   destination;
▶      var service = southbound[x].
   service_type;
▶      var status = southbound[x].status;
▶      var time = southbound[x].depart_
   time;
▶      time = time.substring(11, 17);
▶      output += "<td>" + trainID + "</
   td><td>" + time + "</td><td>" +
   destination + "</td>";
▶      output += "<td>" + service + "</
   td><td>" + status + "</td>";
▶      output += "</tr>";
▶  }
▶  output += "</table>";
```

Example 4-38: The code for creating the southbound train table is very similar to the code for creating the northbound train table.

15 Set *southbound* to the array of southbound train elements, as we did with *northbound*.

16 Begin the table using the same column names as in the *northbound* table.

17 Loop through each element in *southbound*.

18 Have each loop iteration create a table row that consists of the data for each southbound train. Ensure that even and odd rows are styled appropriately.

19 Once the loop is complete, end the table.

The code for the southbound train table is shown in example 4-39. Now that the HTML for the tables is complete and stored in *output*, we can set the inner HTML of the *schedule* **<div>** to *output* in order to display our train information.

```
$("#schedule").html(output);
```

Example 4-39: Set the *schedule* <div> to the value of *output*.

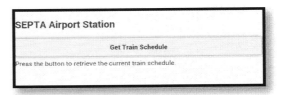

Figure 4-18: The app running on a test device.

20 End *parseJSON()* by setting the HTML of *schedule* to *output*, as shown in example 4-40.

21 The application is complete! Build it and run it on a device or device emulator. When the application loads, the initial screen has a title, a "Get Train Schedule" button, and simple instructions, as seen in figure 4-18.

22 When the user presses the "Get Train Schedule" button, the next trains departing from both northbound and southbound platforms are displayed, as shown in figure 4-19.

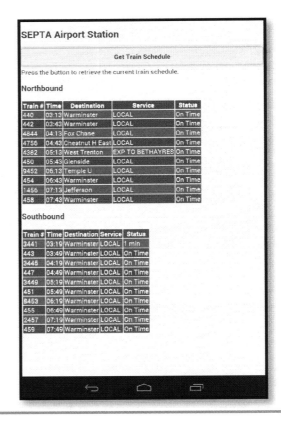

Figure 4-19: Data successfully retrieved and displayed in formatted tables.

Now the complete app will query the Southeastern Pennsylvania Transportation Authority about the trains coming out of the Philadelphia International Airport, retrieve the resulting JSON data, parse it, and display it to the user in a friendly, easy to read set of tables. Anyone who is familiar with SEPTA may also notice that the colors we chose for the table rows are not random, they are the colors of the SEPTA logo. Congratulations! Next time you're in Philadelphia, you'll be able to check up on the train times.

More importantly you now understand how to take a larger set of data, store it in array elements, and loop through those arrays to retrieve the information that you're looking for. In this section we used JSON and jQuery, but the same techniques work with XML data or traditional JavaScript. The output data could be further refined—for example, in the *parseJSON()* function you could have created rows for trains with certain destinations only, or that are leaving within a certain range of times.

Questions for Review

1 What does JSON stand for?

a. JavaScript Simple Object Notation.

b. JavaScript Special Object Notation .

c. JavaScript Object Notation.

d. jQuery Simple Object Notation.

2 How are JSON objects structured?

a. As an array of strings.

b. As key/value pairs.

c. As database tables.

d. There is no set structure.

3 Using jQuery to parse JSON data is not possible.

a. True.

b. False.

4 Which of the following is a good technique to better understand the JSON responses from an API?

a. Contact the API developer for clarification.

b. Use a JSON visualizer.

c. Print it out and use scissors and glue to create a JSON collage.

d. Post a question to an online forum like Stack Exchange.

CHAPTER 04 LAB EXERCISE

There is a huge variety of data sources available to application developers. For this exercise, you are going to use alternative fuel station location data provided freely by the US Federal Government. The API address is located at: *https://api.data.gov/nrel/alt-fuel-stations/v1/nearest.json?*

The parameters for this API are "api_key" and "location." For "api_key" you can either sign up for an API Key at *https://api.data.gov* or enter the value "DEMO_KEY." The "location" parameter can take a variety of different location types, but for this exercise use a ZIP Code.

1 Create a UI that asks the user to enter a ZIP Code. Don't worry about validation at this point, although if you were planning on deploying an app like this you would need to validate that a proper ZIP code was entered.

2 In JavaScript, set up an XMLHttpRequest object to communicate with the API using AJAX.

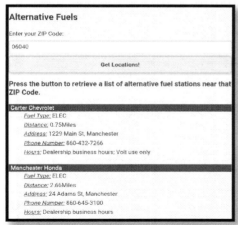

3 Using the data entered by the user, build a connection string to communicate with the API using AJAX. The response will be in JSON.

4 Parse the JSON and display the results to the user in a clear, easy-to-read format. Only show stations that are open to the public. Ensure that you display at least the station's name, its distance from the input ZIP Code, the type of fuel it provides, contact information, and hours of operation.

Chapter Summary

In this chapter, you worked with one of the most fundamental aspects of mobile application development: communicating with a server. The ubiquity of mobile devices means that people now have access to the information they need, when they need it. It's usually impractical and often impossible to store that information locally, so for most mobile applications to be useful they must communicate with a remote server. Understanding how to facilitate that communication—and being able to create code that can handle the most common methods of communication, XML and JSON—is integral to the development of mobile applications.

You have now moved from dealing with a single, simple, JSON response, to requesting a specific response using queries, to parsing a large XML response, and finally to parsing a large, complex JSON response. You've also learned about using AJAX with JavaScript and jQuery.

In order to work with more complicated data sets you can expand on the techniques that you have used in this chapter.

In the next chapter, we will discuss how to create an application that will store data, both locally and on a server.

Storing Data

CHAPTER OBJECTIVES:

- You will learn how to use Web Storage to store data locally.

- You will understand how remote data storage functions on a server.

5.1 Storing Data with store.js

HTML was not initially designed to be able to store information. As the web developed and the technology that powers it evolved, the use of web applications became more widespread. More advanced applications required that information be stored locally, so a variety of methods were developed to facilitate persistent local storage. The problem with the methods was that they came from a variety of sources, were specific to individual browsers, or they required additional third-party plug-ins.

With HTML5, the problem of persistent local storage was solved using the Web Storage specification. All modern browsers support it, including mobile browsers. Web Storage is persistent across page loads, web navigation, and browser loads, and it is never transmitted to any remote servers. The data stored using Web Storage is saved as named key/value pairs.

There are limitations to Web Storage. Because Web Storage is based on a browser, it is not persistent for a web application used across different browsers on the same device. Similarly, the data will not persist if a browser is deleted and reinstalled. The data stored as key/value pairs is stored as a string type, meaning that numeric types will be converted to a string when stored with Web Storage. There is also a 5 MB limit for web application data stored as Web Storage. It is important to keep these limitations in mind when using Web Storage. A floating point number that is converted from a float to a string for use with Web Storage, for example, will require a different amount of memory.

Despite these limitations, Web Storage is a very useful tool for PhoneGap applications. Although the data is stored by a web browser it is not affected by the user clearing their web cache or history, and it will persist across application updates. Web Storage is a solid solution to storing user options or application preferences.

Web Storage is built in to HTML5, but rather than using vanilla JavaScript we will use a library called store.js. store.js was created by Marcus Westin and simplifies the implementation of Web Storage.

store.js can be found at https://github.com/marcuswestin/store.js. Download the store.min.js file. You will save it in the project's "js/" folder.

Create a new, empty PhoneGap application template named MusicList. The MusicList project will have users enter an artist and song title, and it will store that information locally. When requested, the user can output a list of the artist and song titles that they had previously entered into the application.

Ensure that store.min.js is saved in the project's "www/js/" folder. The "www/js/" folder should contain main.js, and store.min.js.

```
▸  <head>
▸  ...
▸      <script src="js/store.min.js"></
   script>
▸      <script src="js/main.js"></script>
▸  ...
▸  </head>
```

Example 5-1: Link to the store.min.js file.

1 First, in index.html, link to store.min.js. In example 5-1 we have placed the link before the link to our main.js file.

2 Next, create the HTML for the user interface. This HTML will be in the **<body>** element, within the *container* **<div>** that we have been using. The content will need a heading with an appropriate title, an input box with a label for the artist, an input box with a label for the song title, and three buttons. One will add a song to the list, one will display the list, and one will clear the list. Finally, create an empty **<div>** named *listArea* to contain the output list. This HTML is shown in example 5-2.

```
▸  <div id="container">
▸  <h1>My Favorite Songs</h1>
▸  <label for="artist">Artist</label>
▸  <input type="text" id="artist" />
▸  <label for="song">Song</label>
▸  <input type="text" id="song" />
▸  <button id="btnAdd">Add To List</
   button>
▸  <button id="btnDisplay">Display List</
   button>
▸  <button id="btnClear">Clear List</
   button>
▸  <div id="listArea"></div>
▸  </div> <!-- container -->
```

Example 5-2: The user interface HTML for MusicList.

3 The HTML is complete. As with the SEPTA Airport trains application that we built in the previous chapter, the MusicList application will output a table. Like before, we will style the even and odd rows of the table differently. In mainAppStyles. css, add the table rules shown in example 5-3. We have used the **border-collapse** property for style and readability.

4 All that is left to do now is to craft the JavaScript that will power the application. Following the same pattern that we have through the book, in main.js, test that the device is ready by adding an event listener to the document using **window.onload**. If the device is ready, run an *init()* function. That function should initialize the three buttons that we have created. This code is shown in example 5-4.

If you are testing on Chrome, the "deviceready" event will never fire, so we have added a call to *init()*. If you are testing this application on a device and not on the Chrome emulator, comment-out the call to *init()*.

```css
.odd {
    background-color: #ccc;
}
.even {
    background-color: #aaa;
}
table {
    width: 100%;
    border-collapse: collapse;
}
th, td {
    padding: 5px;
    border: 1px solid black;
}
```

Example 5-3: The CSS to style the eventual output table.

```javascript
window.onload= function() {
    document.
addEventListener('deviceready', init,
false);
    init();
}

function init() {
    document.getElementById('btnAdd').
addEventListener('click', addSong,
false);
    document.
getElementById('btnDisplay').
addEventListener('click', displayList,
false);
    document.
getElementById('btnClear').
addEventListener('click', clearList,
false);
}
```

Example 5-4: Initialize the button event listeners.

```
▸   function addSong()
▸   {
▸   }
▸
▸   function displayList()
▸   {
▸   }
▸
▸   function clearList()
▸   {
▸   }
```

Example 5-5: The three empty functions.

```
▸   function addSong()
▸   {
▸       var artist = document.
    getElementById('artist');
▸       var song = document.
    getElementById('song');
▸
▸       store.set(song.value, artist.
    value);
▸
▸       artist.value = "";
▸       song.value = "";
▸   }
```

Example 5-6: The addSong() function adds a song and artist to the persistent local storage.

5   The three buttons call three separate functions, addSong(), displayList(), and clearList(). Create those functions now, as shown in example 5-5.

6   First, we will create addSong(), shown in example 5-6. This will set the variables, artist and song, to the artist and song <input> elements from index.html. Note that we are not setting it to the value of those elements, but rather to the elements themselves. Once the values are stored, use the **store.set()** function from store.js to store song.value and artist.value. These values are now stored as a key/value pair with song.value as the key and artist.value as the value.

In a key/value pair, the key has to be unique. An artist may have multiple songs so the artist name is not unique and so cannot be the key.

7   The final two lines of the addSong() function reset the values of the artist and song <input> elements so the user can enter more data.

8   Example 5-7 demonstrates the *displayList()* function used to display our saved data. First, we will create a boolean variable, *oddRow*, set to "False." It might seem counterintuitive to initialize *oddRow* as "False" because row one will be an odd number, but remember that *oddRow* will be tested for the first row that is dynamically created, not the first row that is printed.

9   Next, create *output,* a string to hold the HTML code to be inserted into the *listArea* **<div>**. The HTML will be a table with the first row having the column headings, "Artist" and "Song."

10   Next, loop through the stored data. We have used the store.js **forEach** loop to iterate through every element in *store*. It sets the key/value pair's key to *key* and value to *val*, and then runs a function that creates either an odd or even table row. That row is appended to *output* and the value of *oddRow* is reversed.

11   Finally, after the loop is finished, append a close **<table>** tag to *output*, and set the inner HTML of the *listArea* **<div>** to *output*.

```javascript
function displayList()
{
    var oddRow = false;
    var output = "<table>"
    output += "<tr
class='odd'><td>Artist</td><td>Song</
td></tr>"
    store.forEach(function(key, val) {
        if(oddRow)
        {
            output += "<tr
class='odd'><td>" + val + "</td><td>"
+ key + "</td></tr>";
        } else
        {
            output += "<tr
class='even'><td>" + val + "</td><td>"
+ key + "</td></tr>";
        }
        oddRow = !oddRow;
    });
    output += "</table>";
    document.
getElementById('listArea').innerHTML =
output;
}
```

Example 5-7: *displayList()* uses a **forEach()** loop to iterate through all of the data saved in the persistent local storage.

```
function clearList()
{
    document.
getElementById('listArea').innerHTML =
"";
    store.clear();
}
```

Example 5-8: *clearList()* clears both the persistent local storage and the <div> element that displayed the list output.

12 The final function, *clearList()*, sets the inner HTML of the *listArea* **<div>** to an empty string and uses the **store.clear()** function to remove all values from the persistent local storage, as shown in example 5-8.

13 Load the complete application on either a Chrome emulator or mobile device. You can enter text, save it to the persistent local storage, and then display it in a well formatted table, as shown in figure 5-1.

Close the application, reopen it and click the "Display List" button. You'll see that it will retain the information until you explicitly instruct the application to clear the data.

Figure 5-1: The MusicList application creates a list of artists and song names.

In this section you've created a simple application that uses persistent local storage to retain user-entered information. By leveraging the functions of HTML5 to store simple user data, Web Storage avoids hardware-specific storage implementations and does not require additional permissions from the user. We have shown how to use this feature by storing a list of artists and songs, however there are a number of other potential uses.

In the previous chapter we discussed receiving and parsing JSON. JSON objects can be represented as simple strings, so Web Storage could be used to store JSON objects that you do not expect to change very often, or that you want the user to have access to while offline.

It is also worth noting that there are other storage solutions available for mobile applications created with PhoneGap, but they vary depending on the target platform. WebSQL, a flavor of SQL, is available on Android and iOS devices but not on Windows Phones or Firefox OS powered devices. IndexedDB is available for Windows Phones and Firefox OS devices, but not iOS or Android.

In the next section we will look at using PhoneGap to store data on a server, rather than on the local device.

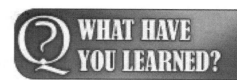

Questions for Review

1 What is the size limit for persistent local storage using Web Storage?

   a. 640kB

   b. 10MB

   c. 5MB

   d. There is no limit.

2 Data stored using Web Storage persists across which of the following scenarios? Select all that apply.

   a. Page refresh.

   b. Browser/Application restart.

   c. Browser/Application uninstallation and reinstallation.

   d. Application update.

3 Why is it possible to store JSON objects with Web Storage?

   a. Web Storage saves data in JSON format.

   b. JSON objects can be represented as simple strings, those strings can be stored by Web Storage.

   c. JSON objects are simple strings.

   d. It is not possible to store JSON objects with Web Storage.

4 Using Web Storage on a mobile requires special permissions.

   a. True.

   b. False.

5.2 Storing Data on a Server

In the previous section we learned how to use Web Storage for persistent local storage on a device. In this section, we will look at a simple method of storing data on a server.

One of the prerequisites to storing data on a server is having access to a server. Historically, supporting a large number of users with back end servers would have been a difficult and expensive proposition, but today there are many server options available to application developers, like Amazon Web Services' (AWS) Simple Storage Service. For testing purposes, however, you can use a server that you are already running or you can set up a local web server.

If you aren't already running a test web server or you do not currently have a local server set up on your development machine, one of the easiest ways to set up a testing environment is using an AMP application stack. AMP stands for Apache, MySQL, and PHP. You can set up all of the services individually, but there are software bundles that are designed to streamline the process. For example, Windows users can install the freely available WampServer software and have a local web server up and running in minutes. A good resource to find the appropriate software bundles is Wikipedia's list of AMP packages, at *http://en.wikipedia.org/wiki/List_of_Apache-MySQL-PHP_packages*. It's important to note, however, that some available packages are specifically intended for testing purposes, and as such may not be appropriate for a release server.

When you have your testing server set up, make a note of its IP address. On Windows, use the command "**ipconfig**" and look for the "IPv4 Address." On Linux or Mac, use the command "**ifconfig**" and look for the "inet addr" entry that is not the Local Loopback.

It's important to note the IP address of the test server—even if it is the development machine—because when you test your application on a device, real or virtual, that device will no longer be able to use "http://localhost" to access your local server. When testing, your testing device must be connected to the same local network as your test server. If your test device is a mobile phone, for example, verify that it is connected to your Wi-Fi network and not your data provider's mobile network to ensure that it communicates with the appropriate test server.

With the test server up and running it is time to prepare a simple PHP file to receive and store test data. PHP is a free, widely used server scripting tool that powers a substantial amount of webpages. The PHP file that we create should be placed in the "/www" directory of the test server that you have set up. We have placed it in the root directory as "/www/get_test.php," but it can be placed in a subdirectory, such as "/www/php/get_test.php."

PHP files can be edited in Brackets in the same manner as HTML, CSS, and JS files.

```php
<?php
    header('Access-Control-Allow-
Origin: *');

    $file = fopen("bands.csv", "w");
    fputcsv($file, $_REQUEST);
    fclose($file);

    echo "Data written: [" . implode(",
", $_REQUEST) . "]";
?>
```

Example 5-9: A brief sample PHP server script that will store information remotely.

1 Create the "get_test.php" file in the "/www" folder of your test web server and open it in your text editor.

2 Example 5-9 shows the entire PHP file. Without going into too much detail, it contains opening and closing tags, a header to allow access from all origins (important if you intend to test the application from Chrome before you install it on a device), and code that writes the information in $_REQUEST to the file "bands.csv." It then responds with the text "Data Written." The variable $_REQUEST is an associative array of the contents of the URL query string that we will create in JavaScript.

The PHP file that we just created is very basic and is for example purposes only. It will take the data in the $_REQUEST array and turn it into a CSV file. CSV files store tabular data as plain text, with a special character separating each value. There is no official standard for the CSV file, though there is a *de facto* standard and the format is widely supported. You will be able to open the bands.csv file that is produced by the PHP as a spreadsheet with Excel, or as a plain text file with any text editor. You can even open it in Brackets.

The simplest way to test your PHP file is to simply open it in a web browser with a query string appended to the URL. The PHP does not parse the URL's query string before it inserts it directly into bands.csv, so any valid query string will result in bands.csv being written.

Enter "http://localhost/get_test.php?query=test&query2=test2" into your browser. You should see the response text, "Data written: [test, test2]," in the browser window. Open bands.csv in Brackets or your text editor of choice, and it should contain the plain text data, "text,text2."

The simple PHP works! While this server script would never be sufficient for a production environment, it is enough to demonstrate how to save user data from an HTML5 mobile application.

3 Now we will create our PhoneGap project. As we have been doing, start a new project from the standard template and name it ServerData. Prepare index.html and main.js for editing.

4 In index.html, create a header and input fields and labels for *song, band, year*, and *rating*. Finally, create a "Send Data" button and an empty *response* **<div>**. Your HTML should look similar to example 5-10.

```
<h1>Song Data</h1>
<label for="song">Song</label>
<input type="text" id="song" />
<label for="band">Band</label>
<input type="text" id="band" />
<label for="year">Year</label>
<input type="text" id="year" />
<label for="rating">Rating</label>
<input type="text" id="rating" />
<button id="btnSendData">Send Data</button>
<div id="response"></div>
```

Example 5-10: The HTML code for our server data testing application.

```
var xmlhttp;

window.onload= function()
{
    document.
addEventListener('deviceready', init,
false);
    init();
}

function init()
{
    document.
getElementById("btnSendData").
addEventListener('click', sendData,
true);
}
```

Example 5-11: In main.js verify that the device is ready and create an *init()* function.

```
xmlhttp = new XMLHttpRequest;
xmlhttp.onreadystatechange =
function() {
    if (xmlhttp.readyState == 4 &&
xmlhttp.status == 200)
    {
        document.
getElementById("response").innerHTML =
xmlhttp.responseText;
    }
};
```

Example 5-12: Within *init()* prepare the *xmlhttp* variable as an **XMLHttpRequest** object and set its **onreadystatechange** property.

Now, open your main.js file. In this file, we will be creating a URL with a query string appended to it, like we did when creating the demonstration apps in chapter four. Also like those demonstration apps, we will be using AJAX to communicate.

5 Create an *xmlhttp* variable, verify that the device is ready, and create an *init()* function. This process will likely be familiar to you now. The code is shown in example 5-11.

6 Within the *init()* function, prepare *xmlhttp* for use by initializing it as an **XMLHttpRequest** object and set its **onreadystatechange** property to a function that will set the inner HTML of the *response* **<div>** to the response text of the AJAX request, as shown in example 5-12. The response text will be the text that our PHP script outputs to the browser window when it is run. Note that we have used "responseText" instead of "responseXML" because the data that is being returned is plain text, not XML or JSON data.

```
function sendData()
{
    var song = document.
getElementById("song").value;
    var band = document.
getElementById("band").value;
    var year = document.
getElementById("year").value;
    var rating = document.
getElementById("rating").value;

    var url = "http://192.168.0.109/
get_test.php?song=" + song + "&band="
+ band + "&year=" + year + "&rating="
+ rating;
    xmlhttp.open("GET", url, true);
    xmlhttp.send();
}
```

Example 5-13: The *sendData()* function builds a URL and uses it in a GET request to communicate with the PHP script on the test server.

7 The event listener added to *btnSendData* calls the *sendData()* function. Example 5-13 shows that function. It creates a set of variables, *song*, *band*, *year*, and *rating*, from the values input by the user in the application. Note that it does not do any validation of the user input data.

8 Once the variables have been set up, a *url* variable is created using the location of our get_test.php file. The query string is built from the user data that was stored in step 7, and sent with AJAX. Note that the IP address in *url* must reflect the IP address of the test server that is hosting get_test.php.

9 The application can be tested either in Chrome or on a device. It will accept user input information about a song, send that data to a server, and then save that information on a server. In figure 5-2 song information has been entered and the server has responded with "Data Written: " followed by the song information.

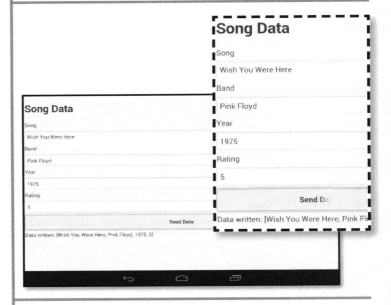

Figure 5-2: The application running on a mobile device communicates with the test server.

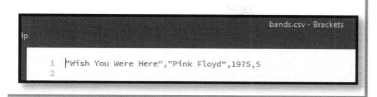

Figure 5-3: The CSV file in Brackets.

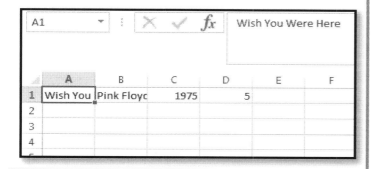

Figure 5-4: The same CSV file in Excel.

10 After testing the application and verifying that the server has responded, you can open the bands.csv file to verify that data was written to it correctly. Opening the file up in brackets will show a plain text, comma separated list, as in figure 5-3. The file can also be opened as a spreadsheet, shown in Excel in figure 5-4.

This set up—server side PHP and client side JavaScript—is a simple way to demonstrate saving user data on a server. The resulting file could be further processed on the server, or it could simply be stored for later retrieval by the end user, or data stored in persistent local storage could be backed up on the server in case the user suffers client side data loss.

In a production environment both the PHP and JavaScript would be more robust to ensure data security and integrity, but the core concept remains the same.

Questions for Review

1 Which of the following is required to use server storage?

    a. An official server license.

    b. A degree in computer science.

    c. A server.

    d. A hosting plan provided by Google, Apple, or Amazon.

2 What is PHP?

    a. A website scripting language usually used for client-side applications.

    b. A commonly used server-side scripting language.

    c. A network encryption protocol.

    d. A low level programming language like C++ or Java.

3 Who maintains the CSV standardization format?

    a. The W3C.

    b. The International Organization for Standardization.

    c. There is no official CSV standard.

    d. Microsoft

4 Once data is stored on a server, it is immutable.

    a. True.

    b. False

CHAPTER 05 LAB EXERCISE

In this exercise we will modify the exercise from chapter four. Ensure that the exercise code is working as intended before beginning this lab.

In this lab you will give your user the option of storing the data that was returned from the remote API in their local Web Storage using store.js. When the application runs, locally stored data will be available for the user to load, or they can request new data from the remote server.

1 Ensure that all of the required files are linked in your index.html.

2 Modify the UI to include a "Save Results" button at the bottom of a set of search results.

3 Display a "Load Results" button in two circumstances—if there is a saved location when the application loads, and after the user saves a location.

4 When "Load Results" is pressed, load the previously saved data in the same manner as server data.

Note that store.js will automatically parse a string into JSON when the **get()** method is called and it will automatically stringify JSON when the **set()** method is called.

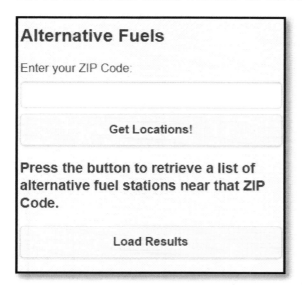

Chapter Summary

In this chapter we have learned a few techniques to store user data. You have stored data locally, using Store.js, and you have learned the basics of storing data remotely on a server. These techniques will allow you to store user data using PhoneGap, but they will also work when designing any HTML5-enabled web app.

In the next chapter we will look into using HTML5 to play media using the W3C standards and a PhoneGap-specific implementation.

Audio and Video

CHAPTER OBJECTIVES:

- You will understand how the HTML5 audio and video standards work.

- You will learn how to use JavaScript to control HTML5 audio and video elements.

- You will learn how to use PhoneGap's media object to create a cross-platform compatible audio application.

- You will use PhoneGap plug-ins to access the hardware camera of a mobile device.

6.1 Playing Audio and Video

Images have been an integral part of websites and website design for a very long time, but integrated audio and video has only become prevalent relatively recently. With the amount of bandwidth available to many consumers today, streaming audio and video is now common. HTML5 introduced a standardized method of including video and audio with webpages and web apps.

PhoneGap supports the HTML5 audio and video standards, allowing you to easily utilize audio and video in your application. Using audio and video in HTML5 is remarkably simple—there is an **<audio>** tag and a **<video>** tag—but there are a few important points to mention before we create a demonstration.

If you're building an application that showcases media that you've created, then you're probably well aware of the rabbit hole that is container formats, audio encoding, and video encoding. If not, then the very short explanation is that the video files we are accustomed to using, such as MP4, are containers for encoded audio and video files. Media compatibility is based on the type of container file and the encoding formats of the contained audio and video files. There is no single combination of container, audio format, and video format that is natively compatible with all popular web browsers and mobile devices.

In order to create multi-platform media for your application you will need a video converter, such as the free Miro Video Converter at *http://www.mirovideoconverter. com*. The HTML5 **<audio>** and **<video>** tags allow for multiple media source files. The browser will play the first compatible file.

To demonstrate media playback in PhoneGap, let's create a simple example app. Create a new PhoneGap project based on our template and call it AudioVideo.

1   First, we'll play an audio file. Find an audio file, such as an MP3, and place it an "/ assets" folder within the project's "/www" folder, as in figure 6-1.

Name	Date modified	Type
assets	1/16/2015 11:38 AM	File folder
css	1/15/2015 2:46 PM	File folder
img	12/23/2014 12:05 ...	File folder
js	1/15/2015 2:46 PM	File folder
res	1/15/2015 2:46 PM	File folder
index.html	1/16/2015 11:40 AM	Chrome HTML Do...

Figure 6-1: Create an assets folder in "/www"

NOTE FOR ANDROID:

This chapter presents the HTML5 standard for audio elements, however, the WebView in Android versions prior to 5.0 DOES NOT SUPPORT the HTML5 audio standard. PhoneGap builds native apps based on a mobile device's WebView, so HTML5 audio WILL NOT WORK on PhoneGap applications running on Android 4.4 and earlier. Section four will cover using the PhoneGap media object to play audio on earlier versions of Android.

```
<audio controls>

</audio>
```

Example 6-1: The outline of an **<audio>** element.

```
<audio controls>
    <source src="assets/01_Mr_Roboto.
mp3">
    <source src="assets/01_Mr_Roboto.
ogg">
</audio>
```

Example 6-2: Passing multiple files as the media source will give your application redundancy. Note that a space character may work when testing the audio on a desktop browser, but it might not work on a mobile device. Ensure that there are no spaces in the source file's name.

2 In this section we will be using the built-in media controls available on a mobile device or browser. Once you have an assets folder and an audio file to play, open index.html and create an **<audio>** tag as shown in example 6-1.

Note that we have set an attribute, **controls**, with no value. That attribute instructs the browser to use the default media controls with the chosen media file.

3 Within the **<audio>** element, create two **<source>** tags, as shown in example 6-2. The device will move through the source elements linearly until it finds an audio source that it can play. In our example, we have two versions of the song "Mr. Roboto" by the band Styx. Initially there is an MP3 file, followed by an OGG file. If the MP3 is incompatible, then the OGG will be played. We have included both versions of the file in the "/www/assets" folder. Also note that the titles use underscore characters in place of spaces.

Figure 6-2: The default audio controls in a Chrome emulator.

Figure 6-3: The default audio controls on a Nexus 7.

4 When you run the application in a Chrome device emulator, shown emulating a Google Nexus 7 in figure 6-2, you'll see a standard media control bar.

5 Running the application on an actual device (like a Google Nexus 7, as shown in figure 6-3) presents a similar media control bar — although on a physical device the control bar does not have a volume option. This is because volume on a mobile is assumed to be handled by the device itself.

```
▸  <video controls>
▸      <source
   src="assets/02OnRangeWyoming.mp4">
▸      <source
   src="assets/02OnRangeWyoming.ogv">
▸  </video>
```

Figure 6-4: The **<video>** element HTML.

6 In order to display video instead of audio, simply replace the **<audio>** tag with the **<video>** tag, and then link to the source video files in exactly the same manner. Example 6-4 shows the HTML.

7 Test the application on a device or with the Chrome emulator. Depending on the size of your source video file and the resolution of your device, you may notice a problem. Figure 6-5 demonstrates this.

Figure 6-5: A large video extends past the edge of the screen.

```
►  <video style="width: 100%" controls>
►      <source
   src="assets/02OnRangeWyoming.mp4">
►  <source src="assets/02OnRangeWyoming.
   ogv">
►  </video>
```

Example 6-3: The **<video>** element with inline CSS to set its width.

Figure 6-6: The video now takes up only the available space. Note the default Android video player controls.

8 You may recall solving a similar problem in chapter three. The solution here is very similar. The **<video>** tag is much like the **<img>** tag, including in the implementation of its **width** and **height** CSS attributes. Modify the code to match example 6-3. Note that the CSS included with the inline **style** attribute could also be placed within **<style>** tags or in an external CSS file.

9 Test the resulting application. On a Google Nexus 7, the video now matches available width whether in portrait or landscape mode, as in figure 6-6. Note that the *container* **<div>** element's border is visible behind the video. This is because, as you may recall from chapter three, a percentage value in a CSS width or height attribute is based the width or height of the containing element—in this case *container*—and not the width or height of the device screen.

In this section you learned how easy it is to include media elements in a PhoneGap application. In the next section, we will create custom controls to manage the playback of a media file, instead of relying on the built-in media controls.

Questions for Review

1 What is the HTML5 standard video format for web applications?

    a. .OGV

    b. .MP4

    c. There is no set standard format.

    d. .AVI

2 How is a video file structured?

    a. It is an encoded video file.

    b. It is an uncompressed video file.

    c. It is a container file for uncompressed video and encoded audio.

    d. It is a container file for encoded video and audio.

3 What is required to play HTML5 audio in a web browser?

    a. An <audio> element with the "controls" attribute.

    b. Any <audio> element.

    c. An <audio> element with controls defined by JavaScript.

    d. A third-party audio plug-in utility, like a Flash player.

4 The Android 4.4 WebView is HTML5 audio standards compliant.

    a. True.

    b. False.

6.2 Controlling Media with JavaScript

In the previous section we learned how to use HTML5 and the built-in browser controls to play media files. In this section we will learn how to override the built-in media controls and use our own, instead.

In a desktop environment, overriding the default media controls will primarily be a style choice. A user with a mouse and keyboard can easily manipulate the browser controls for audio and video. On a mobile device, however, the situation is different.

Video consumption on a mobile device using the default playback mechanism is very effective, but controlling an audio file can be more difficult. The default play, pause, and seek buttons are very small and are not very easy to touch. Wouldn't it be better to have some nice, wide buttons to press? In this section, that's what we'll create.

For this section you can build on from the previous section's AudioVideo project. We will only be concerned with the audio player, though, so ensure that you have the **<audio>** element set up in your index.html file.

① First, we will be overriding the default controls. In your index.html, you can remove the **controls** attribute. However, the default control mechanism includes a progress bar and displays the song's elapsed time, so for right now it is better to keep the default control and instead add our new controls. Above the default control, add three buttons: *btnPlay*, *btnPause*, and *btnStop*. Title them "Play," "Pause," and "Stop." This is shown in example 6-4.

```
<button id="btnPlay">Play</button>
<button id="btnPause">Pause</button>
<button id="btnStop">Stop</button>
<audio id="audioFile" controls>
    <source src="assets/01_Mr_Roboto.
mp3">
    <source src="assets/01_Mr_Roboto.
ogg">
</audio>
```

Example 6-4: The HTML for our simple player controls. Note that the **<audio>** element has been given the id *audioFile*.

2 The buttons that we've just created will be powered by JavaScript. In main.js, prepare an initialization function that runs once the device is ready, as we have been doing. This *init()* function will add event listeners to the buttons that will each call functions that act on the **<audio>** element, *audioFile.* To ensure that *audioFile* is accessible throughout the script, create a global variable outside of *init()* and assign it the value of our audio file once *init()* is called. This is shown in example 6-5.

3 Once the variables are initialized in main.js. we can begin coding our functions. First, create a *playAudio()* function, as shown in example 6-6. In order to begin playback, we simply have to call the *play()* method from the **<audio>** element. Our *init()* function stored our **<audio>** element, *audioFile*, in the variable *audioFile*, so all our *playAudio()* function needs to do is call *audioFile.play()*.

```
var audioFile

window.onload = function()
{
    document.
addEventListener('deviceready', init,
false);
}

function init()
{
    var btnPlay = document.
getElementById('btnPlay');
    var btnPause = document.
getElementById('btnPause');
    var btnStop = document.
getElementById('btnStop');

    btnPlay.addEventListener('click',
playAudio, false);
    btnPause.addEventListener('click',
pauseAudio, false);
    btnStop.addEventListener('click',
stopAudio, false);

    audioFile = document.
getElementById('audioFile');
}
```

Example 6-5: Initializing our variables in main.js.

```
function playAudio()
{
    audioFile.play();
}
```

Example 6-6: Playing our audio file.

```
function pauseAudio()
{
    audioFile.pause();
}
```

Example 6-7: Pausing our audio file.

```
function stopAudio()
{
    pauseAudio();
    audioFile.currentTime = 0;
}
```

Example 6-8: Stopping our audio file by pausing playback and setting the *currentTime* property to zero.

Figure 6-7: The application running on an emulated Nexus 4 screen.

4 Pausing the audio file is just as simple as playing it. Example 6-7 shows the *pauseAudio()* function, which calls the *audioFile.pause()* method.

5 Stopping playback is only slightly more complicated. There is no *stop()* method in the **<audio>** element, so we will have to determine what "stop playback" means to our users and code for that. It's generally accepted that when a "Stop" button is pressed, playback will cease and the media will be reset to the beginning. The **<audio>** element's *currentTime* property sets or returns the playback position in seconds. To reset playback, we can set *audioFile.currentTime* to zero. Therefore, to create a "Stop" button that acts as users expect it to act, we first pause playback then set *currentTime* to zero, as shown in example 6-8.

6 Figure 6-7 shows the application running on an emulated Nexus 4. The buttons are much easier to press than the default control.

HTML5 makes it simple to use JavaScript to control media playback. In the next section, we will continue to build on this example by creating a fully functioning music player using JavaScript and HTML5.

Questions for Review

1 Which of the following are good reasons to override the default media controls?

    a. Ease of use for mobile users.

    b. To implement a specific, consistent style.

    c. Better integration with your application.

    d. All of the above.

2 How would you stop playback using JavaScript?

    a. Use the audio element's *stop()* method.

    b. Reset the audio element by deleting it from the DOM and recreating it.

    c. Pause the audio playback and set its playback position to the start of the file.

    d. Once started, audio file playback cannot be stopped.

3 You cannot use both the built in controls and custom controls for media playback.

    a. True.

    b. False.

4 What is the proper syntax to play an audio file named "myAudio?"

    a. audio.play(myAudio);

    b. myAudio.play();

    c. myAudio.play;

    d. myAudio.playback.start();

6.3 Building a Complete Music Player

This section will build on the previous section to create a complete, fully functional music player. It will feature a selectable list of songs, full playback options through play, pause, and stop buttons, and volume control.

In order for this example to work you will need media files to play. If you do not have any music or other audio files on your computer, you can find free tracks at the Wikimedia commons, *http://commons.wikimedia.org*. Also, many operating systems include sample music tracks. When you see a reference to a music tracks in this section, replace the file names with the names of the audio files that you are using.

Create a project called MusicPlayer that is based on our template, and open the index.html file.

1 As with the previous example program in this chapter, you need to place your media files in your project's "/www/assets" folder.

2 First, create the media player's interface in HTML. It will require "Play," "Pause," and "Stop" buttons, a volume slider, a list of tracks, and an elapsed time display.

3 Example 6-9 shows the HTML for the buttons and the volume slider. Note that the audio player has no **controls** attribute. Also, the volume **<input>** element is a *range* type and uses the jQuery **data-highlight** attribute.

```
<audio id="player">
    <source src="assets/01_Mr_Roboto.
mp3"></source>
</audio>
<button id="btnPlay">Play</button>
<button id="btnPause">Pause</button>
<button id="btnStop">Stop</button>
<label for="rngVolume">Volume</label>
<input type="range" id="rngVolume"
min="0" max="1" step=".01"
value=".5" data-highlight="true"
onchange="changeVolume()" />
```

Example 6-9: The HTML for the **<audio>** element and the buttons is familiar, but the **<input>** element includes a jQuery attribute, **data-highlight**.

```
<ul data-role="listview" data-
inset="true">
   <li data-role="list-
divider">Songs</li>
   <li><a href="#"
onclick="changeSong('01_Mr_
Roboto')">01 Mr. Roboto</a></li>
   <li><a href="#"
onclick="changeSong('03_Dont_Let_It_
End')">03 Don't Let It End</a></li>
   <li><a href="#"
onclick="changeSong('04_High_
Time')">04 High Time</a></li>
</ul>
<div data-role="footer">
   <output id="timeOut">Elapsed
Time:</output>
</div>
```

Example 6-10: The HTML for the song list uses jQuery for a clear, consistent style.

Figure 6-8: The HTML user interface on a Nexus 4.

4 Below the volume control we will list the available tracks. The HTML is shown in example 6-10. Note that you will need to modify the calls to *changeSong()* in each **onclick** attribute of the **<a>** elements to reference the audio files that you are using. For example, if your first track is called "Song_1" then the first **<a>** element will be:

```
<a href="#"
onclick="changeSong
('Song_1')">Song 1</a>
```

This list is styled using jQuery **data-role** attributes. If you are unfamiliar with jQuery, there is extensive documentation available *http://jquerymobile. com*.

5 You can test the layout in Chrome. Figure 6-8 shows the application running in an emulated Google Nexus 4. Notice how jQuery styles the volume slider to highlight the volume level. Also, the list title is an HTML **<li>** element, but using jQuery's *list-divider* for its **data-role** attribute clearly differentiates it from the other **<li>** elements. Finally, the **<output>** element is styled as a jQuery footer.

6 Now that the HTML is in place, we move on to the JavaScript. The main.js file for this application starts similarly to the example in the previous section, but with the addition of new globally scoped variables *rngVolume*, for the volume adjuster, and *intv*, for the timer. We will explain those variables in more depth shortly.

7 In example 6-11 you can see the global variable declarations, the **window.onload** function, and the initialization function. Within *init()* we set the *player* global variable to the *player* **<audio>** element, and we also set the *rngVolume* variable to the *rngVolume* **<input>** element. The button assignments set up the framework for the play, pause, and stop buttons in the same manner as in the previous section's example.

8 Now we can begin to create shells for the functions we need to create. From the HTML and *init()* function, we know we will need *playMusic()*, *pauseMusic()*, *stopMusic()*, *changeVolume()*, and *changeSong()* functions.

```javascript
var player;
var rngVolume;
var intv;

window.onload = function() {
    document.
addEventListener('deviceready', init,
false);
}

function init()
{
    player = document.
getElementById('player');
    var btnPlay = document.
getElementById('btnPlay');
    var btnPause = document.
getElementById('btnPause');
    var btnStop = document.
getElementById('btnStop');
    rngVolume = document.
getElementById('rngVolume');

    btnPlay.addEventListener('click',
playMusic, false);
    btnPause.addEventListener('click',
pauseMusic, false);
    btnStop.addEventListener('click',
stopMusic, false);
}
```

Example 6-11: The start of our main.js file.

```
►   function playMusic()
►   {
►       player.play();
►       startTimer();
►   }
►
►   function pauseMusic()
►   {
►       player.pause();
►   }
►
►   function stopMusic()
►   {
►       pauseMusic();
►       player.currentTime = 0;
►       stopTimer();
►   }
```

Example 6-12: The JavaScript code for the "Play," "Pause," and "Stop" buttons.

```
►   function changeVolume()
►   {
►       player.volume = rngVolume.value;
►   }
►
►   function changeSong(song)
►   {
►       stopMusic();
►       player.src = "assets/" + song +
►   ".mp3";
►       playMusic();
►   }
```

Example 6-13: Changing the volume and the song are simple with JavaScript and the HTML **<audio>** element.

9 We can begin by creating the *playMusic()*, *pauseMusic()*, and *stopMusic()* functions. They are very similar to those same functions from the previous section, with two small differences. In example 6-12, note that we have included a call to a *startTimer()* function in *playMusic()*, and a call to a *stopTimer()* function in *stopMusic()*. We did this because we need to update the HTML within the *timeOut* **<output>** element when music is playing, but not when the music is stopped. We will control this timer with *startTimer()* and *stopTimer()*.

10 The *changeVolume()* function simply sets the volume of the *player* to the value of the *rngVolume* **<input>** element. This works because an **<audio>** element has a **volume** attribute that is a value between zero and one, so a *range* type **<input>** element with a **min** attribute set to *0* and a **max** attribute set to *1* will always have a compatible value. The *changeSong()* function simply calls *stopMusic()*, changes the source of *player*, and then calls *playMusic()*.

11 Now that the buttons are set up, we will move on to the timer. Four functions, shown in example 6-14, will power the elapsed time tracker, *startTimer()*, *stopTimer()*, *updateTime()*, and *secsToMins()*.

12 The *startTimer()* function creates an **interval** using **setInterval()**. An interval will call a function or evaluate an expression every set number of milliseconds. In this case, we are calling *updateTime()* every 1000 milliseconds, or every second. The **setInterval()** method returns an ID value for the interval that has been set, which we have stored as *intv*. The *stopTimer()* function passes this ID to the **clearInterval()** method which stops the interval.

13 The *updateTime()* function is called every second while the interval is active and it sets the inner HTML of the *timeOut* **<output>** element to the value of "Elapsed Time: " plus the current time value of the **<audio>** element, in seconds. The actual value returned from the **<audio>** element needs to be converted to a better format, though. This is what *secsToMins()* is for.

```
function startTimer()
{
    intv = setInterval(updateTime,
1000);
}

function stopTimer()
{
    clearInterval(intv);
    updateTime();
}

function updateTime()
{
    document.
getElementById('timeOut').innerHTML =
    "Elapsed Time: " + secsToMins(player.
currentTime);
}

function secsToMins(seconds)
{
    var minutes = Math.
floor(seconds/60);
    var theSeconds = seconds - minutes
* 60;
    if(theSeconds > 9)
    {
        return minutes + ":" + Math.
round(theSeconds);
    } else
    {
        return minutes + ":0" + Math.
round(theSeconds);
    }
}
```

Example 6-14: The functions that control the output of the elapsed track time in the application.

```
▸  function secsToMins(seconds)
▸  {
▸      var minutes = Math.
   floor(seconds/60);
▸      var theSeconds = seconds - minutes
   * 60;
▸      if(theSeconds > 9)
▸      {
▸          return minutes + ":" + Math.
   round(theSeconds);
▸      } else
▸      {
▸          return minutes + ":0" + Math.
   round(theSeconds);
▸      }
▸  }
```

Example 6-15: The *secsToMins()* function formats the seconds value before we use it in our application's output.

14 The value returned from an **<audio>** element's **currentTime** property is in seconds, but with a much higher degree of precision than we need. The *secsToMins()* function takes that value and, using JavaScript math functions, converts it to a readable format that we can use in our application. A simple if/else conditional ensures consistency by placing a "0" in front of the elapsed number of seconds if that number is lower than "9."

Now when you run the application, you'll see that you can play songs, pause and resume playback, stop to reset playback, and choose other songs to play. You are also able to control the volume and keep track of the elapsed time. Congratulations, you've just made an MP3 player!

In this section we have reinforced what we learned about the **<audio>** element and used our knowledge of JavaScript to create a fully functioning MP3 player that can be deployed to a mobile device.

In the next section we will modify the media player we have just built to ensure that it is compatible with the majority of Android devices. We will also learn how to install and use PhoneGap plug-ins.

Questions for Review

1 What is an effective way of changing the source of an HTML5 audio element?

   a. Remove it from the DOM and create a new audio element with the desired source.

   b. You cannot change the source of an audio element, you need to ensure that all of the audio files you want to play have their own audio elements.

   c. Modify the **src** attribute of the audio element.

   d. Use the *setSource()* method.

2 Which of the following will return the current play time of an audio file?

   a. The **currentTime** property.

   b. The *getCurrentTime()* method.

   c. The **position** property.

   d. The **currentPosition** property.

3 How is the volume of an audio element represented?

   a. As a percentage value.

   b. As an integer value between 0 and 100.

   c. As a value between 0 and 1.

   d. As either "low," "med-low," "med," "med-high," or "high."

4 How often does a JavaScript interval run?

   a. Every second.

   b. Every 1000 milliseconds.

   c. As often as you instruct it to.

   d. Every 100 milliseconds.

6.4 Using the PhoneGap Media Object

In section one of this chapter we mentioned that the Android WebView does not support the HTML5 audio standard in versions prior to 5.0. PhoneGap builds native applications that use a device's WebView, so PhoneGap applications running on Android devices earlier than 5.0 will not play HTML5 audio elements.

The bane of many web developer's lives has always been compatibility. Features that are simple to implement in one web browser running on a certain platform may be completely absent from another platform. Creating a consistent experience across platforms is a problem that standards are meant to solve, however, slow adoption by some players means that many "standards" exist in name only.

When you're designing an application you have a target audience in mind. That target audience informs many of the decisions that you make in the development process, including the decision to use PhoneGap. This target audience will also inform your decision to use the HTML5 audio standard—thus limiting the reach of your application—or the PhoneGapmedia object.

The PhoneGap media object was designed to ensure consistent functionality across devices that do not adhere to the HTML5 audio standard. It is not as simple as using HTML5 **<audio>** tags, and it has quirks that need to be worked around, but it will ensure that your application can run on a wider variety of devices.

The PhoneGap media object requires two additional PhoneGap plug-ins, the Media plug-in and the File plug-in. Create a new PhoneGap project that is a copy of the music player. We will start by installing the required plug-ins.

```
▸   phonegap plugin add org.apache.
    cordova.media
```

Example 6-16: The command to install the PhoneGap media plug-in.

1 Using the command-line interface, navigate to the project directory. The installation command for the media plug-in is shown in example 6-16.

2 After the Media plug-in is installed, add the File plug-in using the command in example 6-17.

Plug-ins in PhoneGap increase its functionality by giving you access to specific device features only when you need them. This allows you to keep your application streamlined and uncluttered while tailoring it with the features you require. The plug-ins are installed in the project's "plugins/" directory.

3 Open the index.html file. We will modify the existing application to work with the PhoneGap media object. There is only one change that needs to be made in the HTML file, and that is to remove the reference to the **<audio>** element. The contents of the body of your HTML should match example 6-18.

The PhoneGap media object only exists in JavaScript and does not have an associated HTML element.

```
phonegap plugin add org.apache.
cordova.file
```

Example 6-17: Installing the PhoneGap file plug-in.

```
<div id="container">
<button id="btnPlay">Play</button>
<button id="btnPause">Pause</button>
<button id="btnStop">Stop</button>
<label for="rngVolume">Volume</label>
<input type="range" id="rngVolume"
min="0" max="1" step=".01"
value=".5" data-highlight="true"
onchange="changeVolume()" />
<ul data-role="listview" data-
inset="true">
    <li data-role="list-
divider">Songs</li>
    <li><a href="#"
onclick="changeSong('01_Mr_
Roboto')">01 Mr. Roboto</a></li>
    <li><a href="#"
onclick="changeSong('03_Dont_Let_It_
End')">03 Don't Let It End</a></li>
    <li><a href="#"
onclick="changeSong('04_High_
Time')">04 High Time</a></li>
</ul>
<div data-role="footer">
    <output id="timeOut">Elapsed
Time:</output>
</div>
</div> <!-- container -->
```

Example 6-18: The HTML for our updated player.

```
var rngVolume;
var intv;
var media;
var increment = false;

var startTime;
var pauseTime = 0;
var elapsed = 0;

window.onload = function() {
    document.
addEventListener('deviceready', init,
false);
}

function init()
{
    var src = cordova.file.
applicationDirectory + "www/assets/01_
Mr_Roboto.ogg";
    media = new Media(src);

    var btnPlay = document.
getElementById('btnPlay');
    var btnPause = document.
getElementById('btnPause');
    var btnStop = document.
getElementById('btnStop');
    rngVolume = document.
getElementById('rngVolume');

    btnPlay.addEventListener('click',
playMusic, false);
    btnPause.addEventListener('click',
pauseMusic, false);
    btnStop.addEventListener('click',
stopMusic, false);

    rngVolume.value = .5;
    changeVolume();
}
```

4 The rest of our work will be done in the main. js file. Open that now.

5 First, we created and initialized some new global variables. Example 6-19 shows the updated global variables, and the updated *init()* function.

6 We have removed the *audio* variable and replaced it with *media*. This will be our media object. We have added a boolean variable *increment* set to "false." This will determine if we are currently incrementing our "Elapsed Time" timer. We have also added the variables *startTime*, *pauseTime*, and *elapsed*. These will be used to track how long the song has been playing.

Example 6-19: New global variables and an updated *init()*.

The first thing that is done in the new *init()* function is the creation of the PhoneGap media object. A PhoneGap media object requires an absolute URI to the media that will be accessed. With HTML5 **<audio>** elements we had been able to use relative URIs, but because the PhoneGap media object does not exist as an HTML element we cannot use a URI that is relative to the HTML file. Using an absolute URI requires knowing the path to our PhoneGap's application directory, however this directory will change depending on the device that is running the application. PhoneGap's file plug-in solves this problem.

The file plug-in provides us with a property, "cordova.file.applicationDirectory," that has as its value the directory that the PhoneGap application is running in. As you can see in the following code from the *init()* function, we use this property to assign the variable *src* the absolute URI of our media file, and then use the *src* variable to create the Media object:

```
var src = cordova.file.applicationDirectory + "www/assets/01_Mr_Roboto.
ogg";
media = new Media(src);
```

The *init()* function also has the reference to the *player* element removed and a call to the *changeVolume()* function added. The button assignments and the assignment of the *rngVolume* variable remain the same.

7 The changes to most of our music functions are minor. Example 6-20 shows the original *playMusic()* function on top, and the updated *playMusic()* function below. Notice that *player.play()* was changed to refer to the Media object with *media.play()*.

```
function playMusic()
{
    player.play();
    startTimer();
}
```

```
function playMusic()
{
    startTimer();
    media.play();
}
```

Example 6-20: The original (top) and updated *playMusic()*.

```
function playMusic()
{
    startTimer();
    media.play();
}

function pauseMusic()
{
    pauseTimer();
    media.pause();
}

function stopMusic()
{
    stopTimer();
    media.stop();
}
```

Example 6-21: The updated button functions.

```
function changeVolume()
{
    media.setVolume(rngVolume.value);
}
```

Example 6-22: Changing the volume with a media object.

```
function changeSong(song)
{
    stopMusic();
    var src = cordova.file.
applicationDirectory + "www/assets/" +
song + ".ogg";
    media = new Media(src);
    playMusic();
}
```

Example 6-23: The updated *changeSong()* function.

8   Example 6-21 shows *playMusic()*, *pauseMusic()*, and *stopMusic()*. Notice that, like *player.play()* changing to *media.play()*, *player.pause()* was changed to *media.pause()*. The *stopMusic()* function was changed more dramatically, though, because unlike the HTML5 **<audio>** element, the PhoneGap media object has a **stop()** method.

9   The *changeVolume()* function was also modified. The PhoneGap media object does not have a directly accessible *volume* property like the HTML5 **<audio>** element, but it does have a **setVolume()** method. We call this method in *changeVolume()* to appropriately set the volume.

10   The updated *changeSong()* function, shown in example 6-23, follows the same pattern as the original, however instead of simply changing the value of the audio source, *media* is assigned a new media object which is instantiated with the updated *src* value. Note that we again use the file plug-in.

The changes made to get media playing with a working volume control in PhoneGap utilizing PhoneGap media objects are, as we have demonstrated, relatively simple. Duplicating the functionality of the elapsed time tracker, however, is more difficult.

PhoneGap media objects do have a parameter that tracks the position of a media file, _position, however, the parameter is not automatically updated during media playback. The result is that the track position cannot be quickly referenced—as the HTML5 **<audio>** element's currentTime parameter can be—to determine how much time has elapsed since playback began. The solution provided by PhoneGap is the getCurrentPosition() method, which updates the value of _position and then returns that value. The problem with using getCurrentPosition() is that it takes an inconsistent amount of time to execute, resulting in an elapsed time tracker that occasionally skips seconds. To solve that problem, we will create a timer that works independently of the media object.

The timer will set a start time when the startTimer() function is called and will then determine the elapsed time by subtracting that starting time from the current time when the updateTime() function is called. This timer will use the increment, startTime, pauseTime, and elapsed global variables that were created earlier.

11 The startTimer() function will initiate our timer and set the update interval, however, we only want this to happen if we are not already incrementing our timer. Example 6-24 shows the code. Note that startTime is set to the result of the **getTime()** method of a new **Date()** object. This returns the number of milliseconds that have elapsed since midnight, January 1st, 1970. The intv variable is set as an interval that runs updateTime() every second, as in the original app.

```
function startTimer()
{
    if (!increment)
    {
        startTime = new Date().
getTime();
        intv = setInterval(updateTime,
1000);
        increment = true;
    }
}
```

Example 6-24: The updated startTimer() function.

```
  ▸   function pauseTimer()
  ▸   {
  ▸       pauseTime = elapsed;
  ▸       clearInterval(intv);
  ▸       increment = false;
  ▸   }
```

Example 6-25: *pauseTimer()* pauses the incrementing of the "Elapsed Time: " display in the HTML.

```
  ▸   function updateTime()
  ▸   {
  ▸      if(increment)
  ▸      {
  ▸             elapsed = new Date().
      getTime();
  ▸             elapsed -= startTime;
  ▸             elapsed += pauseTime;
  ▸      }
  ▸      elapsed = elapsed / 1000
  ▸      document.getElementById('timeOut').
      innerHTML = "Elapsed time: " +
      secsToMins(elapsed);
  ▸   }
```

Example 6-26: The *updateTime()* function updates the "Elapsed Time: " display in the HTML.

12 The *pauseTimer()* function, shown in example 6-25, first sets the value of *pauseTime* to the amount of playback time that has currently elapsed, and then clears the interval. Finally, it sets the value of *increment* to "false." With *increment* set to "false" the play button will cause the *startTime* value to be reset, so in order for the timer to be accurate we need to know how long the song had been playing before the timer was reset.

13 The *updateTime()* function, shown in example 6-26, will first determine if the elapsed time is being incremented. If it is, it will set *elapsed* to the current time, find the difference between the current time and the time that playback started, and then add the amount of time that had elapsed before a *pauseTimer()* function call reset the timer. This results in the value of *elapsed* being the number of milliseconds that the song has been playing.

14 The *updateTime()* function then converts *elapsed* to seconds, and sets the inner HTML of *timeOut* to the amount of time that has elapsed since playback started.

```
function stopTimer()
{
    pauseTimer();
    elapsed = 0;
    pauseTime = 0;
    updateTime();
}
```

Example 6-27: The updated *stopTimer()* function.

15 The *stopTimer()* function, shown in example 6-27, first uses the *pauseTimer()* function to clear the interval and set *increment* to "false," and then resets *elapsed* and *pauseTime* to their initial values. Finally, it calls *updateTime()* to update the elapsed time display.

16 The *secsToMins()* function has not been changed, but it can be seen in example 6-28.

```
function secsToMins(seconds)
{
    var minutes = Math.
floor(seconds/60);
    var theSeconds = seconds - minutes
* 60;
    if(theSeconds >= 10)
    {
        return minutes + ":" + Math.
round(theSeconds);
    } else
    {
        return minutes + ":0" + Math.
round(theSeconds);
    }
}
```

Example 6-28: The *secsToMins()* function did not need to be changed.

With the changes we made, the media player application will now function on Android devices running an operating system version lower than 5.0.

Until this section we have been using standards-compliant HTML5 and creating applications that would run on a wide variety of devices from a number of different manufacturers. However, in this section we learned that even using the established standards we can come across application-breaking incompatibilities that affect a huge number of potential users. At the time of this writing, Android 5.0 is being used by just over 1% of Android users. In order to ensure that our application would work on the majority of Android devices, we had to make modifications that were trivial in some cases but substantial in other cases.

As a developer, you need to understand who your potential audience is and what capabilities their devices have. In this case, it made sense to modify the code to increase compatibility, but as you continue developing you will find yourself in a position where you're weighing ease of development against limiting your potential audience. The HTML5 **<audio>** implementation works and it is quicker and easier to use than the PhoneGap media object. If Android 5.0 had a larger market share, would it have been worthwhile to create a version of the application that used the PhoneGap media object? At what point would the extra work involved in ensuring application compatibility cease being worthwhile? That's a question that you, as developer, will have to ask yourself.

In this section we also learned how to install PhoneGap plug-ins. In the next section, we will use another plug-in to access the camera that is available on most mobile devices.

Questions for Review

1 The PhoneGap media object is functionally identical to the built-in HTML5 audio and video elements.

   a. True.

   b. False.

2 How would you stop media playback using the PhoneGap media object?

   a. Pause the playback and set the playback to the beginning of the file.

   b. Use the media object's *stop()* method.

   c. Pause the playback and reload the media element.

   d. Use the HTML5 *stop()* method.

3 When should you use the PhoneGap media object instead of the HTML5 audio element?

   a. Always.

   b. Never.

   c. When developing for Android.

   d. When it makes sense for your users.

4 What date does the JavaScript **Date()** object originate on?

   a. Midnight, January 01, 1900.

   b. Midnight, January 01, 2000.

   c. Noon, January 01, 1900.

   d. Midnight, January 01, 1970.

6.5 Using the Onboard Camera

In the previous section we learned about plug-ins. In this section, we will use another plug-in to access the camera that is built in to most mobile devices. In order to test the application we're building here, you will need to run it on an actual device.

The application will feature a simple HTML interface with a button that will allow the user to take a picture. When the button is pressed, the device's native camera application will be launched. Once the user takes a picture, the resulting image will be returned to the application.

Create a new project called "Smile" based on the template that we have been using.

① First, install the camera plug-in using the command-line interface, as shown in example 6-29.

```
▶  phonegap plugin add org.apache.
   cordova.camera
```

Example 6-29: The command to install the PhoneGap camera plug-in.

② The index.html file for this project will be very simple. It will include a button to take a picture, a **<div>** for formatting, and an empty **<img>** element to hold the resulting image. Example 6-30 shows the HTML.

```
▶  <div id="container">
▶  <button onclick="takePic()"
   id="btnCam">Take Picture</button>
▶  <div id="result" id>
▶  <img id="resultImg"></img>
▶  </div>
▶  </div> <!-- container -->
```

Example 6-30: The index.html for the Smile project.

3 This project will include some CSS styling, so open the mainAppStyles.cs file. After the standard *container* style we have the app start with the *btnCam* element hidden. Once the "deviceready" event fires in JavaScript, we will show the button. We do not want the user to be able to press the button to take a picture until we have verified that the device, which includes the camera, is ready.

4 Next, the *result* **<div>** element is styled to size the image and center it horizontally. The *resultImg* style resizes the image to be 100% of the size of its parent element, not 100% of its own size. Without this styling, the resulting image would be too large to display on the application screen.

5 In main.js, set up the device ready listener as shown in example 6-32, and create a global variable to hold the options that we will pass to the phone's camera. Those options will be assigned in the *init()* function.

```css
#container {
    margin: 5px;
}
#btnCam {
    display: none;
}
#result {
    margin-left: auto;
    margin-right: auto;
    width: 90%;
}
#resultImg {
    width: 100%;
}
```

Example 6-31: CSS to style the resulting image.

```javascript
var cameraOpts;

window.onload = function() {
    document.
    addEventListener('deviceready', init, false);
}
```

Example 6-32: The global variable *cameraOpts* will contain the camera options that we pass to the phone's camera application.

```
function init()
{
    var btnCam = document.
getElementById('btnCam');
    btnCam.style.display = "block";

    camerOpts = {
        quality : 100,
        destinationType : Camera.
DestinationType.FILE_URI,
        sourceType : Camera.
PictureSourceType.CAMERA,
        allowEdit : false,
        encodingType : Camera.
EncodingType.JPG,
    };
}
```

Example 6-33: The camera button is displayed in the *init()* function, which is called when the device is ready.

```
function takePic()
{
    navigator.camera.
getPicture(cameraSuccess, cameraFail,
cameraOpts);
}
```

Example 6-34: The *getPicture()* function from the camera plug-in is called in our *takePic()* function.

6 The *init()* function, in example 6-23, first displays the camera button, and then sets the options that we will pass to the phone's camera.

• *quality* sets the quality of the picture, from 0 to 100.
• *destinationType* determines what the camera will return—in this case, it will return an absolute URI to the picture's location.
• *sourceType* sets the source of the picture. Instead of the camera, the source can be the device's built-in photo library.
• *allowEdit* determines whether or not the image can be edited before it is selected.
• *encodingType* chooses the encoding of the returned image, either JPEG or PNG.

There are more possible camera options. The full list is available from the PhoneGap camera API documentation.

7 The *takePic()* function, shown in example 6-34, calls the **getPicture()** method to launch the native camera application with the set camera options. If the picture is successful, then *cameraSuccess()* is called. If not, *cameraFail()* is called.

8 The camera plug-in's **getPicture()** method either returns a photo if it is successful or an error message if it is not successful. When we call the **getPicture()** method, we need to instruct the application what to do if it either succeeds or fails. The *cameraSuccess()* function handles success, and the *cameraFail()* function handles failure. They are shown in example 6-35.

9 If the device's camera successfully takes a picture, the *cameraSuccess()* function sets that picture as the source of the *resultImg* **<img>** element in index.html.

10 If the device's camera fails to take a picture, the *cameraFail()* function displays the failure message in an alert window.

11 Figure 6-9 shows the application running before and after taking a picture.

```
function cameraSuccess(imageData)
{
    var result = document.
getElementById('resultImg');
    result.src = imageData;
}

function cameraFail(message)
{
    alert("Error: " + message);
}
```

Example 6-35: The *cameraSuccess()* and *cameraFail()* functions handle the success and fail states of the camera plug-in's **getPicture()** method.

Figure 6-9: The application before taking a picture, left, and after taking a picture, right.

12 If the user cancels the camera application then **getPicture()** fails, returning an error. This is handled by the *cameraFail()* function which pops up an Alert with the failure message, shown in figure 6-10.

Figure 6-10: The *cameraFail()* function pops up an alert message.

In this section you have used the built-in camera on your device to take a picture and display it in your application. When you're working with device hardware, it's important to keep in mind the differences between devices and to understand that even though multiple devices can accomplish the same task, they may go about it in very different ways. The PhoneGap documentation has notes about the quirks and idiosyncrasies of each supported device platform—for example, when taking a picture with an iOS device, PhoneGap recommends setting the quality option to a value below 50 in order to avoid memory errors.

Questions for Review

1 Camera functionality is built into the default PhoneGap project.

    a. True.

    b. False.

2 How do you extend PhoneGap functionality with plug-ins?

    a. Use the command line interface plug-in installation command.

    b. Go to the PhoneGap website and download the appropriate plug-in.

    c. Go to the plug-in's website and download its installation file.

    d. Code the plug-in yourself.

3 Which of the following are options for the image format returned by the camera plug-in?

    a. .PNG

    b. .GIF

    c. .TIF

    d. .JPG

4 If the camera plug-in's *getPicture()* method is not successful, what happens?

    a. It fails silently.

    b. It returns an error message.

    c. It calls a specified function.

    d. Both B and C.

CHAPTER 06 LAB EXERCISE

In this lab exercise you will combine the PhoneGap Camera plug-in and the PhoneGap Media plug-in to create an application that records five seconds of audio, takes a picture, and then displays the picture while the recording audio is playing back. The user interface will display contextually appropriate buttons.

1 Create the HTML. It should have three buttons and a space for instructions. One button will be for recording audio, one will be for taking a picture, and one will be for playing back the audio while displaying the picture. Hide the buttons when the application starts, and once the device is ready, display only the "Record" button and appropriate instructions.

2 Read the PhoneGap Media plug-in documentation and use the Media object's **startRecord()** and **stopRecord()** methods to create an audio file. Note that you will have to release the operating system's audio resources after you have recorded a file. When the file is recorded, display the "Picture" button and appropriate instructions.

3 Use the Camera plug-in to allow the user to take a picture with their mobile device. Once the picture is taken, display it as a thumbnail. Once the picture has been recorded, display the "Show and Tell" button and appropriate instructions.

4 When the user touches the "Show and Tell" button, display the full picture while simultaneously playing back the audio file.

Chapter Summary

In this chapter, you have learned how to use PhoneGap and HTML5 to play media files, as well as how to use the hardware camera available on nearly every modern mobile device to take pictures. You have also learned that the standard HTML5 implementation is not always supported and that you will have to work around the peculiarities of certain devices if you want your application to be truly multi-platform.

PhoneGap is an exceptional tool for a developer looking to release a multi-platform application. It integrates skill sets that many developers already have — experience with existing web technologies — and makes them applicable to new and emerging device ecosystems. However, it is still a tool and it still has limitations. In order to fully apply your knowledge of PhoneGap and HTML5 mobile development you need to understand those limitations and how to work around them.

The camera application that we demonstrated in this chapter uses a hardware component that is very common on modern devices. In the next chapter, we will use another feature based on hardware components that exist on many modern devices, geolocation. We will explore how to find the user's physical location, how to display that location on a map, and how to work with a compass.

Chapter 7

Geolocation

CHAPTER OBJECTIVES:

- You will learn how to use the geolocation plug-in.
- You will better understand the PhoneGap plug-in architecture.
- You will use Google's Map API to locate a user on a map.
- You will learn how to access a user's heading from their device's compass.

7.1 Intro to Geolocation

One of the most interesting and useful features of modern mobile devices is geolocation. A modern mobile device knows where you are, and this knowledge has opened up a world of possibilities for application developers and users. Mapping applications can show you where you are and how to get to your destination, weather applications are able to give you relevant forecasts and information, and restaurants or businesses can advertise their services to nearby customers.

Geolocation on mobile devices is done by utilizing different technologies that provide varying degrees of accuracy. Many devices have an onboard GPS chip, which uses GPS satellites to determine location with what could potentially be a very high degree of accuracy. Nearby Wi-Fi networks can also provide location information, as can cellular network towers.

PhoneGap uses the W3C HTML5 standards in its geolocation implementation. If you choose to use location information in your PhoneGap applications, remember that there are important user privacy concerns to consider. It is important to be upfront with your users about why you are asking for their locations, what you will use their location information for, and how long you will store the information.

To test the geolocation features of PhoneGap, create a new project called WhereAmI, based off of our established template.

1 The HTML in the index.html file for this application will be very simple. We need a button, "Get Location," that will call the *getLocation()* function when it is pressed. We also need a **<div>** element with the id *result* to store the resulting location information. The HTML is shown in example 7-1.

```
<div id="container">
    <button id="btnLocation"
onclick="getLocation()">Get Location</
button>
        <div id='result'></div>
    </div> <!-- container -->
```

Example 7-1: The content of index.html.

```
#btnLocation {
    display: none;
}
```

Example 7-2: Set *btnLocation* to be invisible when the page loads. We will make it visible in the *init()* function in main.js.

```
var options;

window.onload = function()
{
    document.
addEventListener('deviceready', init,
false);
}

function init() {
    document.
getElementById('btnLocation').style.
display = "block";

    options = {
        maximumAge: 3000,
        timeout: 5000,
        enableHighAccuracy: true
    };
}

function getLocation()
{
    navigator.geolocation.
getCurrentPosition(success, failure,
options);
}
```

Example 7-3: The main.js file starts by calling an *init()* function once the device is ready. The *getLocation()* function uses the geolocation plug-in.

2 As with our camera application from the previous chapter, we do not want the "Get Location" button to be available until after we know that the user's device is ready, so in the mainAppStyles.css file, set its **display** property to *none*, as in example 7-2.

3 Example 7-3 shows the start of main.js. You'll notice that there are structural similarities between this application and the camera application from the previous section. Namely, the use of a global *options* variable that is set in the *init()* function, displaying the **<button>** element only once the device is ready, and the syntax of the geolocation call itself.

4 Within the *getLocation()* function you'll see the call to the geolocation plug-in's **getCurrentPosition()** method. As with the camera's **getPicture()** method, **getCurrentPosition()** has two callback functions, one for success and one for failure, and an options parameter.

5 The *options* assignment in *init()* is shown again in example 7-4. It sets the following options:

```
options = {
    maximumAge: 3000,
    timeout: 5000,
    enableHighAccuracy: true
};
```

Example 7-4: The geolocation options.

• *maximumAge* determines the maximum valid age, in milliseconds, of a location. As set, it will return a position object that is no more than 3 seconds old.
• *timeout* sets how long the device will wait for a position object. As set it will return an error if it takes longer than 5 seconds to return a valid position.
• *enableHighAccuracyUl* instructs the geolocation plug-in to use the most accurate possible location data. This will usually be GPS positioning data.

6 Example 7-5 shows the *success()* function that runs when the geolocation's **getCurrentPosition()** method successfully returns a position object. The position object has the coords and timestamp properties. In *success()*, we parse the position object and create variables to hold the latitude, longitude, altitude, and accuracy properties from the position's coords property, as well as a variable to hold the timestamp property.

```
function success(position)
{
    var lat = position.coords.
latitude;
    var long = position.coords.
longitude;
    var alt = position.coords.
altitude;
    var accuracy = position.coords.
accuracy;
    var timeS = position.timestamp;

    var output = "<strong>Latitude:</
strong> " + lat;
    output +=
"<br/><strong>Longitude:</strong> " +
long;
    output +=
"<br/><strong>Altitude:</strong> " +
alt;
    output += "<br/><strong>Accuracy:
</strong> " + accuracy;
    output += "<br/><strong>Time
Stamp: </strong> " + timeS;

    document.getElementById('result').
innerHTML = output;
}
```

Example 7-5: A successful call to **getCurrentPosition()** executes this function.

```
function failure(message)
{
    alert("Error: " + message.
message);
}
```

Example 7-6: The *failure()* function alerts the user to the error message from a failed location request.

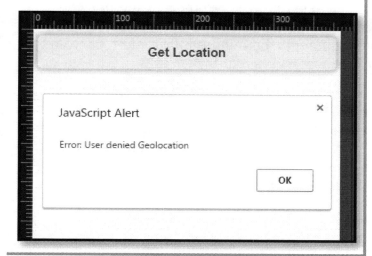

Figure 7-1: An error produced by Chrome on the desktop.

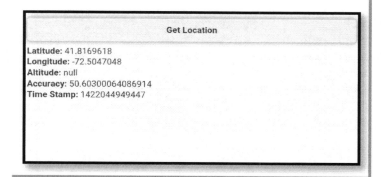

Figure 7-2: Geolocation working on a mobile device.

7 Once the successfully returned position's properties are parsed into variables, those variables are used to create the *output* variable as an HTML string. The inner HTML of the *result* **<div>** is set to the value of *output*.

8 In the event of a failure the *failure()* function—shown in example 7-6—is called. This function alerts the user to the reason for the failure. Note that the geolocation plug-in has an error message object with a message property that contains text, as opposed to the camera plug-in's error message from the previous chapter.

9 You can run the application from your desktop browser (just remember to explicitly call the *init()* function) and you'll likely see an error message, as shown in figure 7-1. Geolocation is a W3C standard, so most standards-compliant browsers will attempt to return a location object. When you run the application on a device, you should see a result like the one shown in figure 7-2.

When you run the application on your mobile device, you'll see latitude and longitude values returned to you. That's your location! At least, it's as near to your location as your mobile device can determine. You can plug those values into Google Maps and it should match your physical location.

There are a few things to note when you're working with locations. First, and most obvious, is that the PhoneGap HTML5 geolocation does not always return the most accurate positioning data. The *accuracy* value that was returned by the position object is the accuracy of the location in meters, and it can sometimes be in the hundreds. This means that the location data may be hundreds of meters off from a user's actual location, even when we request high accuracy.

This accuracy problem occurs because while the degree of accuracy returned from a mobile device increases over time, the HTML5 geolocation standard will return the first valid position object that it receives from the hardware. A simple way to test this is to run our application on a freshly booted device and note how high the *accuracy* value is. It may be over 1000 meters. Reboot the device again, ensure that the GPS is turned on, and open the built-in map application. Once you see that the map application has an accurate location, open our geolocation application and run it again. You should see that the *accuracy* value is much lower, perhaps as low as two or three meters. The reason for the dramatically increased accuracy is because the device had already been tracking its location due to the map application, and so had an accurate position object available to send to the PhoneGap HTML5 geolocation request.

It's also important to note that the position object will return a null value for data that is unavailable. This is especially common with altitude data. When you're designing your application, ensure that essential location data is validated before you use it.

Even with this caveat, the location awareness of modern devices opens up a world of possibilities for application developers. In the next section, we will look at using the information returned from the location object to display a map of the user's position.

WHAT HAVE YOU LEARNED?

Questions for Review

1 Which of the following is important to consider when using geolocation?

a. End user privacy concerns.

b. Accuracy level required for your application.

c. Both A and B.

d. No additional considerations are needed.

2 When your application calls **getCurrentPosition()**, which of the following is returned?

a. The most accurate position object.

b. The oldest cached position object.

c. The first valid position object.

d. The newest cached position object.

3 Which of the following can provide location information?

a. GPS.

b. WiFi networks.

c. Cellular networks.

d. All of the above.

4 When you use the enableHighAccuracyUI option, the location object will always be based on the highly accurate GPS location.

a. True.

b. False.

7.2 Displaying a Map

In the previous section we learned how to obtain a location object that contains accurate geospatial coordinates from device hardware. In this section we will use those coordinates to display a map centered on the device's location.

To create the map that we will display in the application, we will use Google's Map API. In order to use the Map API, you will need an API key. If you have used Google's APIs before and already have a Public API access Key for browser applications, then you only need to activate the Google Maps JavaScript API v3 on your account and you're ready to go. If not, you'll have to create an API key.

1   First, access the Google Developers Console at *https://console.developers.google.com*. If you have not used the developer's console before, you will be prompted to create a new project, as shown in figure 7-3.

Figure 7-3: The Google Developers Console

2   Choose the option to create a new project and give it a name. Once you choose to create a project, you will have to wait while it is built. When it is finished building, you should be looking at a dashboard similar to the one shown in figure 7-4.

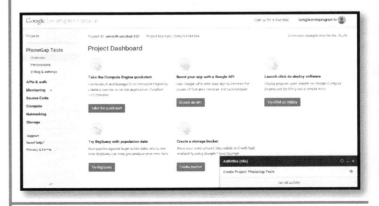

Figure 7-4: The main page for a new project.

Figure 7-5: Google's API list.

Figure 7-6: Choose the Google Maps JavaScript API v3.

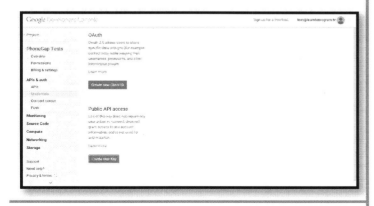

Figure 7-7: The API credentials menu.

3 Select the APIs option from the menu, shown in figure 7-5, and find the Google Maps JavaScript API v3.

4 Activate the API by clicking on the "STATUS" button. You will see a message, as shown in figure 7-6, verifying that you want to add the API.

Now that the Google Maps API is active for your Google Developer account, you can create an API key that will allow you to use the API in PhoneGap applications.

API keys identify you to Google when calls are made to a Google API. This allows Google to know who is using their resources.

5 To create an API key, select the "Credentials" option, shown in figure 7-7. Our application will not need to access Google user's account information, so choose to create a "Public API access" key.

6 Once you've chosen to create a new key, you'll have to choose the type of key that you need. The key options, shown in figure 7-8, are Server, Browser, Android, or iOS. Although you may think that you need an Android or iOS key because you're developing a mobile application, remember that PhoneGap runs in a device's native WebView, which is a type of browser. Choose the "Browser Key" option.

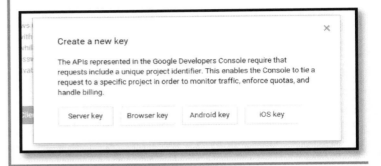

Figure 7-8: The types of API key you can generate.

7 Once you've chosen the key type you will be prompted to list referrers that are permitted to use your API key, shown in figure 7-9. When a web application attempts to use your API key to access Google APIs, Google will compare the site that referred the request to this list of allowed referrers. If the site is on the list, then the API request will be allowed. If not, the API request will be denied. When creating a PhoneGap application, your users will be accessing the API from their mobile device, not a referrer, so you need to allow all referrers. To do so, just leave the field blank.

Figure 7-9: Leave the referrers field blank to allow all referrers.

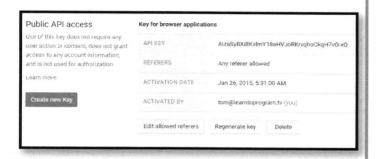

Figure 7-10: An example API key. Keep yours private.

```
<script src="https:/maps.googleapis.
com/maps/api/js?key=[INSERT YOUR KEY
HERE]"></script>
```

Example 7-7: The link to the Google Map APIs. Note that you should replace [INSERT YOUR KEY HERE] with the API key you created in your Google Developer account.

```
<button id="btnLocation"
onclick="getLocation()">Get Location</
button>
<button id="btnClear"
onclick="clearScreen()">Clear</button>
<div id="result"></div>
<div id="map-canvas"></div>
```

Example 7-8: The HTML to create our simple user interface.

⑧ Once you've chosen to create the API key you'll see it displayed on the "Credentials" screen, as in figure 7-10. Note that you need to keep your API key private.

Now that your API key is set up and you've activated the Google Maps JavaScript API v3 for your Google account, we're ready to create our application. This app will build on what we created in the previous section, so you can modify the WhereAmI app instead of creating a new PhoneGap project.

⑨ First, in index.html, link to the Google Map APIs with your API key by including a **<script>** element link in the header. This link is shown in example 7-7.

⑩ Next, modify the user interface. We will reuse the "Get Location" button, but we will add a "Clear" button to remove the map that we generate, and we will also add a **<div>** element to hold the map, called *map-canvas*. This HTML is shown in example 7-8.

```
#btnLocation {
    display: none;
}
#map-canvas {
    height: 600px;
    width: 100%;
}
```

Example 7-9: The CSS sizes the map that we will display.

11 Before jumping into the JavaScript and building all the moving parts, open mainAppStyles.css. We're going to add a style element to our map to size it. The map will fill the **<div>** that it is loaded into, so we will size that **<div>**, *map-canvas*, as in example 7-9. Note that *btnLocation*.

12 Now open main.js. You'll note that it begins identically to the previous section. Once the device is loaded, an *init()* function displays the *btnLocation* button, and the *getLocation()* function is run with the callback functions *success()* for a successful execution, *failure()* for an unsuccessful execution, and the options stored in the global variable *options*.

The changes will occur in the what we do with the *success()* and *failure()* functions. *success()* will have to not only display the coordinates, but also use the Google Maps API to create and display a map.

```
var options;

window.onload = function()
{
    document.
addEventListener('deviceready', init,
false);
}

function init() {
    document.
getElementById('btnLocation').style.
display = "block";
    options = {
        maximumAge: 3000,
        timeout: 5000,
        enableHighAccuracy: true
    };
}

function getLocation()
{
    navigator.geolocation.
getCurrentPosition(success, failure,
options);
}
```

Example 7-10: The JavaScript begins identically to the previous example app.

```
function success(position)
{
    var lat = position.coords.
latitude;
    var long = position.coords.
longitude;

    var output = "<strong>Latitude:</
strong> " + lat;
    output +=
"<br/><strong>Longitude:</strong> " +
long;

    document.getElementById('result').
innerHTML = output;

    var mapOptions = {
        center: {lat: lat, lng: long},
        zoom: 18
    };

    var map = new google.maps.
Map(document.getElementById('map-
canvas'), mapOptions);
    var marker = new google.maps.
Marker({
        position: {lat: lat, lng:
long},
        map: map
    });
}
```

Example 7-11: *success()* creates and displays the map.

```
function failure(message)
{
    alert("Error: " + message.
message);
}
```

Example 7-12: *failure()* displays the error message.

13 The *success()* function, shown in example 7-11, creates the map that we intend to display. First, it uses the position object that the **getCurrentPosition()** method returned to populate *lat* and *long* variables with coordinate information, and then it displays those coordinates in the *result* **<div>**, as we did in the previous section. Then, it creates a *mapOptions* variable with the Google Maps API options that will generate our map. Note that we have simply used the **center** attribute to define the center of the map as being the position objects latitude and longitude, and then we set the **zoom** attribute to "18."

14 The map is actually created with the *map* variable. We pass the element that we intend to use as the map's target, *map-canvas*, and the options to the map. Then, we create a *marker* variable which will draw a marker on the map at the *lat* and *long* position.

15 Example 7-12 shows the *failure()* function. As in the previous section, it displays the error message.

```
function clearScreen()
{
    document.getElementById('map-
canvas').innerHTML = "";
    document.getElementById('map-
canvas').style.backgroundColor =
"white";
    document.getElementById('result').
innerHTML = "";
}
```

Example 7-13: The *clearScreen()* function.

16 The final function, *clearScreen()*, shown in example 7-13, clears the output data that has been displayed to the user.

17 Now, when you run the application and choose the "Get Location" button, you'll see your location coordinates displayed above a map centered on those coordinates, with a marker pinpointing exactly where you are, as shown in figure 7-11. Remember that when testing this application, you have to run it on either an emulated device or a physical device. It will not work in the Chrome mobile emulation mode.

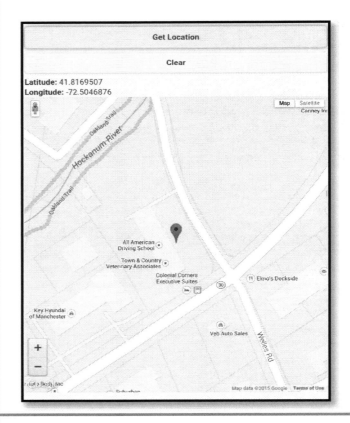

Figure 7-11: The app running on a Google Nexus 7.

Congratulations, you now have a basic mapping application! Using your phones location data and freely available APIs from Google, you're able to create a location-aware application for your users.

The Google Maps JavaScript API v3 has a large set of features and options that allow you to customize the map to fit your application. The API documentation is available at *https://developers.google.com/maps/documentation/javascript/*.

In the next section, we will look at using the compass on a mobile device by creating a simple compass application.

Questions for Review

1 How much does Google charge for access to their Google Map API?

    a. $10 a month.

    b. $0.01 per API call.

    c. Your eternal soul.

    d. Nothing for most users.

2 What should you do with your Google API key?

    a. Post it online for anyone to use.

    b. Put it in a screenshot in a book for anyone to see.

    c. Keep it private.

    d. Nothing, just generate new ones whenever you need them.

3 The size of a map displayed using the Google Maps API is determined by options passed to the API.

    a. True.

    b. False.

4 Maps created using the Google Maps API automatically insert a marker at the origin location.

    a. True.

    b. False.

7.3 Working with the Compass

In this chapter we have been demonstrating the location aware capabilities of modern mobile devices by using PhoneGap's geolocation plug-in. In this section, we will use another PhoneGap plug-in, the device orientation plug-in, to create an application that displays the user's current heading.

As with the plug-ins we have used so far in this book, the device orientation plug-in adds specific, requested functionality to PhoneGap. The base PhoneGap installation does not include the complete code to interact with all of the features offered by a mobile device. This is because most applications do not need to access all of a phone's features. Adding that code to a simple application like the Chuck Norris Joke Generator would create extraneous data that neither we nor our users need. Plug-ins allow us to specifically target a PhoneGap project to a specific usage scenario.

For this section, create a new PhoneGap project named Compass that is based on the template we have been using. This simple application will feature "Start Compass" and "Stop Compass" buttons and a display **<div>** to contain the resulting compass heading. The compass heading that will be returned to us from the mobile device will be represented in degrees, from zero to 360.

① First, add the plug-in to the PhoneGap project. Navigate to the Compass project directory, and use the "phonegap add plugin" command to add the device orientation plug-in, as shown in example 7-15.

```
phonegap plugin add org.apache.
cordova.device-orientation
```

Example 7-14: The console command to install the device orientation plug-in.

2 In the index.html file the user interface requires two buttons, "Start Compass" and "Stop Compass," a "Compass Heading" heading text, and an empty **<div>** element to contain the result. The HTML is shown in example 7-16.

```
<button id="start"
onclick="startCompass()">Start
Compass</button>
<button id="stop"
onclick="stopCompass()">Stop Compass</
button>
<h2>Compass Heading:</h2>
<div id="result"></div>
```

Example 7-15: The HTML code for our compass application.

3 In the mainAppStyles. css file, hide the *start* and *stop* buttons by setting their display to "none," as in example 7-16.

```
#start, #stop {
    display: none;
}
```

Example 7-16: mainAppStyles.css hides *start* and *stop*.

4 In main.js create three global variables, *compass*, *options*, and *result*. Have an *init()* function run once the device is loaded, as we have been doing. Within that *init()* function, display the *start* and *stop* buttons and set the value of the global variable *result* to the *result* **<div>** element.

In *init()* we also set the options that we will use when the application communicates with the compass, as we did with the options for the geolocation plug-in. In this case, shown in example 7-18, we only set one option, frequency, to the value "500." That refers to how often, in milliseconds, we want to refresh the heading data.

```
var compass;
var options;
var result;

window.onload = function() {
    document.
addEventListener('deviceready', init,
false);
}

function init(){
    document.getElementById('start').
style.display = "block";
    document.getElementById('stop').
style.display = "block";
    result = document.
getElementById('result');
    options = { frequency: 500 };
}
```

Example 7-17: The beginning of main.js.

```
function startCompass()
{
    compass = navigator.compass.
watchHeading(success, compassError,
options);
}

function stopCompass()
{
    navigator.compass.
clearWatch(compass);
    result.innerHTML = "";
}

function success(heading)
{
    result.innerHTML = "<strong>" +
heading.magneticHeading + "</strong>";
}

function compassError(error)
{
    alert("Compass Error: " + error.
code);
}
```

Example 7-18: The *startCompass()*, *stopCompass()*, *success()*, and *compassError()* functions control the starting, stopping, and display of the compass heading information.

5 The *startCompass()* function runs when the user touches the "Start Compass" button. It uses the **watchHeading()** method of the **compass** object to retrieve heading data, which executes the callback function *success()* when it successfully receives heading information, *compassError()* when it does not, and takes *options* as an argument. **watchHeading()** will return heading data until we clear it.

6 The *stopCompass()* function uses the **clearWatch()** method to stop receiving heading data. It also clears the inner HTML of the *result* **<div>**.

7 The *success()* function takes the heading object that is returned from the compass plug-in and displays its **magneticHeading** property in the *result* **<div>**.

8 Finally, the *compassError()* function is called when **watchHeading()** encounters an error. It simply alerts the user to the error's error code.

9 When you run your application and press the "Start Compass" button, you will see your heading displayed in the *result* **<div>**, as seen in figure 7-12.

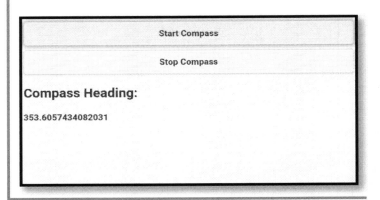

Figure 7-12: The application returning heading information.

You now have a simple application that will display to your user the direction that they are facing. As with a traditional compass, zero degrees represents North, 90 degrees represents East, 180 degrees represents South, and 270 degrees represents West. You can use this information to visualize a user's direction in any number of ways.

Questions for Review

1 How does the heading object represent a heading?

a. Using mils.

b. Using degrees.

c. Using N/S/E/W.

d. Graphically.

2 How often does the compass object return a heading object when using the **watchHeading()** method?

a. Every second.

b. Every 500 milliseconds.

c. Every 100 milliseconds.

d. As often as requested by the "frequency" option parameter.

3 What direction are you facing if your device displays a heading of 45?

a. North.

b. Northeast.

c. Southeast.

d. West.

4 The clearWatch() method from the compass object will stop the object from returning heading objects.

a. True.

b. False.

CHAPTER 07 LAB EXERCISE

In this lab exercise we will build on the exercise from chapter five. In that exercise, we had an application that returned a list of alternative fuel stations based on a ZIP code. In this exercise, we will add a button to allow the user to return a list of alternative fuel stations based on their current location.

The API that was used can dynamically understand different types of location data, including latitude and longitude coordinates. They can be used in place of ZIP codes when calling the API.

1   Modify index.html to include a button that lets users get a list of alternative fuel stations based on their current location.

2   Wire that button to a function that will access the PhoneGap Geolocation plug-in and find the device's current latitude and longitude. Use that position information to create an API call to the remote server.

Alternative Fuels

Enter your ZIP Code:

Get Locations!

Load Saved Results

Press the button to retrieve a list of alternative fuel stations near that ZIP Code.

OR

Press the button below to retrieve a list of alternative fuel stations based on your current location

Get Locations Near Me!

3   Display the list of alternative fuel stations returned from the latitude and longitude API call. Modify the output HTML so that it reflects whether the information is based off of a ZIP code or nearby locations.

Alternative Fuels

Enter your ZIP Code:

[   ]

Get Locations!

Load Saved Results

Press the button to retrieve a list of alternative fuel stations near that ZIP Code.

OR

Press the button below to retrieve a list of alternative fuel stations based on your current location

Get Locations Near Me!

Nearby

De Cormier Nissan
> *Fuel Type:* ELEC
> *Distance:* 0.26Miles
> *Address:* 30 Tolland Tpke, Manchester
> *Phone Number:* 860-643-4165
> *Hours:* Dealership business hours

DECORMIER NISS
> *Fuel Type:* ELEC
> *Distance:* 0.30Miles
> *Address:* 30 Tolland Turnpike, Manchester
> *Phone Number:* 888-758-4389
> *Hours:* 24 hours daily

Chapter Summary

So far you have used PhoneGap plug-ins to access device orientation, geolocation, the device's camera, the file system, and media controls. All of the documentation for these APIs can be found on PhoneGap's website, *http://docs.phonegap.com/en/ edge/cordova_plugins_pluginapis.md.html*. From here, you can browse through the APIs that we have used and explore them in more detail, or you can look at other features that you could add to your future applications.

As you use more plug-ins to access more features of an end user's mobile device, it is important to remember that you are asking to be entrusted with personal information. It's important to respect your users, and the best way to do that is to clearly and forthrightly disclose what information your application collects, what it does with that information, and why your app requires it..

In the next chapter we will continue to use features of mobile hardware by accessing the accelerometer. We will obtain accelerometer readings and we will explore how to use the accelerometer for user input.

Working with the Accelerometer

CHAPTER OBJECTIVES:

- You will understand how accelerometers work.
- You will learn how to access accelerometer data.
- You will discover how to use the accelerometer as an input device.

8.1 Obtaining Accelerometer Readings

In this chapter we will use another hardware sensor that is available on all modern mobile devices, the accelerometer. An accelerometer is a sensor that measures acceleration along a given axis. On your phone or mobile device, the accelerometer returns acceleration data for an X, Y, and Z axis in meters per second squared.

In order to visualize this, place your mobile phone or tablet on a flat surface and look at it from above. The axis running from the bottom of the device to the top is the Y axis. The axis running from the left of the device to the right is the X axis.

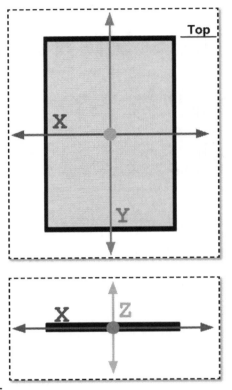

Now, look at your device from the bottom edge. The axis running up and down, perpendicular to the X and Y axes, is the Z axis.

Right now, if your phone or tablet is laid on a flat surface, the accelerometer is registering approximately 9.81 on the Z axis. This is because it is measuring the effect of gravity on the device along its Z axis. If you were to hold your device against a flat wall, so that the bottom edge of the device was closest to the floor and the top edge of the device was closest to the ceiling, the accelerometer would register 9.81 on the Y axis. If you then rotated the device by 90 degrees, so that the right side of the device was closest to the ceiling and the left side of the device was closest to the floor, the accelerometer would register 9.81 on the X axis.

By measuring the forces being applied to these three axes, the accelerometer lets you know how a device is positioned in space. In this chapter we will first learn how to access those values, and then we will demonstrate using them to control an object on the screen.

First, create a new PhoneGap project named Accel using our standard template. We will install the device motion plug-in in order to access the accelerometer data.

```
▸  phonegap plugin add org.apache.
   cordova.device-motion
```

Example 8-1: Installing the device motion plug-in.

```
▸  <div id="result">
▸      <strong>X: </strong><output
   id="xOut"></output><br/>
▸      <strong>Y: </strong><output
   id="yOut"></output><br/>
▸      <strong>Z: </strong><output
   id="zOut"></output><br/>
▸  </div>
```

Example 8-2: The HTML will display the accelerometer data.

```
▸  var xOut;
▸  var yOut;
▸  var zOut;
▸
▸  window.onload = function () {
▸      document.
   addEventListener("deviceready", init,
   false);
▸  };
▸
▸  function init()
▸  {
▸      xOut = document.
   getElementById('xOut');
▸      yOut = document.
   getElementById('yOut');
▸      zOut = document.
   getElementById('zOut');
▸  }
```

Example 8-3: The start of main.js.

1 In the Accel project directory, use the "phonegap plugin add" command to add the device motion plug-in, as shown in example 8-1.

2 Once the plug-in is installed, open the index.html file. Create a *result* **<div>** that contains a set of **<output>** elements named *xOut*, *yOut*, and *zOut* to hold the data returned from the accelerometer, as shown in example 8-2.

3 Next, open main.js. First, create three global variables, *xOut*, *yOut*, and *zOut*. Then, launch an *init()* function when the device is ready. Within that *init()* function, set the global *xOut*, *yOut*, and *zOut* variables to the *xOut*, *yOut*, and *zOut* HTML elements. This is shown in example 8-3.

4 Still in the *init()* function, shown in example 8-4, create an *accel* variable. Set this variable to the **watchAcceleration()** method of the **accelerometer** object. The **watchAcceleration()** method follows a similar pattern to other PhoneGap methods we have used. There are two callback functions—here assigned to *success()* and *accelError()*—and an options parameter. In this case, we have set the options parameter in the method call itself, rather than as a separate variable.

watchAcceleration() will poll the accelerometer every set number of milliseconds. We have set that poll to occur every 1000 milliseconds, or every second, with the *frequency* value.

5 The *success()* function takes the accelerometer data from the X, Y, and Z axis of an accelerometer object and uses that data to populate the *xOut*, *yOut*, and *zOut* HTML elements. The *accelError()* function alerts the user to an error. This is shown in example 8-5.

```
function init()
{
    xOut = document.
getElementById('xOut');
    yOut = document.
getElementById('yOut');
    zOut = document.
getElementById('zOut');

    var options = { frequency: 1000 };
    var accel = navigator.
accelerometer.
watchAcceleration(success, accelError,
options);
}
```

Example 8-4: The complete *init()* function.

```
function success(accel)
{
    var x = accel.x;
    var y = accel.y;
    var z = accel.z;

    xOut.innerHTML = x;
    yOut.innerHTML = y;
    zOut.innerHTML = z;
}

function accelError(error)
{
    alert("Accelerometer Error");
}
```

Example 8-5: The *success()* and *accelError()* functions.

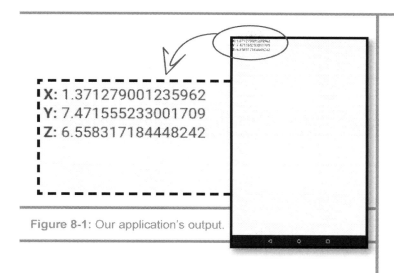

X: 1.371279001235962
Y: 7.471555233001709
Z: 6.558317184448242

Figure 8-1: Our application's output.

6 When you run the program on your test device, you'll see output similar to what is shown in figure 8-1.

Now you can see the accelerometer's readings for each axis. Place your device on a flat surface again, as you did at the beginning of this section. You should see that the X and Y values are near zero, and the Z value is approximately 9.81. Don't worry if the readings are not exact.

Pick up your device and hold it directly in front of you with the top of the device pointing up. The Y value should approach 9.81, and the Z value should have been reduced to approximately zero. As you move the device, notice how all of the values change. Using these three values, it is possible to determine the exact orientation of the device. It is also possible to use those values to control elements that are displayed on the screen.

In the next section we will use the X and Y values to move an object around the screen. Imagine a marble balanced on your device (I do not recommend actually balancing a marble on your device) and consider how it would move as you changed your device's position. This will inform how we use the accelerometer values in the next section. Hold your mobile device flat, so that X and Y are as near to zero as you can make them, and rotate the device on the Y axis, and then on the X axis. As you rotate on the Y axis you will see the value of X increasing or decreasing, and as you rotate on the X axis you will see the value of Y increasing or decreasing.

Questions for Review

1 What are the values returned from the accelerometer measuring?

   a. Rotational forces acting on the device.

   b. Gravitational forces acting on the device.

   c. Movement of the device.

   d. The direction that the device is pointing.

2 If you rotate your device on its X axis, which return value will change?

   a. X.

   b. Y.

   c. Z.

   d. Both Y and Z.

3 How often does the watchAcceleration() method return data?

   a. Once per second.

   b. Every 500 milliseconds.

   c. As set in the options.

   d. Once, when first called.

4 Why does a device at rest on a table register approximately 9.81 on its Z axis?

   a. It is registering Earth's gravity.

   b. It has not been properly calibrated.

   c. It is broken and should be returned.

   d. It is registering its height above the floor.

8.2 Using the Accelerometer for Input

In the previous section we learned how to access the accelerometer and obtain its readings. We learned that those accelerometer readings allow us to determine the orientation of our mobile device, and we experimented with changing the device's orientation while watching how the accelerometer readings changed. In this section we will use that knowledge to make the device orientation control a graphic on our device's screen. In this way, we will demonstrate how to use the orientation of the device as a means for user input.

In order to create and move a simple graphic we will use the HTML5 **<canvas>** element. For those who do not have experience using the **<canvas>** element, it is a bitmap canvas that can be used to render graphics on an HTML page. We will not delve too deeply into the specifics of the **<canvas>** element, however, it is a very useful tool for creating games or other graphically demanding applications with HTML5.

The graphic that we move will behave in a similar manner to our theoretical balanced marble in the previous section. As we tilt the device right, it will move right. Tilt the device forward and it will move forward. One problem that you might already be considering is that a device's screen orientation changes based on the device's position, so by controlling our application with the device's position we run the risk of unexpectedly changing the screen orientation during normal use. To solve that problem, we will use a third-party plug-in.

To create this section's application you can either create a copy of the previous section's Accel project or directly modify that project.

1 First, we will use the Screen Orientation Plug-in from Yoik, available at *https://github.com/yoik/cordova-yoik-screenorientation*. Example 8-6 shows the installation command. Note that it is identical to a first-party plug-in installation command.

```
▶   phonegap plugin add net.yoik.cordova.
    plugins.screenorientation
```

Example 8-6: Install a plug-in to control screen orientation in our application.

2 Because this application is based on the previous section's application, the device motion plug-in is already installed. Open the index.html file and create a single **<canvas>** element, as shown in example 8-7.

The **<canvas>** element will contain graphics that will be defined in JavaScript, so nothing further needs to be created in HTML.

```
<div id="container">
    <canvas id="myCanvas"></canvas>
</div> <!-- container -->
```

Example 8-7: The HTML code to create an empty **<canvas>** element.

3 In mainAppStyles.css, modify the default *container* **<div>** that we have been using as per example 8-8. We are using the **<canvas>** element to display the output of this application, so we no longer need the standard *margin* value. Also, we want to ensure that it uses all available space, so set *height* and *width* to 100%.

```
#container {
    margin: 0px;
    width: 100%;
    height: 100%
}
```

Example 8-8: Style the *container* **<div>** to encompass the entire device screen.

4 Before you begin writing the JavaScript code, find a small, simple, square graphic to use in this program. We found a 50x50 pixel graphic, but any small square graphic will do. If you cannot find one, you can simply make a 50x50 pixel colored square in any drawing software.

```
var ctx;
var monster;
var monsterPosX=0;
var monsterPosY=0;
```

Example 8-9: The global variables that we will use in this application.

```
window.onload = function () {
    document.
addEventListener("deviceready", init,
false);
    screen.lockOrientation('portrait-
primary');
    var c = document.
getElementById('myCanvas');
    ctx = c.getContext("2d");
    ctx.canvas.width = window.
innerWidth;
    ctx.canvas.height = window.
innerHeight;
    monsterPosX = window.innerWidth /
2 - 25;
    monsterPosY = window.innerHeight /
2 - 25;
    displayMonster();
};
```

Example 8-10: The function called by the **window.onload** event.

5 In main.js first create a set of global variables, *ctx*, *monster*, *monsterPosX*, and *monsterPosY*, as shown in example 8-9. The *ctx* variable will hold the drawing context of our **<canvas>** element. This context is an object that provides the methods and properties we will use to draw graphics. The *monster* variable will hold information about our monster graphic, most importantly its data source. Finally, the *monsterPosX* and *monsterPosY* variables will hold the current position on the screen of *monster*.

6 The function called by the **window.onload** event is much larger than it has been in previous sections. Its use here is to initialize the context object and set up the application's initial state. It is shown in example 8-10.

7 First, the *init()* function is called once the device is ready. Next, we use the Screen Orientation plug-in to lock the orientation to "portrait-primary" mode.

8 After the orientation is set, we initialize a variable to hold the **<canvas>** HTML element. Once that is done, we set the *ctx* global variable to the 2D context of the **<canvas>** element. This allows us to use the methods and properties associated with the HTML5 canvas 2D object. At the moment, the only context available is 2D, however, there are plans to eventually add a 3D context.

9 Once *ctx* is established we can set its width and height to fill the screen. Then, we set *monsterPosX* and *monsterPosY* to the center of the screen, but offset them by half of the pixel size of our image. Positioning of elements is done according to their top left corner, so our offset ensures that when we display *monster* it will be drawn in the center of the screen.

10 Finally, we call the *displayMonster()* function. This function, shown in example 8-12, sets the *monster* variable as an **Image** object, sets its source to the "monster.gif" file, and, when that file is loaded, draws *monster* to *ctx* at location *monsterPosX, monsterPosY*.

```
window.onload = function () {
    document.
addEventListener("deviceready", init,
false);
    screen.lockOrientation('portrait-
primary');
    var c = document.
getElementById('myCanvas');
    ctx = c.getContext("2d");
    ctx.canvas.width = window.
innerWidth;
    ctx.canvas.height = window.
innerHeight;
    monsterPosX = window.innerWidth /
2 - 25;
    monsterPosY = window.innerHeight /
2 - 25;
    displayMonster();
};
```

Example 8-11: The function called by the **window.onload** event.

```
function displayMonster()
{
    monster = new Image();
    monster.onload = function()
    {
        ctx.drawImage(monster,
monsterPosX, monsterPosY);
    }
    monster.src = "monster.gif";
}
```

Example 8-12: The *displayMonster()* function.

```
function init() {
    var accel = navigator.
accelerometer.
watchAcceleration(success, accelError,
{ frequency: 50});
}
```

Example 8-13: The *init()* function.

```
function success(accel)
{
    ctx.canvas.width = ctx.canvas.
width;
    monsterPosX -= accel.x;
    monsterPosY += accel.y;
    ctx.drawImage(monster,
monsterPosX, monsterPosY);
}
```

Example 8-14: The *success()* function.

11 You certainly noticed that the *init()* function was called by the **window.onload** event. This function, shown in example 8-13, starts watching the accelerometer using the **watchAcceleration()** method, as it did in the previous section. The key difference is that here the frequency is much higher. That higher frequency will create a much more responsive experience for the end user.

12 The **watchAcceleration()** method calls the *success()* function, shown in example 8-14, when it receives data from the accelerometer. The first thing that *success()* does is clear the screen by resetting *ctx*. A context will be reset whenever its width or height are set. Once the screen is clear, we modify *monsterPosX* by the subtracting value of the accelerometer's X axis reading and then modify *monsterPosY* by adding the value of the accelerometer's Y axis reading. X is subtracted and Y is added due to the values that are returned from the accelerometer. If we added X, then the graphic would move to the left when the screen was tilted right.

13 Finally, the *accelError()* function simply alerts the user that there was an error with the accelerometer.

```
function accelError(error)
{
    alert("Accelerometer Error");
}
```

Example 8-15: The *accelError()* function.

When you run the application on a device you'll see your image in the center of the screen and it will move as you would expect when you tilt your device.

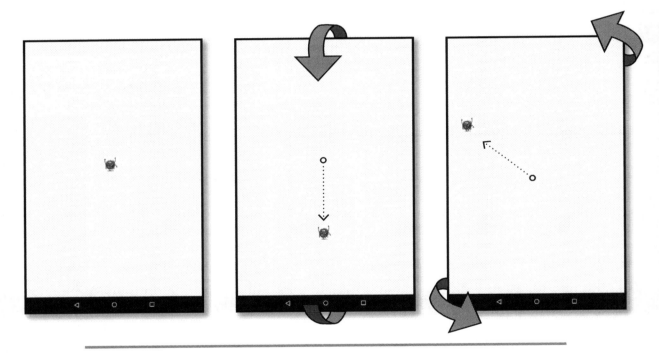

Figure 8-2: The graphic begins in the center of the screen, but when the device is tilted it moves around as though it were rolling.

The implementation here isn't perfect, but it does show how easy it is to use the accelerometer of a modern mobile device as a key part of the user interface.

Questions for Review

1 When using a canvas element, what different contexts are available?

   a. The 2D and 3D contexts.

   b. Only the 2D context.

   c. Only the 3D context.

   d. The 5D context, as combination of the 2D and 3D contexts.

2 Why is it important to poll the accelerometer more often in this application than it was in the previous section?

   a. In order to obtain a more accurate reading.

   b. In order to obtain a more valid reading.

   c. In order to make the application feel more responsive to the user.

   d. There is not reason to poll the accelerometer more frequently in this application.

3 There is no way to stop the screen orientation from changing when using this application.

   a. True.

   b. False.

4 The canvas element is used to render graphics on an HTML page.

   a. True.

   b. False.

CHAPTER 08 LAB EXERCISE

1 Using the command line, create a new PhoneGap application called Accelerate.

```
● ● ●                    🖿 Desktop — bash — 80×24
Last login: Thu Feb 19 14:00:28 on ttys000
Mark-MacBook-Pro:~ marklassoff$ cd Desktop/
Mark-MacBook-Pro:Desktop marklassoff$ phonegap create Accelerate
Creating a new cordova project with name "Hello World" and id "com.phonegap.hell
oworld" at location "/Users/marklassoff/Desktop/Accelerate"
Using custom www assets from https://github.com/phonegap/phonegap-app-hello-worl
d/archive/master.tar.gz

Mark-MacBook-Pro:Desktop marklassoff$ ▊
```

2 Add the necessary PhoneGap accelerometer libraries as demonstrated in this chapter. Enter the project on the command line by typing `cd Accelerate`.

Enter the following into the command line to access the necessary PhoneGap libraries: `cordova plugin add org.apache.cordova.device-motion`

```
● ● ●                    🖿 Accelerate — bash — 80×24
Mark-MacBook-Pro:Desktop marklassoff$ cd Accelerate/
Mark-MacBook-Pro:Accelerate marklassoff$ phonegap plugin add org.apache.cordova.
device-motion
Fetching plugin "org.apache.cordova.device-motion" via plugin registry

npm
  http GET http://registry.cordova.io/org.apache.cordova.device-motion

npm http
  200 http://registry.cordova.io/org.apache.cordova.device-motion

Mark-MacBook-Pro:Accelerate marklassoff$ ▯
```

3 Remove unnecessary files from the application template as demonstrated in this chapter. Also remove any unnecessary code from the index.html file. In the body of the document, create the following HTML:

```
<div id="out"></div>
```

4 Add a <style> element in the head of your document. To center the output <div> we just created, add the following CSS code inside the style element:

```
#out {
    width: 50%;
    margin: 0 auto;
    height: 100px;
    font-size: 2.5em;
}
```

5 Using Javascript, create an initialization sequence that runs a function named init() once the 'deviceready' event occurs. You'll want to start with the following Javascript code:

```
window.onload= function()
{
    document.addEventListener();
}
```

Note that this code is incomplete and you'll need to fill in the missing code to launch the init() function when the 'deviceready' event occurs.

6 Write the necessary code to activate the accelerometer and obtain readings every 50 - 100 milliseconds. In the "success" callback function associated with the accelerometer. watchAcceleration(), you're going to need to work with the X and Y values returned by the accelerometer. Make sure you code the "error" callback function to display an error message, should the unit fail to obtain accelerometer readings.

7 Referring to the diagram, use the "out" logical division to display which direction(s) the unit is rotated.

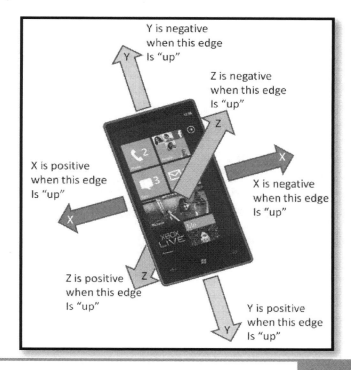

Y is negative when this edge Is "up"

Z is negative when this edge Is "up"

X is positive when this edge Is "up"

X is negative when this edge Is "up"

Z is positive when this edge Is "up"

Y is positive when this edge Is "up"

If the X value returned by the accelerometer is positive, display "LEFT". If the X value is negative, display "RIGHT". Use the Y value returned by the accelerometer to display "TOP" or "BOTTOM". You may ignore the Z value for the purpose of this exercise. The X and Y value will react simultaneously, so you will have to display both axes in the logical division.

8 Test and debug if you do not get the expected result.

9 You will notice that the accelerometer is VERY sensitive to any movement at all. Adjust your code to create a reasonable "buffer" so that the unit can be held in your hands and only intentional movements result in output displayed in the logical division. You want to make the unit less sensitive to very slight tilts along either the X or Y axis. You can do this by adjusting the values at which the device reacts to the tilt. Examine the entire range of values as you tilt the device 360 degrees. Experiment until the effects of minor movements are dampened and the user can accurately make the LEFT, RIGHT, TOP, and BOTTOM values appear.

Chapter Summary

In this chapter you have accessed your mobile device's built-in accelerometer, displayed the acceleration values, learned how the accelerometer works, and created a simple application that leveraged the accelerometer as a control input.

Now, you can determine where a device is in the world using geolocation, its direction using the compass, and its orientation using the accelerometer. The sensors included on modern mobile devices can provide developers with a remarkable amount of data to use when creating applications and user interfaces.

So far, the user interfaces that we have created have been basic. Instead of creating complicated interfaces, we have focused on exposing the features available on mobile devices. In the next few chapters we will talk about creating more advanced user interfaces using the jQuery Mobile framework.

Interfaces with jQuery Mobile

CHAPTER OBJECTIVES:

- You will learn what the jQuery Mobile Framework is and why it is useful.

- You will understand how to implement a customized version of the jQuery Mobile Framework for your project.

- You will create jQuery Pages, Toolbars, and Navbars.

- You will use jQuery to create mobile Buttons and Switches.

9.1 jQuery Mobile Basics

When we created our template project we included a link to the jQuery Mobile Framework through a Content Delivery Network, or CDN. In case you've forgotten, here is the code that created that link:

```
<link rel="stylesheet" href="http://code.jquery.com/mobile/1.4.3/jquery.mobile-1.4.3.min.css" />
<script src="http://code.jquery.com/jquery-1.11.1.min.js"></script>
<script src="http://code.jquery.com/mobile/1.4.3/jquery.mobile-1.4.3.min.js"></script>
```

This code has appeared in all of our applications so far. A CDN is a website that provides content—in this case the jQuery Mobile Framework—for other webpages or web applications to use. For a standard web application or webpage that targets users who have to be online, a CDN can be a valuable resource. When developing and testing a mobile PhoneGap application, CDNs are also a useful resource. However, because in order to use the content delivered by a CDN a user must be online, PhoneGap applications that may be used offline cannot rely on a CDN.

The jQuery Mobile Framework is a resource, based on the standard jQuery library, that provides webpage and application components that work across a range of mobile devices. Explaining the entirety of the jQuery Mobile Framework could be a complete course in itself, but in this chapter we will cover a few basic aspects that can improve our PhoneGap applications.

We have primarily been using jQuery Mobile in our applications for visual effects. Most commonly, you have seen buttons formatted for a mobile device due to the jQuery Mobile Framework. Also, the formatting of our Media Player from chapter six relied on the jQuery Mobile Framework.

jQuery doesn't only offer visual improvements, but it includes a complete event system that compliments and enhances standard JavaScript. You have seen some of the jQuery event system in chapter four when we parsed JSON objects. Later, in chapter 10, we will take a look at other, mobile-centric jQuery events that can enhance your application.

The best way to get acquainted with the jQuery Mobile Framework is to visit their website, at *http://www.jquerymobile.com*. The goal of jQuery is to simplify the development of webpages and web applications - and, therefore, PhoneGap applications - by simplifying and standardizing common tasks and by introducing a common, consistent design language that is optimized for mobile usage. If you only use jQuery to enhance the style of your application without ever touching on the event system, it will still save you time and effort.

Figure 9-1: The jQuery Mobile website.

Figure 9-2: The link to the jQuery Mobile CDN.

1 Go to the jQuery Mobile website, *http://www.jquerymobile.com*, shown in figure 9-1.

2 To access the CDN, click on "Download" and scroll down the page. The valid link to the jQuery CDN is shown in figure 9-2. The download page also offers a number of other alternatives to the CDN link.

When you're developing or testing an application, using the CDN is often the easiest and fastest way to use the full suite of features available with the most up-to-date jQuery Mobile. However, you may prefer to download the complete jQuery Mobile Framework, host it locally, and have your application link to the local version. This ensures that you can continue development whether or not you have internet access.

Downloading the complete jQuery Mobile Framework for development can be helpful, but it is a requirement if you want to implement jQuery Mobile in a PhoneGap application that can be used offline. Although the full framework seems relatively small, clocking in at approximately seven and a half megabytes, for mobile applications where every byte counts (often in a literal sense as more and more data providers are tracking bandwidth use) including the complete framework is wasteful.

The best way to use the jQuery Mobile Framework when developing PhoneGap applications is to only download the aspects of it that are required for your application. Fortunately, this is simple to do using the jQuery Mobile Download Builder.

3 The Download Builder, found at *http://www.jquerymobile.com/download-builder/* and shown in figure 9-3, allows you to pick and choose exactly which jQuery Mobile modules you will need to use. Once you have selected what you are interested in—for example, the slider, transitions, and the listview—you will be able to download a customized version of jQuery. Note that it will automatically select dependencies for anything you've selected.

Figure 9-3: The Download Builder site.

4 Once you're ready, select the "Build My Download" button, shown in figure 9-4.

Note that the Download Builder is still alpha software and, as such, it is your responsibility to ensure that it works with your app.

Figure 9-4: When you're ready, click "Build My Download."

The default theme and styling of jQuery is effective and visually appealing, however as your application moves closer to production you'll want to personalize it to suit your style or brand. This can be done through custom CSS, graphical assets, or other means, but jQuery Mobile offers a tool that may handle much of the groundwork for you: the ThemeRoller tool.

Available at *http://themeroller.jquerymobile.com/*, the ThemeRoller tool is a GUI tool to color and style page elements. The styles are then stored as a CSS file that can be downloaded and used in conjunction with jQuery Mobile.

Figure 9-5: The jQuery Mobile ThemeRoller.

5 The ThemeRoller makes it simple to select and modify the colors and styles of jQuery Mobile elements. It's a quick way to modify the standard jQuery look and feel so that your application more accurately reflects your creative vision or brand. The ThemeRoller website is shown in figure 9-5.

6 Once you've created a theme that you're happy with, choose to download it as a zip file. You'll be presented with a pop up that explains how to integrate your theme into your site, and shows you how to modify it later using the ThemeRoller tool. This is shown in figure 9-6.

Figure 9-6: Saving your ThemeRoller theme.

7 The amount of features available with jQuery Mobile can be overwhelming to new developers. A good way to develop an understanding of what is available and how it can be used is through the online demos that are available at *http://demos. jquerymobile.com/1.4.5/*, shown in figure 9-7. The menu on the left allows you to navigate the demos available, and the main content pane explains them in detail.

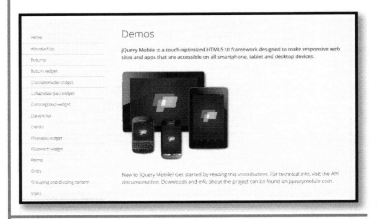

Figure 9-7: The jQuery Mobile Demos page.

8 For further information about jQuery Mobile and implementing it with your project, visit the API documentation page at *http://api.jquerymobile.com/*, shown in figure 9-8. As we have seen throughout this book, API documentation is an invaluable resource for understanding how an API works and how to utilize it in your application. The jQuery API documentation provides detailed explanations and examples for the framework.

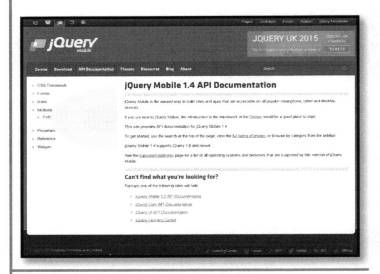

Figure 9-8: The jQuery Mobile API documentation.

The jQuery Mobile Framework, and jQuery itself, are valuable and useful tools for PhoneGap developers. Using jQuery is not required for PhoneGap development, however, it does offer a suite of tools that will make life much easier. jQuery has become a de facto standard in web development as an extension of JavaScript; although everything that you do with jQuery can be done using standard JavaScript, you'll find that using jQuery can save you time and effort.

In this section we have touched on what's offered by the jQuery Mobile Framework. In the next section we'll see how the jQuery Mobile Framework provides a new way to create pages and parse traditional HTML. Later in this chapter we'll talk about creating more useful and mobile-focused toolbars and buttons with jQuery.

Questions for Review

1 Which of the following is a key part of the jQuery Mobile Framework?

a. An event system.

b. A JavaScript compiler.

c. Custom server architecture.

d. Desktop-first design methodology.

2 jQuery Mobile is compatible with JavaScript.

a. True.

b. False.

3 What is the best option for implementing jQuery on a mobile device?

a. Always use the jQuery CDN.

b. Use a local copy of the complete jQuery Mobile.

c. Use a customized local copy of jQuery Mobile.

d. Host your own jQuery CDN.

4 Everything that can be done with jQuery can also be done with JavaScript.

a. True.

b. False.

9.2 jQuery Mobile Pages

Early in the book we discussed two methods of displaying content, using multiple HTML content files and using a single HTML file with JavaScript controlled dynamic content. jQuery Mobile provides another method of organizing content in pages.

The examples in this section will demonstrate jQuery functionality that is independent of PhoneGap. They can be completed and tested using only the Chrome mobile screen emulator.

```
▸  <meta name="viewport"
   content="width=device-width, initial-
   scale=1">
▸  <link rel="stylesheet" href="http://
   code.jquery.com/mobile/1.4.5/jquery.
   mobile-1.4.5.min.css" />
▸  <script src="http://code.jquery.com/
   jquery-1.11.1.min.js"></script>
▸  <script src="http://code.jquery.com/
   mobile/1.4.5/jquery.mobile-1.4.5.min.
   js"></script>
```

Example 9-1: The content of the HTML **<head>** element.

```
▸  <div data-role="page" id="first">
▸     <div data-role="header">
▸          <h1>Page I</h1>
▸     </div> <!-- Header -->
▸     <div role="main" class="ui-
   content">
▸          <p>Page Content</p>
▸     </div> <!-- Main -->
▸     <div data-role="footer">
▸          <h3>(c)LTP Media</h3>
▸     </div> <!-- Footer -->
▸  </div> <!-- first -->
```

Example 9-2: A basic jQuery Mobile page.

1 First, link to the jQuery CDN in your **<head>** element and add the **<meta>** tag shown in example 9-1.

2 jQuery Mobile uses the **data-role** attribute to identify elements within the **<body>**. The parent **data-role** is the *page* role, and it should be placed in a **<div>** element, as shown in example 9-2.

3 Children of the *page* role are *header*, *main*, and *footer*. The *header* role contains header information, the *main* role contains the page content, and the *footer* role contains footer information. These are shown in example 9-2. Note that the *main* role is defined using the **role** attribute, not the **data-role** attribute.

Below is a complete jQuery page, including the link to the jQuery CDN.

```
<!DOCTYPE html>
<html>
<head>
    <title>jQuery Mobile Test</title>
    <meta name="viewport" content="width=device-width, initial-scale=1">
    <link rel="stylesheet" href="http://code.jquery.com/mobile/1.4.5/
jquery.mobile-1.4.5.min.css" />
    <script src="http://code.jquery.com/jquery-1.11.1.min.js"></script>
    <script src="http://code.jquery.com/mobile/1.4.5/jquery.mobile-
1.4.5.min.js"></script>
</head>
<body>
    <div data-role="page" id="first">
        <div data-role="header">
            <h1>Page I</h1>
        </div> <!-- Header -->
        <div role="main" class="ui-content">
            <p>Page Content</p>
        </div> <!-- Main -->
        <div data-role="footer">
            <h3>(c)LTP Media</h3>
        </div> <!-- Footer -->
    </div> <!-- first -->
</body>
</html>
```

If you load the above content in your Chrome mobile device emulator, you will see a simple test page, shown at right. You'll notice that the **<div>** that was given the *header* role is styled in a specific manner, as is the **<div>** that was assigned the *footer* role. The page content, assigned the *main* role and given the **class** *ui-content* is also styled to differentiate it from the rest of the page and to promote readability.

You may be thinking that HTML already has a **<head>** tag. The difference is that jQuery roles define the *header* as a layout element, whereas the HTML **<head>** tag is a container for head elements, but is not displayed.

```
<div data-role="page" id="second">
    <div data-role="header">
            <h1>Page II</h1>
    </div> <!-- Header -->
    <div role="main" class="ui-
content">
            <p>Page 2 Content</p>
    </div> <!-- Main -->
    <div data-role="footer">
            <h3>(c)LTP Media</h3>
    </div> <!-- Footer -->
</div> <!-- second -->
```

Example 9-3: The HTML for the second content page.

```
<div role="main" class="ui-content">
    <p>Page Content</p>
    <a href="#second">Second Page</a>
</div> <!-- Main -->
```

Example 9-4: A link from the first content page to the second.

```
<div role="main" class="ui-content">
    <p>Page Content</p>
    <a href="#first">First Page</a>
</div> <!-- Main -->
```

Example 9-5: A link from the second content page to the first.

4 A single HTML file can have multiple jQuery pages. Add a second page, shown in example 9-3, to your HTML file below your first page. Note that it is nearly identical to the first page, except for a change to the *page* **<div>**'s id.

5 Load the page in Chrome and you'll see that only the first page is being displayed even though the second page exists in the HTML file. This is because jQuery Mobile treats each element with the *page* **data-role** as a distinct content page.

6 Add a link, shown in example 9-4, from the first page to the second page and then add another link, shown in example 9-5, from the second page back to the first page.

7 You'll notice now, when you click on the links, you can navigate between the two pages. Also, note that as the different pages load there is a subtle fade effect. jQuery Mobile includes page transition effects, and this fade is the default effect.

8 On many mobile devices you may want to keep the header and footer visible over content, even as that content can be scrolled. Include a few paragraphs of Lipsum text in the page content (enough to require the page to be scrolled) and view the results, shown in figure 9-9. You'll notice that the header is visible, but the footer is now at the bottom of the content text.

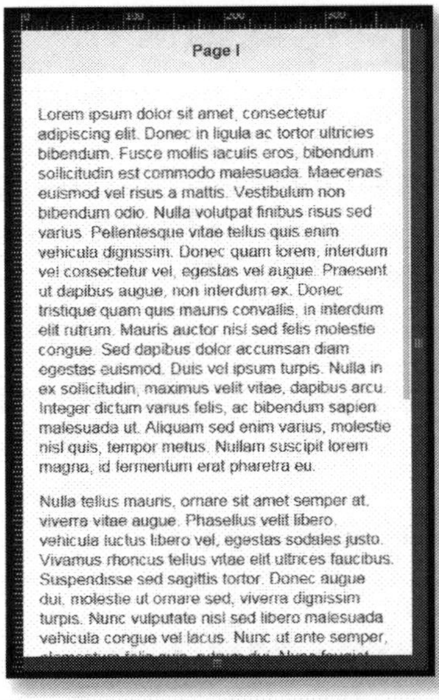

Figure 9-9: With length text the footer is pushed off of the page view.

9 Include a **data-position** attribute in the opening **<div>** tag for the *header* and *footer* data roles. Set to *fixed*, as shown in example 9-6. Now, when you load the page in Chrome, both the header and footer will be visible, and will remain visible as you scroll through the content.

```
<div data-role="header" data-position="fixed">
```

```
<div data-role="footer" data-position="fixed">
```

Example 9-6: Setting the header and footer to a fixed position.

Using pages in jQuery Mobile to define content keeps the user experience responsive and consistent while implementing a logical layout paradigm.

In the next section, we will expand on this jQuery layout by looking into toolbars, and we will explain how the header and footer that we just created are actually jQuery Mobile toolbars.

Questions for Review

1 What is a requirement of jQuery Pages?

    a. Multiple HTML files for content pages.

    b. Custom JavaScript to load page content.

    c. Usage of jQuery data-roles.

    d. A jQuery-enabled server.

2 A jQuery Mobile Page uses the HTML **<head>** element as a default header.

    a. True.

    b. False.

3 How is a footer implemented in jQuery Pages?

    a. With the **<footer>** element.

    b. With the **<foot>** element.

    c. With the "footer" data-role.

    d. With the "foot" data-role.

4 The jQuery Mobile Page structure cannot be used without the jQuery Mobile Framework.

    a. True.

    b. False.

9.3 jQuery Mobile Toolbars

In the previous section we created a pair of simple jQuery Mobile pages with headers and footers. Those headers and footers are also jQuery Mobile toolbars. Toolbars are not limited to containing only simple text; they can also contain buttons and navbars. In this section, we will enhance our header by adding link buttons to it, and then we will see how to include a navbar to allow quick navigation around our app.

We will continue from the example in the previous section. First, we are going to add another page of content, and then we will add buttons to our header.

1 First, remove the linking **<a>** tags from the content, and then add a third page to your HTML file, as shown in example 9-7. It is identical to the first two pages, with the *page* **<div>**'s id value changed and some of the header text changed.

2 In order to add a button to the header, we will add an **<a>** element with jQuery Mobile-specific classes. The classes that we add will define the button's layout, style, icon, and size. Our buttons will act as "Next" and "Previous" navigation buttons. In the first page we only want a "Next" button, and we want it to navigate to the second page. Add the code from example 9-8 to the header on the first page.

```
<div data-role="page" id="third">
    <div data-role="header" data-
position="fixed">
        <h1>Page III</h1>
    </div> <!-- Header -->
    <div role="main" class="ui-
content">
        <p>Lorem ipsum ... pharetra eu.</p>
        <p>Nulla ... mollis libero.</p>
        <p>Aenean ... facilisis.</p>
    </div> <!-- Main -->
    <div data-role="footer" data-
position="fixed">
        <h3>(c)LTP Media</h3>
    </div> <!-- Footer -->
</div> <!-- Third -->
```

Example 9-7: Add a third page with some Lipsum text.

```
<h1>Page I</h1>
<a href="#second" class="ui-btn ui-
btn-right ui-btn-icon-right ui-icon-
carat-r">Next</a>
```

Example 9-8: The content of the first page's header.

The lengthy class definition uses jQuery Mobile styles to precisely define the icon that we are using for the "Next" button in our header. For a complete description of all of the possible button options, you should check the jQuery website, but we will go over the options that we have chosen here, shown in figure 9-10.

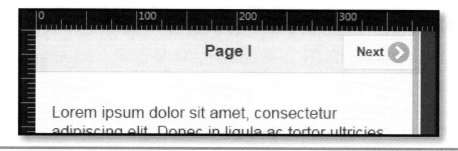

Figure 9-10: The "Next" button with icon.

The "ui-btn" class defines the element as being a user interface button. "ui-btn-right" aligns the button on the right-hand side of its parent element. "ui-btn-icon-right" aligns the icon to the right side of any text in the button element itself. Finally, "ui-icon-carat-r" defines the actual icon to use — in this case, the right-facing carat icon.

```
<div data-role="header" data-
position="fixed">
    <a href="#first" class="ui-btn
ui-btn-left ui-btn-icon-left ui-icon-
carat-l">Previous</a>
    <h1>Page II</h1>
    <a href="#third" class="ui-btn ui-
btn-right ui-btn-icon-right ui-icon-
carat-r">Next</a>
</div> <!-- Header -->
```

Example 9-9: The header of the second content page. It includes a "Previous" button that returns to the first page and a "Next" button that continues to the third page.

3 Page two will have two buttons, a "Previous" button and a "Next" button. The "Next" button will be identical to the "Next" button on page one except that it will link to the third page. The previous button, however, will use the appropriate classes to position the button on the left-hand side of the header and will use the left facing carat icon. The page 2 header is shown in example 9-9.

4 In Chrome, you can view the header for the second page and use it to navigate. The header is shown in figure 9-11.

5 The final piece of navigation is to include a button on the header for the third page. This button, shown in example 9-10, will link back to the second page.

Now, when you view the page in Chrome, you can navigate through all three pages sequentially.

6 Now we will implement a navbar that will allow us to navigate amongst the three pages nonlinearly. This navbar will be appended to the header and it will link to each of the three pages.

A navbar in jQuery Mobile is a specifically formatted unordered list. Up to five list items are displayed evenly across a single row, and those items can contain links, text, or icons. Example 9-11 shows the navbar for the first page. Each list item is a either a static link or a link to another page.

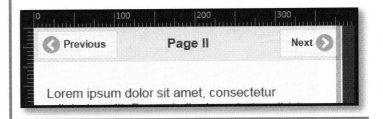

Figure 9-11: The "Previous" and "Next" buttons on the second page.

```
<div data-role="header" data-
position="fixed">
    <a href="#second" class="ui-btn
ui-btn-left ui-btn-icon-left ui-icon-
carat-l">Previous</a>
    <h1>Page III</h1>
</div> <!-- Header -->
```

Example 9-10: The HTML for the third page's header toolbar.

```
<div data-role="navbar">
    <ul>
        <li><a href="#" class="ui-
btn-active ui-state-persist">Page 1</
a></li>
        <li><a href="#second">Page
2</a></li>
        <li><a href="#third">Page
3</a></li>
    </ul>
</div> <!-- navbar -->
```

Example 9-11: The HTML to create the first page's navbar.

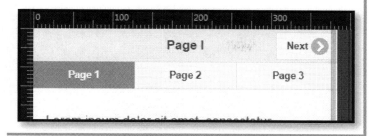

Figure 9-12: The navbar displayed on page one.

```
▸  <div data-role="navbar">
▸     <ul>
▸          <li><a href="#first">Page
   1</a></li>
▸          <li><a href="#"  class="ui-
   btn-active ui-state-persist">Page 2</
   a></li>
▸          <li><a href="#third">Page
   3</a></li>
▸     </ul>
▸  </div> <!-- navbar -->
```

```
▸  <div data-role="navbar">
▸     <ul>
▸          <li><a href="#first">Page
   1</a></li>
▸          <li><a href="#second">Page
   2</a></li>
▸          <li><a href="#" class="ui-
   btn-active ui-state-persist">Page 3</
   a></li>
▸     </ul>
▸  </div> <!-- navbar -->
```

Example 9-12: The navbar for page two, top, and page three, bottom.

⑦ When viewed in Chrome, the page one navbar, shown in figure 9-12, allows a user to quickly jump to any of the three pages. As of now, though, the other two pages do not have the navbar. Add it using the code shown in example 9-12.

⑧ You'll note that each of the three navbars has **class** attributes in the list item that would link back to themselves. The "ui-btn-active" class sets that element as having the active state, giving it the blue background color. The "ui-state-persist" class instructs jQuery to restore the active state whenever the page is shown.

In this section we have presented both a header toolbar and a navbar as a means of navigating through pages using jQuery. Both of those techniques can be used for more than just navigation. The toolbar can be home to a drop down menu, or the navbar can be used to dynamically change page content, as just two examples. The methods of displaying page elements discussed in this section, in toolbars and navbars, are tools that you can use to customize the design and layout of your application.

In the next section, we will examine jQuery buttons in more detail, including how to create toggles or checkboxes.

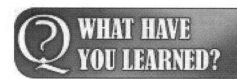

WHAT HAVE YOU LEARNED?

Questions for Review

1 How is a toolbar button defined in jQuery Mobile?

 a. Using data-roles.

 b. With the **<button>** tag.

 c. Using an element's id.

 d. With classes.

2 A toolbar can have a maximum of five buttons.

 a. True.

 b. False.

3 What HTML structure is used to create a navbar?

 a. The **<navbar>** element.

 b. Unordered lists and list items.

 c. Ordered lists and list items.

 d. The **<div>** element.

4 How many items can populate a single-row navbar?.

 a. 3.

 b. 6.

 c. Any number of items.

 d. 5.

9.4 jQuery Mobile Buttons

So far in this book we have primarily been using jQuery to style buttons in our applications. In this section, we will go over jQuery buttons and also create button toggles.

You can continue this section from the previous example and place the button HTML within the content of page one, as will be shown in the examples, or you can create a new HTML file. Either way will work as the examples in this section do not explicitly build on the examples from the previous sections.

1 A button can be created using either the **<button>** element, or by assigning a class to an **<a>** element. Example 9-13 demonstrates both techniques.

```
<a href="#" class="ui-btn">Anchor</a>
<button class="ui-btn">Button</button>
```

Example 9-13: The code to create jQuery buttons.

Notice that both elements are given the "ui-btn" class. That class defines the element as a button. When you view the page, shown in figure 9-13, you can see that both buttons appear identical.

2 Adding interactivity to a **<button>** element is done by using the **onclick** attribute or by adding an event listener in JavaScript. Both techniques have been used in this book to create interactive elements using jQuery buttons.

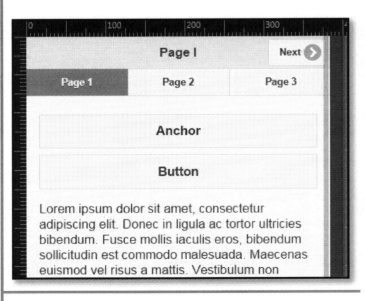

Figure 9-13: Both anchor and button elements display effectively using jQuery.

```
▸  <a href="#" class="ui-btn ui-
   shadow">Anchor</a>
▸  <button class="ui-btn">Button</button>
```

Example 9-14: Applying a shadow to a button.

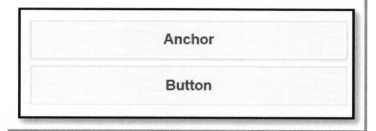

Figure 9-14: The shadow effect is subtle, but noticeable.

```
▸  <a href="#" class="ui-btn ui-
   shadow">Anchor</a>
▸  <button class="ui-btn">Button</button>
▸  <button data-role="none">Native
   Button</button>
```

Example 9-15: Creating a native-style button.

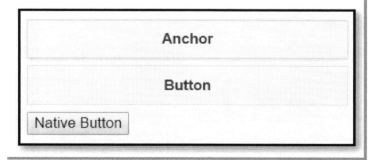

Figure 9-15: The native button compared to jQuery buttons.

③ Buttons can have styles applied to them. Example 9-14 demonstrates applying a shadow to the **\<a>** button, with the **\<button>** button retaining the default style. The results can be seen in figure 9-14.

④ It is also possible to remove the jQuery styling from the **\<button>** element if you need a native-style button. Example 9-15 shows the code to do this, and figure 9-15 demonstrates the result.

The jQuery Mobile Framework is designed to be mobile first, and this is most immediately evident in how buttons are handled. jQuery Mobile buttons rendered on a desktop browser are awkwardly styled, but on a mobile device they substantially increase usability.

```
▸  <div>
▸      <label for="switch">Flip me!</
   label>
▸      <input type="checkbox" id="switch"
   name="switch" data-role="flipswitch"
   />
▸  </div>
```

Example 9-16: The code to create a flipswitch.

⑤ jQuery Mobile provides a mobile optimized implementation of the checkbox, rendered as a switch or *flipswitch*. Example 9-16 shows the code to create a simple flipswitch and figure 9-16 demonstrates the switch in both the "on" and "off" positions.

Figure 9-16: The flipswitch in the off position, left, and the on position, right.

⑥ The text in the switch can be customized. Example 9-17 customizes the text and figure 9-17 shows the result. Anything that can be represented in a binary is a good option for a *flipswitch* in jQuery Mobile.

```
▸  <input type="checkbox" id="switch"
   name="switch" data-role="flipswitch"
   data-on-text="Yes" data-off-
   text="No"/>
```

Figure 9-17: Customizing a flipswitch.

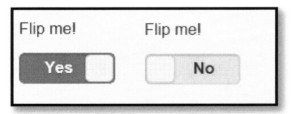

Figure 9-18: Changing from the default options to "Yes" and "No."

Buttons and switches are an easy way to use HTML5 to add interactivity to a webpage, but in the context of a mobile application the default options available are not appropriate. The options available through the jQuery Mobile Framework, on the other hand, are specifically designed to be accessible on mobile devices.

In this section you've learned how to quickly and easily use the jQuery Mobile Framework to add buttons and switches to your application.

Questions for Review

1 Is it possible to use native-style buttons with jQuery Mobile?

    a. Yes.

    b. No.

    c. Yes, but with a custom jQuery Mobile installation.

    d. Yes, but only on desktop systems.

2 What is the primary visual difference between an **<a>** button and a **<button>**-based button?

    a. The **<a>** button has a slight shadow.

    b. The **<button>** button can have rounded corners.

    c. There is no visual difference.

    d. The **<a>** button can be resized, the **<button>** button cannot.

3 Which of the following would be a good candidate for representation with a flipswitch?

    a. Which baseball position a player has.

    b. How often an event occurs.

    c. What percentage of seats on a plane are filled.

    d. Whether a light is on or off.

4 Can you customize the text within a jQuery Mobile flipswitch?

    a. Yes.

    b. No.

Chapter Summary

In this chapter you have scratched the surface of what is available to you the jQuery Mobile Framework. As an extension of JavaScript, jQuery has become an industry standard and the extended jQuery Mobile Framework brings those useful tools to mobile app developers. Even if you only use jQuery Mobile for styling, its mobile-first approach to layout and design will save time and effort when creating PhoneGap applications.

In the next chapter we will peel back a few more layers of the jQuery Mobile Framework and examine forms, listviews, and events.

Chapter 110

Interfaces with jQuery Mobile Part II

CHAPTER OBJECTIVES:

- You will learn about jQuery Mobile forms.
- You will utilize jQuery Mobile Listviews
- You will understand jQuery Mobile events.

10.1 jQuery Mobile Forms

In this chapter we will continue working with the jQuery Mobile Framework. First, we will look at creating forms using HTML5 and jQuery.

HTML5 has introduced new form input types to make data entry more streamlined and convenient. The jQuery Mobile Framework further refines the data entry process by introducing design elements geared towards mobile users. Cumulatively, these tools create a mobile data entry experience that can be best described as "passable."

Mobile devices can broadly be categorized as consumption devices. Certainly there are tools for content creation and creativity on mobiles, but their primary purpose is the display of media, content, and information to be consumed by the user. Data entry on a mobile device is occasionally a necessity, one that should be minimized and streamlined wherever possible. At best, data entry will be awkward and time consuming. At worst, it will be frustrating enough to prompt someone to stop using an application altogether. Careful application of form elements will allow your applications to carefully toe that line.

Although we will be using W3C standard HTML5 and jQuery, the examples in this section should be tested on a device. Create a new PhoneGap project according to our template and open the index.html file.

1 First, create a simple jQuery Page outline to hold the form elements that we will test, shown in example 10-1. The default layout of the content class of a jQuery page will position our content nicely, so we no longer need to use our *container* **<div>**.

```
<div data-role="page" id="first">
    <div data-role="header">
        <h1>Form Test</h1>
    </div> <!-- Header -->
    <div role="main" class="ui-
content">
    </div> <!-- Main -->
</div> <!-- First -->
```

Example 10-1: The jQuery Page outline.

```
▸   <label for="ti">Name</label>
▸   <input type="text" id="ti" />
▸
▸   <label for="mini">Nickname</label>
▸   <input type="text" id="mini" data-
    mini="true" />
```

Example 10-2: Text input types, normal and mini.

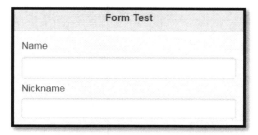

Figure 10-1: Text input boxes styled with jQuery Mobile.

```
▸   <label for="dob">Date of Birth:</
    label>
▸   <input type="date" id="dob" />
```

Example 10-3: Implementing the date input type.

Figure 10-2: Android 5.0's integrated date picker.

2 The simplest form of input is the text field. Text fields in jQuery Mobile are styled to be more convenient for mobile users. There is also an option for a "mini" text field that uses slightly less vertical screen real estate than the traditional text field. These two text fields are shown in example 10-2. Note that the HTML standard **<label>** and **<input>** paradigm is used with jQuery Mobile. Figure 10-1 demonstrates the labels in a Chrome mobile emulator.

3 The HTML5 standard includes a "date" type for **<input>** elements. Support for the "date" type is not consistent across all browsers and platforms, but it is becoming more common. Implementing the date type is as simple as creating an **<input>** element and setting its **type** attribute to "date," as shown in example 10-3.

Figure 10-2 shows the default date picker in Android 5.0. It is important to test the "date" **<input>** type, though, because earlier versions of Android are incompatible with this HTML standard.

```
▸   <label for="fn">Favorite Number</
    label>
▸   <input type="number" id="fn" />
```

Example 10-4: Implementing the number input type.

④ Phone keyboards have implemented very effective text input engines, but entering numbers with the standard keyboard can be challenging. Using the "number" input type, shown in example 10-4, invokes a number pad for input, shown in figure 10-3, instead of the standard keyboard.

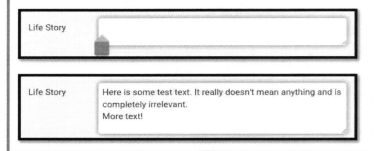

Figure 10-3: The numpad keyboard on Android 5.0.

⑤ Text areas on mobile devices with jQuery Mobile are similar to traditional text areas, however they have an important additional feature — they will automatically expand to fill the content that a user enters into them. This is especially useful on mobile devices where screen real estate is at a premium. Example 10-5 demonstrates a **\<textarea\>** element, and figure 10-4 shows the difference in size between an empty **\<textarea\>** and a **\<textarea\>** with a few lines of text input into it.

```
▸   <div>
▸       <label for="ls">Life Story</label>
▸       <textarea id="ls"></textarea>
▸   </div>
```

Example 10-5: Text areas in jQuery automatically resize.

Life Story

Life Story   Here is some test text. It really doesn't mean anything and is
              completely irrelevant.
              More text!

Figure 10-4: As users enter text, the text area will grow.

```
▸  <label for="rating">Rating:</label>
▸  <input type="range" id="rating" min=0
   max=100 />
```

Example 10-6: The "range" type can be used to create sliders.

Figure 10-5: A jQuery range slider.

```
▸  <fieldset data-role="controlgroup">
▸      <legend>Favorite Band</legend>
▸      <input type="radio" name="bands"
   id="journey" checked="checked" />
▸      <label for="journey">Journey</
   label>
▸      <input type="radio" name="bands"
   id="reo" />
▸      <label for="reo">REO Speedwagon</
   label>
▸      <input type="radio" name="bands"
   id="styx" />
▸      <label for="styx">Styx</label>
▸  </fieldset>
```

Example 10-7: Creating a list of radio buttons.

Figure 10-6: The radio buttons displayed on a mobile device.

6 Using jQuery Mobile also allows us to easily implement a range slider input element. By creating an HTML5 **<input>** element with the "range" type, shown in example 10-6, a simple but effective slider is created, as shown in figure 10-5. Note how the number to the left of the slider updates to accurately reflect the slider's value.

7 In example 10-7 we use an HTML **<fieldset>** element to contain a set of radio buttons. The jQuery Mobile "controlgroup" role groups a set of form buttons together, and we have used it here because we want our radio buttons to be grouped. Setting up the **<label>** and **<input>** elements is simple, but when we display the form elements, shown in figure 10-6, they are rendered in a touch-friendly style. Notice that the radio button is selected if you touch anywhere along the **<label>** text or across the button. It makes using radio buttons much easier on devices with small screens.

8 Finally, we're going to create a select box, also known as a dropdown menu. Example 10-8 demonstrates the HTML to do this. Notice that there are no jQuery Mobile-specific attributes or roles in this example, it is a standard select box. In this case, it is a list of favorite foods. Figure 10-7 demonstrates the select box as implemented by Android 5.0. The exact rendering of the box will vary depending on the platform.

9 As an experiment, comment out the link to the jQuery CDN in the **<head>** element of your index.html file, and then load the application on a mobile device. Figure 10-8, on the facing page, compares the same HTML rendered with and without the jQuery Mobile Framework. You'll immediately notice that the jQuery Mobile version is more aesthetically appealing and usable, whereas the HTML5 version with no additional styling is virtually useless.

```html
<label for="foods"
class="select">Favorite Foods</label>
<select id="foods">
    <option value="cheese">Cheese</option>
    <option value="pizza">Pizza</option>
    <option value="chinese">Chinese</option>
    <option value="chocolate">Chocolate</option>
    <option value="salad">Salad</option>
</select>
```

Example 10-8: The HTML for a select box.

Figure 10-7: The select box rendered on Android 5.0.

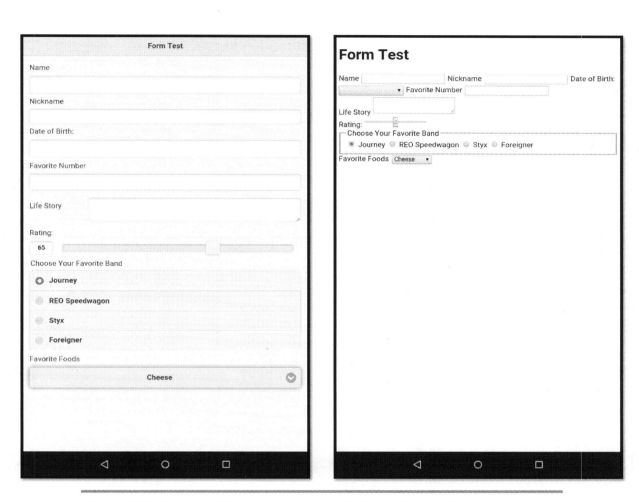

Figure 10-8: The same HTML page rendered with jQuery Mobile, left, and without, right.

If you've done some web development before, you probably know that the example we presented in figure 10-8 isn't entirely fair. No one would only use HTML when styling and laying out a webpage. Instead, you would create custom CSS to control the layout, styling, and display of page elements. However, one of the most useful features of the jQuery Mobile Framework is that this styling has already been created, tested, and implemented.

In this section you've learned how to use standard HTML5 form elements in jQuery. In the next section we will look at using jQuery ListViews.

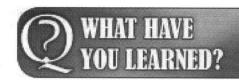

Questions for Review

1 It is safe to assume that if something is contained as part of the W3C HTML5 standard, it is supported by all modern web browsers.

    a. True.

    b. False.

2 What will jQuery Mobile textareas do that standard HTML5 textareas will not do?

    a. Automatically spell-check the text.

    b. Perform text validation.

    c. Resize according to input content.

    d. Nothing, jQuery Mobile textareas exactly match the HTML5 standards.

3 What HTML5 element is used to contain a group of radio buttons?

    a. <fieldset>

    b. <radio>

    c. <buttonfield>

    d. <form>

4 What element defines the choices available in a dropdown menu?

    a. <option>

    b. <choice>

    c. <dropdown>

    d. <dropchoice>

10.2 jQuery Mobile Listvew

In this section we will learn about the basics of the jQuery Listview. The Listview is coded as a standard HTML list element and given a "listview" data role to access an expansive possible set of features. In this section, we will create a standard Listvew, style the list items as links, and then create a filtered list.

The Listvew, and other similar widgets available with jQuery Mobile, solves fairly common layout and display problems in a simple and efficient way. There is a substantial amount of JavaScript powering some of the Listview features that we will use, however, from a design standpoint, only a few lines of HTML are needed along with custom jQuery attributes.

The examples in this chapter can be demonstrated effectively either in a Chrome mobile emulator or on a mobile device.

1 As we did in the previous section, we will contain our example within the content of a jQuery page. Begin with the HTML code shown in example 10-9.

```
<div data-role="page" id="first">
    <div data-role="header">
        <h1>ListView Test</h1>
    </div> <!-- Header -->
    <div role="main" class="ui-content">
    </div> <!-- Main -->
</div> <!-- First -->
```

Example 10-9: The jQuery Mobile Page outline.

2 In the content **<div>**, add a simple **<ul>** element, shown in example 10-10. Give this element the **data-role** attribute "listview," and then add a set of list items. In the example we have used some nearby states.

```
<ul data-role="listview">
    <li>Connecticut</li>
    <li>Vermont</li>
    <li>New Hampshire</li>
    <li>Maine</li>
    <li>New York</li>
</ul>
```

Example 10-10: A simple Listvew.

Figure 10-9: The default Listview style.

```
<ul data-role="listview">
    <li><a href="#">Connecticut</a></
li>
    <li><a href="#">Vermont</a></li>
    <li><a href="#">New Hampshire</a></
li>
    <li><a href="#">Maine</a></li>
    <li><a href="#">New York</a></li>
</ul>
```

Example 10-11: Adding links to list items.

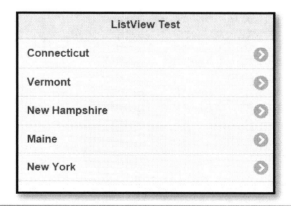

Figure 10-10: The Listview with linked list items.

3 When displayed, this Listview renders in a clear, readable list, as shown in figure 10-9.

4 Adding links to the list items, shown in example 10-11, will cause jQuery to style them differently. Figure 10-10 demonstrates this style. Note the icon displayed on the left side of each list item.

This styling makes it simple to use Listviews for navigation or menu screens. Additional Listview widget components make implementations like collapsible lists easy. Next, we will use a built-in filter to demonstrate how simple it is to create an auto-complete list. This Listview tool will only show those list items that contain pattern matches with user input.

5 In order to create a list that automatically populates according to user input, you first need to create a form with an **<input>** element, shown in example 10-12. The form's class is "ui-filterable" and the **<input>** element is a "search" type.

```
<form class="ui-filterable">
    <input id="ac-input" type="search"
placeholder="Search states..." />
</form>
```

Example 10-12: The input elements for a filtered list.

6 Next, modify the **<ul>** element so that it is set to be a filtered list by setting the **data-filter** attribute to "true," and then set it to reveal list items as they match the filter by setting the **data-filter-reveal** attribute to "true." Now, you need to link this Listview to the user input that will control the filter by setting the **data-input** attribute to the CSS selector for the input form, "#ac-input." The **data-inset** attribute styles the list items to appear inset in the page, instead of spanning the entire page.

```
<ul data-role="listview" data-
filter="true" data-filter-
reveal="true" data-input="#ac-input"
data-inset="true">
    <li><a href="#">Connecticut</a></
li>
    <li><a href="#">Vermont</a></li>
    <li><a href="#">New Hampshire</a></
li>
    <li><a href="#">Maine</a></li>
    <li><a href="#">New York</a></li>
</ul>
```

Example 10-13: Modify the **<ul>** so it's filterable.

7 Test the page now. You will see that as you enter data into the text box, list items that are possible matches will appear. In figure 10-11 you can see the empty input field with no list items shown, then an input field with "n" entered and a filtered list, and finally an input field with "new" entered and a more filtered list.

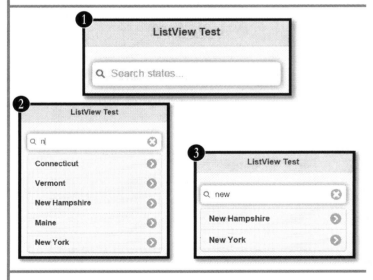

Figure 10-11: The results filter which list items are shown.

Listviews in jQuery have more features that are explained in the jQuery documentation and demonstrated on the jQuery demo page. Using Listviews allows you to create clean, well-organized lists that function consistently across multiple platforms and are optimized for display on a mobile device.

In the next section we will close our overview of jQuery Mobile by looking at the event system and, specifically, some events that are particularly important to mobile developers.

Questions for Review

1 What HTML element does a Listview use for structure?

    a. An unordered list.

    b. An ordered list.

    c. Either an unordered or an ordered list.

    d. The <listview> element.

2 How do you create a jQuery Listvew?

    a. With the "listview" data role.

    b. By setting the "listview" attribute to "true."

    c. With the <listview> element.

    d. With the "list-type" attribute set to "view."

3 How are the list items of a Listview defined?

    a. With the <div> element and the "list-item" data role.

    b. Using the <a> element.

    c. Using the <li> element.

    d. With the <list-item> element.

4 Listviews can be used to create auto-complete functionality without adding JavaScript.

    a. True.

    b. False.

10.3 jQuery Mobile Events

The jQuery Framework includes an event handling system that enhances the standard JavaScript library. For mobile devices, jQuery Mobile further extends the standard event system with mobile-specific events. Hooking into those events with your application is simple and gives a more native feel to the way your users interact with your PhoneGap app.

Some user interactions can be mapped between a mouse-driven environment and a touch environment fairly intuitively. For example, a click can be considered a tap or a click-and-hold can be considered touch-and-hold. Other interactions are not as intuitive. For example, the swipe action that has become a user interface standard on mobile devices does not have a clear counterpart on desktop interfaces. The jQuery Mobile Framework tries to solve that problem by including mobile interactions in the event system, including swipe events.

In this section we will use jQuery Mobile events to create event handlers for mobile user interactions. Create a new PhoneGap project and ensure that it is linked to the jQuery CDN.

```
<div data-role="page" id="first">
    <div data-role="header">
        <h1>Event Test</h1>
    </div> <!-- Header -->
    <div role="main" class="ui-content">
        <button id='btnTapMe'>Tap Me!</button>
        <div id='result'></div>
    </div> <!-- Main -->
</div> <!-- First -->
```

Example 10-14: The HTML code in index.html.

1 The HTML in index.html is very simple. We have created a jQuery Page and populated the content **<div>** with a button that says "Tap Me!" and an empty result **<div>**. The **<button>** has the id *btnTapMe* and the **<div>** has the id *result*. This is shown in example 10-14.

2   In main.js create an *init()* function that runs when the device is ready. In the *init()* function we will use jQuery to add event listeners to the swipe left, swipe right, and tap events.

3   If you haven't used jQuery before then the syntax might seem strange. For the swipe left event, we call *jQuery* and then use standard selectors to find DOM elements, the window object, in this case. The *on* method attaches an event listener—in this case, the "swipeleft" event—and defines the function to call when that event is registered. Here, we have used anonymous functions that set the value of the inner HTML of the *result* **<div>**. The swipe right event is handled the same way.

4   For the "Tap Me!" button's listener we use the same syntax, but the DOM element is obtained using its CSS selector. The event listener is waiting for the "tap" event and when that event is registered the inner HTML of *result* is updated.

You can see the JavaScript and jQuery code in example 10-15.

```
window.onload = function() {
    document.
addEventListener('deviceready', init,
false);
}

function init() {
    jQuery(window).on("swipeleft",
function(event){
        document.
getElementById('result').innerHTML =
"Swipe Left";
    });

    jQuery(window).on("swiperight",
function(event){
        document.
getElementById('result').innerHTML =
"Swipe Right";
    });

    jQuery("#btnTapMe").on("tap",
function(event) {
        document.
getElementById('result').innerHTML =
"Tap Event on Button";
    });
}
```

Example 10-15: The content of main.js includes standard JavaScript and jQuery.

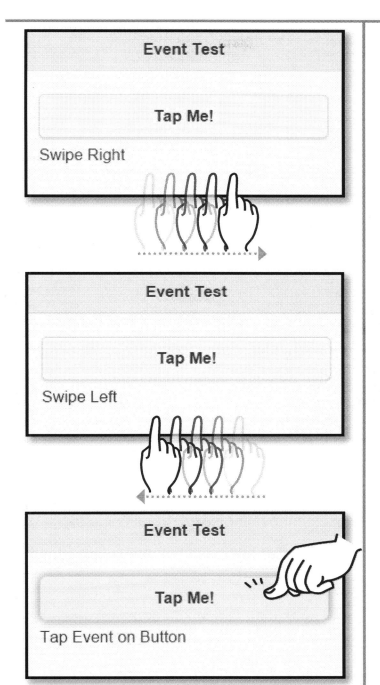

5 The swipe events can be tested in the Chrome mobile emulator (be sure to explicitly call *init()*) by clicking, holding, and moving your mouse left or right, but it is better to test on an actual device.

If you are using an older Android device then you will find that the swipe events don't register as cleanly as native swipe events. This is a known problem due to the older Android WebView, and it has been addressed in newer versions of Android. If you are creating an application that targets Android users who have older versions of the OS, though, you may want to look into alternative methods of handling swipe events.

Figure 10-12 demonstrates the expected output from different touch events.

Figure 10-12: The outputs from swiping left, swiping right, and tapping.

Using jQuery Mobile events to handle user interactions is an effective alternative to using standard JavaScript. Everything that you can do in jQuery can be done in JavaScript, but the jQuery implementations of many common dynamic web elements are convenient, easy to use, and well documented. The jQuery Mobile website has comprehensive documentation for the event system.

That being said, there are limitations to jQuery. The framework does not cover every circumstance and, as we have seen in this section, there are occasional compatibility concerns.

Questions for Review

1 The swipe touch interface element is supported by the HTML5 W3C standard.

    a. True.

    b. False.

2 What is the jQuery event name for swiping to the right?

    a. swipe-right.

    b. swipe_right.

    c. swiperight.

    d. rightswipe.

3 Which of the following desktop user interface actions does not map intuitively to a touch interface action?

    a. Single click.

    b. Click and hold.

    c. Double click.

    d. Right click.

4 Which of the following touch interface actions does not map intuitively to a desktop interface action?

    a. Pinch to zoom.

    b. Multiple finger touch.

    c. Swipe up.

    d. All of the above.

CHAPTER 10 LAB EXERCISE

You will need the files provided at *https://s3-us-west-2.amazonaws.com/labcontent/Lab9_10.zip* before starting these lab exercises. Click the link to download.

1 Using the command line, create a new PhoneGap application called MetroNorthWestport.

```
● ● ●                    ⌂ marklassoff — bash — 80×24
Last login: Thu Feb 19 21:04:31 on console
Mark-MacBook-Pro:~ marklassoff$ phonegap create MetroNorthWestport
Creating a new cordova project with name "Hello World" and id "com.phonegap.hell
oworld" at location "/Users/marklassoff/MetroNorthWestport"

Using custom www assets from https://github.com/phonegap/phonegap-app-hello-worl
d/archive/master.tar.gz

Mark-MacBook-Pro:~ marklassoff$ ▊
```

2 "Clean up" the application template eliminating unnecessary files created, as demonstrated earlier in this book.

3 From the starter.zip file, place the stations.js and trains.js files in your www folder. Replace the existing index.html file with the index.html file provided in the zip.

4 Double-click the index.html file to load it into your browser. Click the button and you'll see a display that looks something like this:

Westport Trains

- Westbound
- **8:33** Final Stop: Grand Central
  Train Number: 1537
- **9:05** Final Stop: Grand Central
  Train Number: 1541

- Eastbound
- **8:40** Final Stop: NH-State St.
  Train Number: 1510
- **9:19** Final Stop: New Haven
  Train Number: 1512

Next Trains

Copyright 2015 | LearnToProgram, Inc.

The application is displaying the next Metro North trains due at the Westport, Connecticut train station.

⑤ The final application user interface should look like the screenshot here:

⑥ Open trains.js and remove the comments from lines 20, 75 and 84-89.

⑦ Examine the following section of the HTML code:

```
    <div id="container">
                <div><h1>Westport
Trains</h1></div>
                <div id="content">
                    <ul
id="trainSchedWest">

<li>Westbound</li>
                    </ul>
                    <ul
id="trainSchedEast" >

<li>Eastbound</li>
                    </ul>
                </div><!-- content
-->
                <button
id="btnNext">Next Trains</button>
                <div id="footer"><p
class="center">Copyright 2015 |
LearnToProgram, Inc.</p></div>
```

Make the necessary additions to use jQuery mobile to adjust the display so it appears more like the completed application above.

⑧ To get the colors correct, use the jQuery theme roller located at *http://themeroller.jquerymobile.com/*. Once you have the colors adjusted to your liking, click the 'Download Theme Zip File' button from the themeroller interface. Follow the instructions to utilize the theme and verify your results in the web browser.

Chapter Summary

In this chapter we have learned more about the jQuery Mobile Framework, an exceptionally useful tool for many web and mobile application developers. We have examined jQuery form styles, used the Listview widget, and used the jQuery Mobile events to register swipe and tap events.

We have also learned about some of the limitations of jQuery. It is important to remember that jQuery is a tool. It is a well-crafted and widely used tool, but it is a tool nonetheless, and no tool is perfect for every situation. The key to implementing the jQuery Mobile Framework, or any other framework or API, is developing a solid understanding of what it can and can't do.

In the next chapter we will return to PhoneGap and look at some additional APIs, including the File API and the Device API.

Other Important PhoneGap APIs

CHAPTER OBJECTIVES:

- You will learn how to use the File plug-in.
- You will understand the Device plug-in.
- You will get experience working with the Contacts plug-in.
- You will use the Notifications plug-in.
- You will learn about the config.xml file.

11.1 PhoneGap File API

In this chapter we will be doing a survey of other useful PhoneGap APIs. First, we will look at the File API.

You may recall the File API from chapter six when we used it in order to build a media player that was compatible with older versions of Android. In this section, we will look more fully at the features of the File API.

The purpose of the File API is to allow you to access the file system of a device outside of the browser environment. In chapter five when we worked with Store. js, we were using storage that was inextricably linked to the webview environment. Using the PhoneGap File API, we can store data permanently on a device's storage space.

To demonstrate this, we will create a simple application that takes a user-input list of values and saves them to a file. When the application is loaded it will look for a previously saved list and, if possible, load that list. The list that we create will be a Comma-Separated Value, or CSV, list. To work with that list we will use a parser which was created by Evan Plaice and is freely available online.

Create a new PhoneGap project based on our template. In order to test the examples in this chapter you need to run the application on your device or in an emulator.

1 First, install the PhoneGap File plug-in using the command shown in example 11-1.

```
▸ phonegap plugin add org.apache.
  cordova.file
```

Example 11-1: Add the plug-in from the command line in the project's directory.

2 Download the CSV parser from https://code.google.com/p/jquery-csv/ and save the minified version to the project's "www/" directory. Link to it in index.html's **<head>** using the code in example 11-2.

```
▸ <script src="jquery.csv-0.71.min.
  js"></script>
```

Example 11-2: The link to the CSV parser.

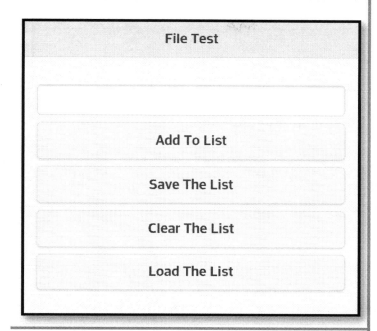

Figure 11-1: The UI of our application.

③ Before we begin accessing the file system we will create the user interface. Figure 11-1 shows how the user interface will look, and example 11-3 demonstrates the code. The HTML shown has been placed inside a jQuery Page element that is not shown.

④ In the HTML we have created an unordered list as a Listview and given it the id *masterList*. We have also created a text input box and a set of buttons: "Add To List" linked to the *addToList()* function, "Save The List" linked to the *saveList()* function, "Clear The List" linked to the *clearList()* function, and "Load The List" linked to the *loadList()* function.

```
‣  <ul data-role="list-view" data-
   inset="true" id="masterList">
‣  </ul>
‣  <input type="text" id="listItem" />
‣  <button id="btnAddToList"
   onclick="addToList()">Add To List</
   button>
‣  <button id="btnSaveList"
   onclick="saveList()">Save The List</
   button>
‣  <button id="btnClearList"
   onclick="clearList()">Clear The List</
   button>
‣  <button id="btnLoadList"
   onclick="loadList()">Load The List</
   button>
```

Example 11-3: The index.html that powers our UI.

5 Before we begin working with the File API we will write the JavaScript to create and display a list. First, we need to have a list and access to the *masterList* **<ul>** element, so create the global variables *list* and *masterList*, as shown in example 11-4. Then, create the *init()* that will run once the device is loaded, also shown in example 11-4. Notice that *init()* sets *masterList* to the appropriate DOM element, but then it also calls the *loadList()* function. This is because we want to automatically load a list when the application first runs.

```javascript
var list = "";
var masterList;

window.onload = function() {
    document.
    addEventListener('deviceready', init,
    false);
};

function init() {
    masterList = document.
    getElementById('masterList');
    loadList();
}
```

Example 11-4: Setting up some global variables and creating the initialization functions.

6 Now we will create the *addToList()* function, shown in example 11-5. This function stores the value entered by a user as the variable *itemToAdd*. Then, if that value is neither empty nor null, it adds it to the *list* global variable and appends a comma. Finally it displays the list using a call to the *displayList()* function before resetting the value of the input HTML element.

```javascript
function addToList() {
    var itemToAdd = document.
    getElementById('listItem').value;
    if (itemToAdd != null && itemToAdd
    != "") {
        list += itemToAdd + ",";
        displayList();
        document.
    getElementById('listItem').value = "";
    }
}
```

Example 11-5: The *addToList()* function.

```
function displayList() {
    var output = "";
    var listArray = $.csv.
toArray(list);
    listArray.pop();
    for(var i = 0; i < listArray.
length; i++) {
        output += "<li>" +
listArray[i] + "</li>";
    }
    masterList.innerHTML = output;
    $(masterList).listview().
listview('refresh');
}
```

Example 11-6: The *displayList()* function.

```
function clearList() {
    list = "";
    displayList();
}
```

Example 11-7: The *clearList()* function.

7 The *displayList()* function is shown in example 11-6. First, *displayList()* creates an output variable, *output*, that will hold the HTML for the new list items. Then, it uses the CSV parser to create an array, *listArray*, from the CSV string that was stored in *list*. The way *list* is created results in a trailing comma, which the CSV parser will understand as signaling a new value. This value results in an empty final array element in *listArray*, which we remove using *listArray.pop()*. Next, we loop through every element of *listArray*, which will be the values in our list, and append them to *output* as HTML list items. Once that has completed, we set the inner HTML of the *masterList* **<ul>** element to the value of *output* and then use jQuery to refresh the *masterList* Listview.

8 The *clearList()* function, shown in example 11-7, is very simple. It sets *list* to an empty string and then uses *displayList()* to display that empty string, thereby clearing *masterList*.

9 That code completes the ability to create a list of values and display them. If you run this application now you will be able to add elements to the *masterList* and have them appear on your device, as shown in figure 11-2. Now that we have a simple string that we can create, parse, and display, we will add functionality to save and load that string to and from the file system.

10 In order to save the list using the File API, we need to create a set of objects to work with the file system. First, we request a file system object. Next, we pass that file system object to a function that either gets or creates a file. Then, we pass a reference to that file to a function that will create a writer object that can write to the file. That writer object is then passed to another function which actually writes to the file.

It seems complicated but it will be clearer as we create the code. The file system is generated, then a file is found on that file system, then a writer is created for that file, and finally the writer writes to the file. Figure 11-3 shows this.

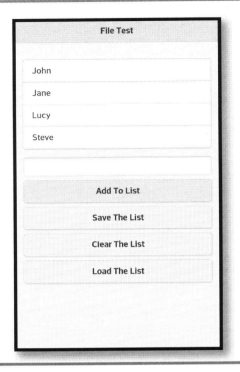

Figure 11-2: The application displaying a list of names.

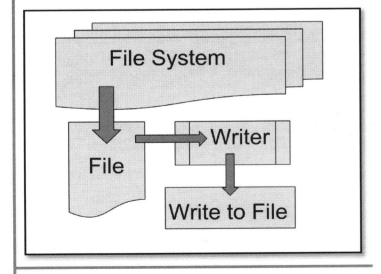

Figure 11-3: An outline of the file writing process.

11 First, when *saveList()*—shown in example 11-8—is called, it requests a file system where the application can store data. The options passed define the type of file system, either persistent or temporary, the requested size of the file system, and two callback functions for a success and a failure. In the event of a successful call, the file system object is passed to the success callback—in our case, defined as *onFS()*.

```
function saveList() {
    window.
requestFileSystem(LocalFileSystem.
PERSISTENT, 0, onFS, onError);
}
```

Example 11-8: The *saveList()* function requests a file system and then passes that file system to *onFS()*.

12 The *onFS()* function, shown in example 11-9, is passed a file system object, *fs*, and calls a method of the file system object, *getFile()*. That method takes a filename—"list. txt" in our case—a set of options, and success and failure callback functions. The options tell the file system whether or not it should create the file if it does not exist, (set to "true" in our example) and whether or not the application should have exclusive access to this file (set to "false" in our application). The success callback function is passed the file entry object that results from the *getFile()* method.

```
function onFS(fs) {
    fs.root.getFile("list.txt", {
create: true, exclusive: false },
onFile, onError);
}
```

Example 11-9: The *onFS()* function takes a file system and gets a specific file entry from it, passing that file entry on to *onFile()*.

13 The *onFile()* function, shown in example 11-10, is called by *onFS()* and is passed a file entry object, *file*. The function calls the *createWriter()* method of the file entry object to create a writer object that is able to actually write data to the file. The *createWriter()* function takes two parameters (both callback functions): *onWriter* for success, and *onError* for failure.

```
function onFile(file) {
    file.createWriter(onWriter,
  onError);
}
```

Example 11-10: The *onFile()* function takes a file entry and creates a writer object for it, passing that object on to *onWriter()*.

14 The *onWriter()* function, shown in example 11-11, is where the file writing actually takes place. It is passed a writer object, *writer*, which has a method, *write()*, that is able to write to the file. Before we call that method, though, we set the *onwriteend* attribute of *writer* to define what to do when its *write()* method completes. In our case, we log a message to the console. Finally, we call the *write()* method with our *list* string variable as a parameter to write our list to permanent storage.

```
function onWriter(writer) {
    writer.onwriteend = function() {
        console.log("File written");
    }
    writer.write(list);
}
```

Example 11-11: The *onWriter()* function writes data to its parent file entry.

```
▸  function loadList() {
▸      window.
   requestFileSystem(LocalFileSystem.
   PERSISTENT, 0, onFSLoad, onError);
▸  }
```

Example 11-12: The *loadList()* function requests a file system and passes that file system on to *onFSLoad()*.

```
▸  function onFSLoad(fs) {
▸      fs.root.getFile("list.txt",
   {create: true, exclusive: false },
   gotFileLoad, onError);
▸  }
```

Example 11-13: The *onFSLoad()* function takes a file system and gets a specific file entry from it, and then passes that file entry to *gotFileLoad()*.

```
▸  function gotFileLoad(theFile) {
▸      theFile.file(readFile, onError);
▸  }
```

Example 11-14: The *gotFileLoad()* function takes a file entry and gets a file object from it, and then passes that file object to the *readFile()* function.

15 Loading the data from a previously saved file follows a similar pattern, only instead of writing to a file we are reading from a file. Start with the *loadList()* function, shown in example 11-13. *loadList()* requests the local permanent file system just as *saveList()* did but, instead passes the file system object to *onFSLoad()*.

16 *onFSLoad()*, shown in example 11-13, uses the *getFile()* method to access "list.txt," again creating it if need be. If successful, *getFile()* calls *gotFileLoad()*.

17 *gotFileLoad()*, shown in example 11-14, is passed a file entry object as *theFile* and then calls that file entry object's *file()* method. This method creates a file object that contains file properties. If it is successful it calls *readFile()* and if it fails it calls *onError()*.

18 In the *readFile()* function, shown in example 11-15, we create a new FileReader object that we name *reader* and set its *onloadend* attribute. The *onloadend* attribute defines what happens when the FileReader object finishes reading a file. In our case, once "list.txt" is read we want to take the result of the read event and set it as the value of the *list* global variable, and then call the *displayList()* function to display the list to the user. To actually read the file we use the FileReader object's *readAsText()* method and pass it the file to be read as a parameter.

19 The final function that we need is the *onError()* function, shown in example 11-16. The *onError()* function simply alerts the user to the error that occurred.

```
function readFile(file) {
    var reader = new FileReader();
    reader.onloadend = function(evt) {
        list = evt.target.result;
        displayList();
    };
    reader.readAsText(file);
}
```

Example 11-15: The *readFile()* function takes a file object and reads data from it.

```
function onError(e) {
    alert(e.code);
}
```

Example 11-16: The *onError()* function alerts the user to an error code.

This may seem complicated, but it follows a basic pattern. First, get the file system. Then, get or create the file. After that, you are able to act on that file. We have shown you how to write to it by creating a writer and how to read from it by creating a reader. The PhoneGap File API documentation goes into much more detail and has a number of examples: *http://docs.phonegap.com/en/edge/cordova_file_file.md.html*

Now, with the completed program, you can use the "Save The List" button to save the list information that has been entered and you can use the "Load The List" button to load the saved information. If you enter data, save the list, and then clear the list — remember that "Clear The List" only removes the information from the *list* global variable, not the "list.txt" file — you can use "Load The List" to bring it back up. Also, when the program starts it will automatically load and display a saved list.

Although we have only stored simple text data in this section, the File API can be used to store other types of data. Check the documentation to see the other options that are available.

Using the File API you are able to store application information permanently on a mobile device. This gives you much more freedom when creating applications, but it also gives you more responsibility. Remember, when you're developing applications you are responsible for informing the user what your application will be doing with their device.

In the next section we will look at the PhoneGap Device API.

Questions for Review

1 In order to save a file to the device storage, what must be done first?

a. The file must be loaded.

b. A file system must be requested.

c. The writer must be initialized.

d. The file must be created.

2 Which of the following is not needed to load a file?

a. A file system request.

b. A file reader.

c. A file object.

d. A file writer.

3 How frequently does the OS delete data stored using the File API?

a. When the device is rebooted.

b. When the application is uninstalled.

c. Never.

d. Every 4-6 weeks.

4 You are only able to use the PhoneGap File API to store text data.

a. True.

b. False.

11.2 PhoneGap Device API

The PhoneGap Device API allows you to quickly and easily access hardware and software information about the device that your application is running on. In this section, we'll create a simple application that outputs that data returned by the Device API.

Create a new PhoneGap project based off of our template. First, we'll have to install the Devices plug-in from PhoneGap.

```
phonegap plugin add org.apache.
cordova.device
```

Example 11-17: Install the plug-in.

```
<div id="result"></div>
```

Example 11-18: In index.html create a *result* <div>.

```
function init() {
    var output = "Model: " + device.
model;
    output += "<br/>Cordova: " +
device.cordova;
    output += "<br/>Platform: " +
device.platform;
    output += "<br/>UUID: " + device.
uuid;
    output += "<br/>Version: " +
device.version;
    document.getElementById('result').
innerHTML = output;
}
```

Example 11-19: When the app initializes, get the device data.

1 Install the plug-in using the command shown in example 11-17.

2 In index.html, just create a simple **<div>** to display some result data, as shown in example 11-18.

3 In the *init()* function of main.js, called through a "deviceready" event listener, as we have been doing, we create an HTML string called *output* that is built using the properties of the device. Those properties are, device.model, device.platform, device.uuid, and device.version. The UUID is a universally unique identifier.

4 When you run the application the *init()* function will get the device information and display it in your *result* **<div>**, as shown in figure 11-4.

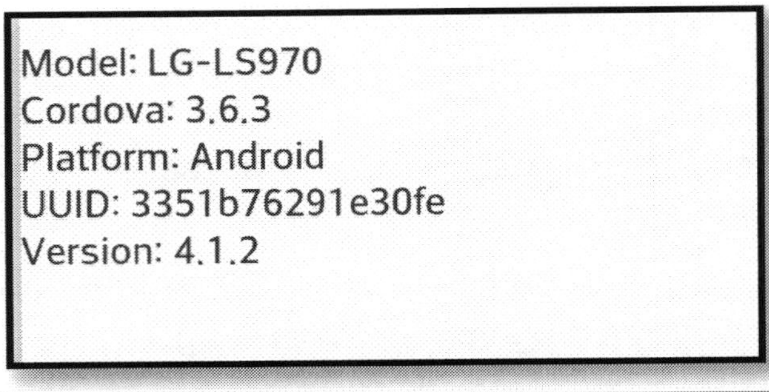

```
Model: LG-LS970
Cordova: 3.6.3
Platform: Android
UUID: 3351b76291e30fe
Version: 4.1.2
```

Figure 11-4: The output from the Device plug-in data on an LG phone running Android 4.1.2.

In chapter six we created a media player using standards-compliant HTML5, but that media player would not work on older Android devices. To rectify that problem, we created another media player that would work on older Android devices. We might want our application to prioritize the HTML5 compliant media player if a device is compatible, and fall back on the media plug-in based player if a device is incompatible. Using the device plug-in we could have made that determination.

Having more information about a device allows you to create a more targeted experience for your user. In this book we have focused on creating simple example applications that explain the core principles of PhoneGap and HTML5 functionality, but even in that context there have been problems with compatibility and function across different mobile devices. Knowing the device that your customer is using to access your application allows you to create a more effective and compelling experience.

In the next section we will look into the Contacts API, which allows you to access a user's contact list.

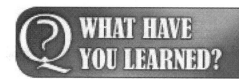

Questions for Review

1 What does the Device API allow you to do?

   a. It is the prerequisite for any other plug-in that needs to use a device element.

   b. Access device information.

   c. Modify device information.

   d. Access the status of hardware sensors.

2 Which of the following is not a property that can be read using the Device plug-in?

   a. device.model.

   b. device.cordova.

   c. device.version.

   d. device.provider.

3 Why would you be interested in device information?

   a. To create a more targeted experience for your user.

   b. To inform the user of their operating system version.

   c. To send metrics to Google or Apple about device usage.

   d. There is no reason to gather device information.

4 What is the UUID device property?

   a. A unique unit identifier.

   b. A universal unit identifier.

   c. The unique universal item design.

   d. A universally unique identifier.

11.3 PhoneGap Contacts API

In this section we will look at another PhoneGap API, the Contacts API. The Contacts API gives you access to a users contact list.

Create a new PhoneGap project from the template and name it ContactsDemo. The demo application will create a contact with a first name, last name, email, and phone number and add that contact to the user's contact list.

1 First, in order to use the Contacts API you need to install the contacts plug-in. Use the command line code from example 11-20 to install the plug-in.

```
phonegap plugin add org.apache.
cordova.contacts
```

Example 11-20: The command to install the plug-in.

2 The application requires a first name, a last name, an email address, and a phone number. Use the HTML code from example 11-21 to create the user interface. Notice the input types that we have chosen for certain data elements in order to facilitate data entry on a mobile device. Also, the **<button>** element calls the *saveContact()* function. Remember that in a production application you would likely want to validate the information before saving it.

```
<label for="first">First</label>
<input type="text" id="first" />
<label for="last">Last</label>
<input type="text" id="last" />
<label for="email">Email</label>
<input type="email" id="email" />
<label for="phone">Phone</label>
<input type="tel" id="phone" />
<button id="btnSave"
onclick="saveContact()">Save To
Contacts</button>
```

Example 11-21: The HTML will allow the user to enter some basic contact information.

```
function saveContact() {
    var first = document.
getElementById('first').value;
    var last = document.
getElementById('last').value;
    var emailAddress = document.
getElementById('email').value;
    var phoneNumber = document.
getElementById('phone').value;

    var newContact = navigator.
contacts.create();
    newContact.displayName = first + "
" + last;
    newContact.nickname = first + " "
+ last;

    var name = new ContactName();
    name.givenName = first;
    name.familyName = last;
    newContact.name = name;

    var email = [];
    email[0] = new ContactField('home'
, emailAddress, true);
    newContact.emails = email;
    var phoneNums = [];
    phoneNums[0] = new
ContactField('home' , phoneNumber,
true);
    newContact.phoneNumbers =
phoneNums;

    newContact.save();
}
```

Example 11-22: The *saveContact()* function.

3 In main.js create the *saveContact()* function, as shown in example 11-22. The *saveContact()* function collects contact information from the HTML and then uses methods of the **contact** object to store that information as a contact in the user's device.

4 First, we create the variables *first*, *last*, *emailAddress*, and *phoneNumber* to hold contact data. Next, we create a new contact object, *newContact*, using the **create()** method. Then, we set the **displayName** and **nickname** properties of that object to be the first and last name of the contact. We create both a display name and a nickname in order to ensure compatibility across different mobile devices.

5 Next, we create a **ContactName** object called *name* and assign its **givenName** and **familyName** properties our contact's first and last names. The **name** property of *newContact* is set to the value of *name*.

6 With the name set, we can move on to the contact's contact information. *saveContact()* is shown again in example 11-23. We have created arrays *email* and *phoneNums*. An array is used so we can pass multiple pieces of contact information to the **contact** object—for example, a home, work, and mobile phone number—without having to make multiple function calls.

7 The actual contact information is stored in a **ContactField** object that is instantiated with a type value— we have used "home," but this can be anything—a the contact's value, and a preference. The preference is a boolean that determines whether or not this contact value is the preferred method of contact.

8 Once the contact information is stored as **ContactField** objects, those objects are set to the **email** and **phoneNumber** properties of *newContact*.

9 The final step is to save the contact information with the **save()** method.

```
function saveContact() {
    var first = document.
getElementById('first').value;
    var last = document.
getElementById('last').value;
    var emailAddress = document.
getElementById('email').value;
    var phoneNumber = document.
getElementById('phone').value;

    var newContact = navigator.
contacts.create();
    newContact.displayName = first + "
" + last;
    newContact.nickname = first + " "
+ last;

    var name = new ContactName();
    name.givenName = first;
    name.familyName = last;
    newContact.name = name;

    var email = [];
    email[0] = new ContactField('home'
, emailAddress, true);
    newContact.emails = email;
    var phoneNums = [];
    phoneNums[0] = new
ContactField('home' , phoneNumber,
true);
    newContact.phoneNumbers =
phoneNums;

    newContact.save();
}
```

Example 11-23: The *saveContact()* function.

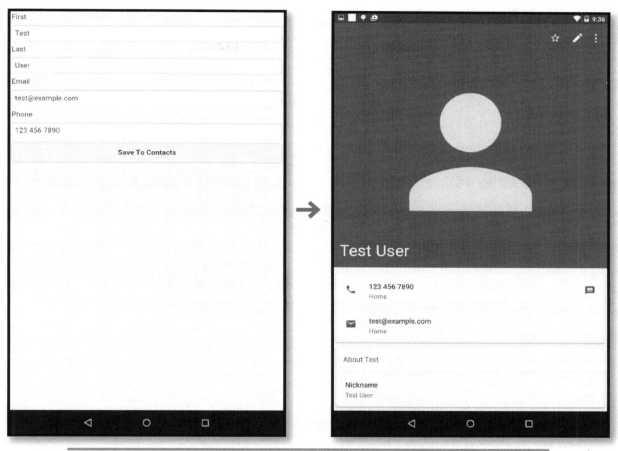

Figure 11-5: Contact information being entered, left, and the newly created contact, right.

Figure 11-5, above, demonstrates a contact being added and the new contact appearing as a member of the contact list.

Using the Contacts plug-in gives you the ability to add substantial convenience to your user's experience, but it also puts a burden of responsibility on your shoulder. Contact information is very personal; it is up to you as a developer to use that information safely and securely.

In the next section we will look into the PhoneGap Notifications API.

Questions for Review

1 How do you access a user's contact information?

    a. With the Contacts API.

    b. By launching the device's default contacts application.

    c. You cannot access a user's contact information.

    d. Through the Device plug-in.

2 Why do we set both the **nickname** and **displayName** properties?

    a. We do not set both properties.

    b. Because every device has both a nickname and a display name.

    c. To ensure compatibility across multiple devices.

    d. In order to give users the option to have either a nickname or a display name.

3 What is the purpose of using arrays to set contact types such as email addresses?

    a. Arrays allow multiple values of the same type to be set simultaneously.

    b. There is no specific purpose, it is arbitrary.

    c. Arrays are not used to set contact types.

    d. Arrays allow multiple types of contacts to be entered simultaneously, such as an email address and a phone number.

4 Arrays are used to set both phone numbers and email addresses.

    a. True.

    b. False.

11.4 PhoneGap Notifications API

In this section we will use the PhoneGap Notifications API to create a native pop-up alert and to access the vibration function of a mobile device. Every mobile operating system handles pop-up notifications somewhat differently, so by using the PhoneGap Notifications API you can ensure that any pop-ups from your application match the accepted system standards. Adding vibration effects brings another level of tactile feedback to your application's notifications.

Create a new PhoneGap project called NotificationsDemo using our standard template. First, we will install the required plug-ins.

---

1 There are two plug-ins that relate to the notification system. The first is the dialogs plug-in. Navigate to your project's directory and install it with the command shown in example 11-24.

```
phonegap plugin add org.apache.
cordova.dialogs
```

Example 11-24: The command to add the dialogs plug-in.

2 The next plug-in to install is the vibration plug-in. Install it using the command shown in example 11-25.

```
phonegap plugin add org.apache.
cordova.vibration
```

Example 11-25: The command to add the vibration plug-in.

3 Now that the appropriate plug-ins are installed, modify your index.html to contain only an empty *container* **<div>**, as shown in example 11-26.

```
<div id="container">
</div> <!--container -->
```

Example 11-26: The empty *container* <div>.

4 Next, in your main.js file, set up an *init()* function to run once the device is ready.

5 In that *init()* function, launch a device notification using the **alert()** method of the **notification** object. The **alert()** method takes up to four properties: an alert message, a callback function to run after the alert has been dismissed, an optional alert box title, and an optional alert box button message. In our example we use the message "You rock!", the callback function *alertDismiss()*, the title "Journey Fan," and the button message "Complete." This is all shown in example 11-27.

6 In *alertDismiss()*, the alert callback function, shown in example 11-28, we will first modify the content of *container* to show that the alert was dismissed, and we will then use the **vibrate()** method of the **notification** object to vibrate the mobile device for a set number of milliseconds. In our example, we have used "1000" milliseconds, or one full second.

```
window.onload = function()
{
    document.
addEventListener('deviceready', init,
false);
}

function init()
{
    navigator.notification.alert(
        "You rock!",     // Message
        alertDismiss,    // Callback
        "Journey Fan",   // Title
        "Complete"       // Button
message
    );
}
```

Example 11-27: The *init()* function.

```
function alertDismiss()
{
    document.
getElementById('container').innerHTML
= "<h2>Alert Dismissed</h2>";
    navigator.notification.
vibrate(1000);
}
```

Example 11-28: The *alertDismiss()* callback function.

Now, when you install this application on a mobile device, it will automatically launch a native OS alert box with your message information. When that alert box is dismissed, the vibration functionality of your device will activate for a set amount of time.

In the next and final section we will look into a few of the key points of the config.xml file in your PhoneGap project.

Questions for Review

1 What plug-ins are required for notifications with vibrations?

    a. Just the Dialog plug-in.

    b. Just the Vibration plug-in.

    c. Both the Dialog plug-in and the Vibration plug-in.

    d. Neither the Dialog plug-in nor the Vibration plug-in.

2 What style does the **alert()** method of the **notification** object use?

    a. The HTML5 standard notification pop-up style.

    b. The webview's native notification pop-up style.

    c. The device's native pop-up style.

    d. A user-defined pop-up style.

3 How long does the mobile device vibrate when the **vibrate()** method is called?

    a. 1 second.

    b. 1000 milliseconds.

    c. As long as the user permits.

    d. For the number of milliseconds passed to the **vibrate()** method.

4 Which **alert()** method parameters are optional?

    a. Message.

    b. Callback function.

    c. Title.

    d. Button Message.

11.5 The config.xml File

Every PhoneGap application has a config.xml file located in the project's root directory. The config.xml file sets application options and controls aspects of an application's behavior. It also sets the title of an application, developer information, and developer contact information.

```
<widget id="tv.learntoprogram.test" version="0.0.1">
    <name>AppName</name>
    <description>
        A description of the application.
    </description>
    <author email="mark@learntoprogram.tv" href="http://learntoprogram.tv">
        Mark Lassoff
    </author>
    <content src="index.html" />
    <access origin="*" />
</widget>
```

Above is an example of a minimum config.xml file. Within the **<widget>** element, the **id** attribute is the application's reverse-domain identifier and a version number. The reverse-domain identifier should be unique. The **<name>** element contains the application's name, the **<description>** element contains the application's description, and the **<author>** element contains the application author's information. Note that the **<author>** element contains attributes, **email** and **href**, that set the author's email address and website address. The **<content>** element's **src** attribute sets the starting page of the application and the **<access>** element's **origin** attribute defines the external domains that the application is authorized to communicate with.

If you view the config.xml file of one of the test PhoneGap applications, you have probably noticed that it is much larger than this minimum config.xml file. That is because the config.xml file created by PhoneGap also contains **<preference>**, **<gap:plugin>**, **<icon>**, and **<gap:splash>** elements. Those elements allow you to set preferences, add functionality, and link to required graphical resources.

The **<preference>** elements in the config.xml file set certain application preferences, including the default orientation, whether or not an application is full-screen, how long the splash screen is displayed for, and others. There are platform-specific preferences that can be set as well to determine with more specificity how an application will perform on the varying platforms that PhoneGap supports. Preferences are usually set according to the following syntax:

```
<preference name="NAME" value="VALE" />
```

The **name** attribute is the name of the preference, and the **value** attribute is its target value.

The **<gap:plugin>** elements determine which plug-ins your application is asking permission to use. When a user installs your application they will be asked to confirm that the application is permitted access to various components of their device hardware. You only want to include plug-ins that you are actually using in your application in your config.xml file. Many users are justifiably suspicious about applications that request too many permissions.

The **<icon>** elements link to the application icons required on each platform. Below is an example of the link to a high dpi Android icon, followed by an example of the link to a similarly sized iOS icon.

```
<icon gap:platform="android" gap:qualifier="hdpi" src="www/res/icon/
android/icon-72-hdpi.png" />
```

```
<icon gap:platform="ios" height="72" src="www/res/icon/ios/icon-72.png"
width="72" />
```

Notice that the Android link has different attributes than the iOS link, even though both icons have the same 72 by 72 resolution.

The **<gap:splash>** elements are similar to the **<icon>** elements, but instead of linking to icons, they link to the appropriate splash screen resources for each platform. PhoneGap's default project includes templates for these icons and splash screens in the "/www/res" directory.

A properly formatted config.xml file is very important when preparing an application for distribution. The complete documentation about the config.xml is available on the PhoneGap website at *http://docs.phonegap.com/en/4.0.0/config_ref_index.md.html*.

Remember to specify an appropriately unique reverse-domain identifier, ensure that all of your contact information is correct, and only request the permissions that your application will actually use.

WHAT HAVE YOU LEARNED?

Questions for Review

1 How should you approach permissions in your application?

a. Request every permission so you can be certain that your application can do anything.

b. Don't request any permissions and just design your application with strict limitations.

c. Only request those permissions that are strictly required, but don't explain why to your users.

d. Only request those permissions that are strictly required and explain why to your users.

2 What should be used as the value of the **<widget>** element's **id** attribute?

a. The name of the application.

b. The name of the developer.

c. A unique reverse-domain identifier for the application.

d. Your favorite number.

3 The format of the **<icon>** element is identical across platforms.

a. True.

b. False.

4 When preparing your application for distribution, properly formatting your config.xml file is an essential step.

a. True.

b. False.

Chapter Summary

In this chapter we have covered additional PhoneGap plug-ins—the File, Device, Contacts, and Notifications plug-ins—and we have discussed the config.xml file.

Throughout this book you have been building example PhoneGap applications with HTML5, CSS, and JavaScript. You have learned about the PhoneGap environment and plug-in system, and you have used modern web technologies to create mobile applications that can be deployed on a number of different platforms. You can now access device hardware functionality on modern mobile systems through a familiar programming environment. Congratulations! You are well on your way to developing and releasing mobile applications!

I hope that you have enjoyed this book. The most important thing to remember as you continue on your path to developing mobile applications with PhoneGap is to treat your users with respect. Through your application, users are giving you access to their personal information and you should not take that responsibility lightly. Handle their information securely and with care, and be upfront with your users about what your application does and why.

ANSWER KEY

Chapter 01

Section 1.1

1. What is PhoneGap?

c. A library that lets developers create native apps with HTML5, CSS, and JavaScript.

2. Which of the following is a requirement in order to use PhoneGap?

c. node.js.

3. PhoneGap contains all of the software required to build an Android .apk file.

b. False.

4. Which of the following is a benefit of using Chrome for app development?

b. Chrome "Device Mode" allows you to see how an app might look on a certain device.

Section 1.2

1. After installation, where can you find the PhoneGap application icon?

d. There is no icon, PhoneGap is a command line tool.

2. When creating a new PhoneGap project, which of the following are created for you?

a. An index.html file.

3. What is the proper command to run a PhoneGap application on an Android emulator?

a. phonegap run android.

4. What is the proper command to install and run a PhoneGap application on a connected iPhone?

c. phonegap run ios.

Chapter 02

Section 2.1

1. PhoneGap applications do not have a specific file structure.

b. False.

2. What is the purpose of the "/platforms" folder in a PhoneGap application project?

c. It contains the code required to build a PhoneGap application for a specific platform.

3. Why do PhoneGap projects have a "/www/res" folder?

a. To contain project resources.

4. What is the purpose of the "/www/plugins" folder?

c. To allow PhoneGap to add plugins to your app when necessary.

Section 2.2

1. Within an application, what does "navigation" mean?

b. Moving through content pages within an app.

2. What is a reasonable method of displaying different content in an application?

c. Create an app that loads multiple files, each of which has different content.

3. How can a single HTML page display multiple content pages?

a. Using JavaScript to dynamically load content.

4. Using JavaScript to dynamically load content is always the best way to create multiple content pages for an app.

b. False.

Section 2.3

1. New HTML5 input types can help ameliorate mobile input problems.

a. True

2. Which of the following is an effective input type for emails on mobile devices?

a. email.

3. When using the tel input type, which of the following will appear for the user?

c. A number pad for phone number entry.

4. When testing emulated layouts in Chrome, it is important to remember which of the following?

a. Chrome cannot emulate the device's keyboard.

Section 2.4

1. Which tag is used for images in HTML5 with PhoneGap?

b. <img />

2. Standard CSS image styles do not work with PhoneGap.

b. False.

3. What is one way to ensure that an image fits the space available in a view?

c. Set the width to 100%.

4. What does the max-width attribute do?

a. Determines the minimum width of an element.

Chapter 03

Section 3.1

1. Which of the following is CSS used for?

b. Determining the presentation of a page.

2. What does the "font-family" attribute determine?

a. The font that an element is rendered in.

3. What is the purpose of the "font-color" attribute?

d. Nothing, "font-color" does not exist.

4. All HTML elements have default styles that cannot be overridden with CSS.

b. False.

Section 3.2

1. The CSS box model includes which elements?

a. Content, border, padding, and margin.

2. What does the width attribute determine?

a. The width of an entire element, including all parts of the box model.

3. Given an element with a set width of 500 pixels, how wide would it be with a 10 pixel border and 10 pixel padding?

b. 540 pixels.

4. Where will an element with "float: left" and "clear: right" display in relation to a following element with "float: right?"

a. On the same line as the following element, on the far left of the page.

Section 3.3

1. What is a media query?

    b. A method of determining properties of the display device so that a page's CSS can be customized.

2. What problem does a media query solve?

    a. Many possible display sizes and resolutions.

3. Media queries can only check for one attribute.

    b. False.

4. Media queries can be used to link different CSS files depending on device specifications.

    b. False.

Chapter 04

Section 4.1 _____

1. What is service-oriented architecture?

    a. Designing an application that interacts with a server to retrieve data that is displayed to the user.

2. Which of the following ready state and status combinations means that your XMLHttpRequest is ready to process?

    d. readyState == 4 && status == 200

3. Why is JSON useful?

    b. It provides a known, consistent format for data transfer.

4. When Chuck Norris does a push-up, he is actually pushing the Earth down.

    a. True.

Section 4.2 _____

1. Using parameterized queries allows your application to do which of the following?

    b. Request specific data from the server.

2. What is the first place to look when determining how to use an API?

    c. The API documentation.

3. The GET method of communication cannot use a string variable for its URL parameter.

    b. False.

4. When designing for mobile, what should you take into consideration?

d. All of the above.

Section 4.3

1. What does XML stand for?

   c. Extensible Markup Language.

2. What is AJAX used for?

   d. Asynchronous communication between a browser and a server.

3. When XML response text is received, what is a method for parsing data from it?

   c. Either A or B.

4. Very few people use XML anymore.

   a. True.

Section 4.4

1. What does JSON stand for?

   c. JavaScript Object Notation.

2. How are JSON objects structured?

   b. As key/value pairs.

3. Using jQuery to parse JSON data is not possible.

   b. False.

4. Which of the following is a good technique to better understand the JSON responses from an API?

   b. Use a JSON visualizer.

Chapter 05

Section 5.1

1. What is the size limit for persistent local storage using Web Storage?

   d. There is no limit.

2. Data stored using Web Storage persists across which of the following scenarios? Select all that apply.

   a. Page refresh.

   b. Browser/Application restart.

   d. Application update.

3. Why is it possible to store JSON objects with Web Storage?

   b. JSON objects can be represented as simple strings, those strings can be stored by Web Storage.

4. Using Web Storage on a mobile requires special permissions.

b. False.

Section 5.2

1. Which of the following is required to use server storage?

c. A server.

2. What is PHP?

b. A commonly used server-side scripting language.

3. Who maintains the CSV standardization format?

c. There is no official CSV standard.

4. Once data is stored on a server, it is immutable.

b. False

Chapter 06

Section 6.1

1. What is the HTML5 standard video format for web applications?

c. There is no set standard format.

2. How is a video file structured?

d. It is a container file for encoded video and audio.

3. What is required to play HTML5 audio in a web browser?

b. Any <audio> element.

4. The Android 4.4 WebView is HTML5 audio standards compliant.

a. True.

Section 6.2

1. Which of the following are good reasons to override the default media controls?

d. All of the above.

2. How would you stop playback using JavaScript?

c. Pause the audio playback and set its playback position to the start of the file.

3. You cannot use both the built in controls and custom controls for media playback.

a. True.

4. What is the proper syntax to play an audio file named "myAudio?"

b. myAudio.play();

Section 6.3

1. What is an effective way of changing the source of an HTML5 audio element?

c. Modify the **src** attribute of the audio element.

2. Which of the following will return the current play time of an audio file?

a. The **currentTime** property.

3. How is the volume of an audio element represented?

c. As a value between 0 and 1.

4. How often does a JavaScript interval run?

c. As often as you instruct it to.

Section 6.4

1. The PhoneGap media object is functionally identical to the built-in HTML5 audio and video elements.

a. True.

2. How would you stop media playback using the PhoneGap media object?

a. Pause the playback and set the playback to the beginning of the file.

3. When should you use the PhoneGap media object instead of the HTML5 audio element?

a. Always.

4. What date does the JavaScript **Date()** object originate on?

d. Midnight, January 01, 1970.

Section 6.5

1. Camera functionality is built into the default PhoneGap project.

b. False.

2. How do you extend PhoneGap functionality with plug-ins?

a. Use the command line interface plug-in installation command.

3. Which of the following are options for the image format returned by the camera plug-in?

a. .PNG

d. .JPG

4. If the camera plug-in's *getPicture()* method is not successful, what happens?

b. It returns an error message.

Chapter 07

Section 7.1

1. Which of the following is important to consider when using geolocation?

c. Both A and B.

2. When your application calls **getCurrentPosition()**, which of the following is returned?

d. The newest cached position object.

3. Which of the following can provide location information?

d. All of the above.

4. When you use the enableHighAccuracyUI option, the location object will always be based on the highly accurate GPS location.

b. False.

Section 7.2

1. How much does Google charge for access to their Google Map API?

d. Nothing for most users.

2. What should you do with your Google API key?

d. Nothing, just generate new ones whenever you need them.

3. The size of a map displayed using the Google Maps API is determined by options passed to the API.

b. False.

4. Maps created using the Google Maps API automatically insert a marker at the origin location.

b. False.

Section 7.3

1. How does the heading object represent a heading?

b. Using degrees.

2. How often does the compass object return a heading object when using the **watchHeading()** method?

d. As often as requested by the "frequency" option parameter.

3. What direction are you facing if your device displays a heading of 45?

b. Northeast.

4. The clearWatch() method from the compass object will stop the object from returning heading objects.

a. True.

Chapter 08

Section 8.1

1. What are the values returned from the accelerometer measuring?

c. Movement of the device.

2. If you rotate your device on its X axis, which return value will change?

d. Both Y and Z.

3. How often does the watchAcceleration() method return data?

c. As set in the options.

4. Why does a device at rest on a table register approximately 9.81 on its Z axis?

a. It is registering Earth's gravity.

Section 8.2

1. When using a canvas element, what different contexts are available?

a. The 2D and 3D contexts.

2. Why is it important to poll the accelerometer more often in this application than it was in the previous section?

c. In order to make the application feel more responsive to the user.

3. There is no way to stop the screen orientation from changing when using this application.

b. False.

4. The canvas element is used to render graphics on an HTML page.

a. True.

Chapter 09

Section 9.1

1. Which of the following is a key part of the jQuery Mobile Framework?

a. An event system.

2. jQuery Mobile is compatible with JavaScript.

a. True.

3. What is the best option for implementing jQuery on a mobile device?

c. Use a customized local copy of jQuery Mobile.

4. Everything that can be done with jQuery can also be done with JavaScript.

a. True.

Section 9.2

1. What is a requirement of jQuery Pages?

c. Usage of jQuery data-roles.

2. A jQuery Mobile Page uses the HTML **<head>** element as a default header.

b. False.

3. How is a footer implemented in jQuery Pages?

c. With the "footer" data-role.

4. The jQuery Mobile Page structure cannot be used without the jQuery Mobile Framework.

a. True.

Section 9.3

1. How is a toolbar button defined in jQuery Mobile?

a. Using data-roles.

2. A toolbar can have a maximum of five buttons.

b. False.

3. What HTML structure is used to create a navbar?

b. Unordered lists and list items.

4. How many items can populate a single-row navbar?.

d. 5.

Section 9.4

1. Is it possible to use native-style buttons with jQuery Mobile?

c. Yes, but with a custom jQuery Mobile installation.

2. What is the primary visual difference between an **<a>** button and a **<button>**-based button?

c. There is no visual difference.

3. Which of the following would be a good candidate for representation with a flipswitch?

d. Whether a light is on or off.

4. Can you customize the text within a jQuery Mobile flipswitch?

a. Yes.

Chapter 10

Section 10.1

1. It is safe to assume that if something is contained as part of the W3C HTML5 standard, it is supported by all modern web browsers.

b. False.

2. What will jQuery Mobile textareas do that standard HTML5 textareas will not do?

c. Resize according to input content.

3. What HTML5 element is used to contain a group of radio buttons?

a. <fieldset>

4. What element defines the choices available in a dropdown menu?

a. <option>

Section 10.2

1. What HTML element does a Listview use for structure?

a. An unordered list.

2. How do you create a jQuery Listvew?

a. With the "listview" data role.

3. How are the list items of a Listview defined?

c. Using the <li> element.

4. Listviews can be used to create auto-complete functionality without adding JavaScript.

a. True.

Section 10.3

1. The swipe touch interface element is supported by the HTML5 W3C standard.

b. False.

2. What is the jQuery event name for swiping to the right?

c. swiperight.

3. Which of the following desktop user interface actions does not map intuitively to a touch interface action?

c. Double click.

4. Which of the following touch interface actions does not map intuitively to a desktop interface action?

d. All of the above.

Chapter 11

Section 11.1

1. In order to save a file to the device storage, what must be done first?

c. The writer must be initialized.

2. Which of the following is not needed to load a file?

d. A file writer.

3. How frequently does the OS delete data stored using the File API?

b. When the application is uninstalled.

4. You are only able to use the PhoneGap File API to store text data.

b. False.

Section 11.2

1. What does the Device API allow you to do?

b. Access device information.

2. Which of the following is not a property that can be read using the Device plug-in?

c. device.version.

3. Why would you be interested in device information?

a. To create a more targeted experience for your user.

4. What is the UUID device property?

d. A universally unique identifier.

Section 11.3

1. How do you access a user's contact information?

a. With the Contacts API.

2. Why do we set both the **nickname** and **displayName** properties?

c. To ensure compatibility across multiple devices.

3. What is the purpose of using arrays to set contact types such as email addresses?

    a. Arrays allow multiple values of the same type to be set simultaneously.

4. Arrays are used to set both phone numbers and email addresses.

    a. True.

Section 11.4

1. What plug-ins are required for notifications with vibrations?

    d. Neither the Dialog plug-in nor the Vibration plug-in.

2. What style does the **alert()** method of the **notification** object use?

    b. The webview's native notification pop-up style.

3. How long does the mobile device vibrate when the **vibrate()** method is called?

    d. For the number of milliseconds passed to the **vibrate()** method.

4. Which **alert()** method parameters are optional?

    b. Callback function.

Section 11.5

1. How should you approach permissions in your application?

    d. Only request those permissions that are strictly required and explain why to your users.

2. What should be used as the value of the **<widget>** element's **id** attribute?

    b. The name of the developer.

3. The format of the **<icon>** element is identical across platforms.

    b. False.

4. When preparing your application for distribution, properly formatting your config.xml file is an essential step.

    a. True.

Appendix

The Box Model

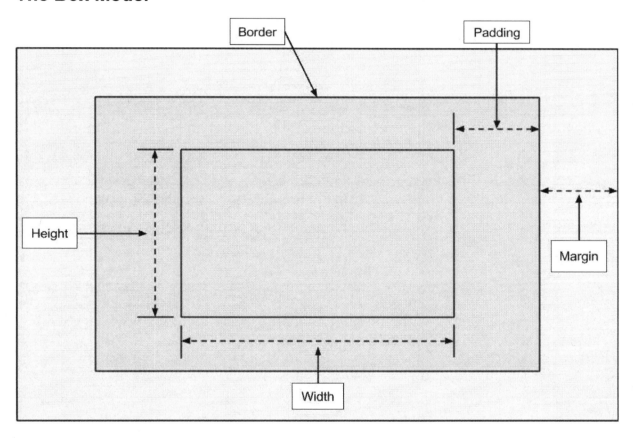

Glossary

Term	Definition
<a>	<a>nchor tag creates links between pages in HTML
<access>	<ul> element whose "origin" attribute defines the external domains the application is authorized to communicate with
<audio>	denotes an audio file
<author>	contains information about the author(s) of an application
<body>	delineates the body section of an HTML document
<button>	creates an interactive button that the user can click on
<canvas>	a surface that allows rendering of raster graphics, bitmaps, animation, and text on an HTML page
<content>	HTML5 tag that denotes primary content in a document
<div>	a tag used to create a container that is normally displayed as a block element within an HTML page
<fieldset>	HTML element that usually contains a group of radio buttons
<footer>	HTML5 tag that denotes the document footer
<form>	HTML tag that denotes a user input form and usually surrounds user input interface elements
<h1>	HTML tag used to denote the most important heading(s) in a document
<head>	delineates the heading section of an HTML document
<html>	usually the root element of an HTML document, this element establishes that a document is written in HTML
<img>	HTML tag used to display an image

Term	Definition
<input>	HTML tag that displays a interface element that allows the user to input data
<label>	HTML5 tag displays a label that a user can edit
<li>	HTML tag that denotes a single item within an ordered or unordered list
<meta>	HTML tag that contains the metadata of an HTML document. This usually includes information about the document itself which is not displayed within the browser window
<navbar>	HTML5 tag used to store elements and text that comprise a navigation bar
<output>	HTML5 tag that denotes the output of a function
<p>	HTML element that denotes a paragraph of content
<preference>	establishes application preferences (like default orientation or full-screen)
<script>	HTML tag that denotes JavaScript content
<source>	stores the source(s) of multimedia files; the device will search linearly through them until it finds a compatible one
<style>	HTML formatting element that usually contains CSS code decribing how individual HTML elements on the page will appear
<table>	HTML element creates a table intended to display tabular data
<textarea>	HTML element that displays a textbox that expands as more text is input
<ul>	HTML element that displays an unordered, or bulleted, list.

Term	Definition
<video>	HTML element that denotes a video file
accelerometer	sensor hardware in most mobile devices that measures acceleration along a given axis
alert()	JavaScript code that sends a user a pop-up message
alertDismiss()	JavaScript function that dismisses a pop-up alert
allowEdit	attribute that determines whether or not element content can be edited before it is selected
border-collapse	CSS style that collapses the borders of an element (a table, for example)
border-radius	CSS style that limits the border radius of an element (a button, for example) to create rounded edges
class	category of CSS selector that can be applied multiple times on a page. In CSS code a class is denoted by a period
clear	CSS rule that specifies the side of a CSS element on which floating elements are not allowed
clearInterval()	JavaScript function that dismisses interval execution of a specified function
clearWatch()	PhoneGap-specific function that prevents the compass and accelerometer objects from sending further heading data
color	CSS rule used to apply color to an element
compass	tool for locating one's bearings in relation to the cardinal directions
compassError()	JavaScript callback function that alerts the user when watchHeading() encounters an error
ContactField	PhoneGap abstraction that stores contact information

Term	Definition
ContactName	PhoneGap abstraction that stores the name of a contact
controls	HTML attribute that instructs the browser to use the default media controls with a media file in an <audio> or <video> element
currentPosition	PhoneGap object that stores a user's coordinates (longitude and latitude)
currentTime	JavaScript property that stores the current time of an audio or video file (seconds)
data-filter	From jQuery, <ul> attribute that sets data to be a filtered list
data-filter-reveal	From jQuery, <ul> attribute that reveals list items as they match the filter
data-highlight	From jQuery, <ul> attribute that allows user input to control the filter
data-inset	From jQuery, <ul> attribute that styles list items to appear inset in the page
Date()	JavaScript object that stores the number of milliseconds elapsed since midnight on 1 January 1970
displayName	PhoneGap abstraction that denotes the name of a contact that will appear onscreen
email	PhoneGap field that stores an email address
enableHighAccuracyUI	instructs a geolocation plug-in to use the most accurate location data (usually GPS positioning data)
encodingType	chooses the encoding of the image returned from the device camera (JPEG or PNG)
familyName	denotes a contact's family name

Term	Definition
float	places an element on the right or left side of its parent element, with the remaining elements flowing around it
font-family	CSS rule type that defines the font that text is displayed in
font-style	CSS rule type that specifies the style of the font (bold, italics, etc.)
font-variant	CSS rule type that is used to specify capitalization attributes (all capitalized or all lowercase, for example)
font-weight	CSS attribute for bolded text
forEach	loop that allows you to loop through all of the nodes of an object. Commonly used with arrays.
get()	prompts store.js to automatically parse a string into JSON
getCurrentPosition()	JavaScript geolocation function that returns a user's coordinates (longitude and latitude)
getPicture()	PhoneGap library function that launches a device's native camera application with specified camera options
getTime()	JavaScript function that returns the number of milliseconds elapsed since midnight on 1 January 1970
givenName	PhoneGap abstraction that denotes a contact's given name
height	CSS rule that determines the height of an element. Can be unreliable with some elements and in some browsers
href	field that stores the destination website address within an <a>nchor tag
ifconfig	Mac/Linux command for finding the IP address of a server (under "inet addr")

Term	Definition
Image()	JavaScript generic image object
innerHTML	property that denotes that HTML code between the opening and closing tag of the element selected
ipconfig	Windows command for finding the IP address of a server (under IPv4 Address)
line-height	CSS rule that expands or reduces the space between lines of text
listview	jQuery user interface widget that renders an organized list
magneticHeading	property returned by PhoneGap's Compass object that returns a heading between 0-359 degrees.
margin-top	CSS rule that renders margin space at the top of an element
max	<input> attribute that defines the maximum volume of an audio file (0 to 1)
max-width	defines the maximum width of an image in CSS (overrides the width attribute)
maximumAge	determines the maximum valid age, in milliseconds, of a location
min	<input> attribute that defines the minimum volume of an audio file (0 to 1)
nickname	PhoneGap abstraction that denotes the display name of a contact
notification	JavaScript object that notifies a user (the alert() method, for example)
onclick	JavaScript event performs a specified action when a user clicks an element

Term	Definition
onreadystatechange	XMLHttpRequest() event that executes every time the readyState property changes value. readyState values range from 0-4.
origin	PhoneGap preference that defines the external domains that a PhoneGap application is authorized to communicate with
parseJSON()	jQuery function that parses JSON content into a generic JavaScript object that may be accessed using the dot notation
phonegap create	command line in PhoneGap that creates a new project
phonegap run	command line in PhoneGap that runs an application on a given platform
phoneNumber	PhoneGap contact field that stores a contact's phone number
position	JavaScript geolocation object that reflects a user's physical location on the earth. Contains latitude and longitude properties
quality	property that sets the quality of a picture, from 0 to 100
readyState	XMLHttpRequest() object property reflects the status of the client side of an XMLHttpRequest (the code "4" indicates it is ready)
set()	method that prompts store.js to automatically stringify JSON
setInterval()	JavaScript method that launches a function or evaluates an expression at a specified time interval expressed in milliseconds
sourceType	property that defines the source of a picture (built-in camera, device library, etc.)

Term	Definition
status	XMLHttpRequest() object property that reflects the HTTP status of a server ("404 page not found," for example)
style	HTML attribute to add CSS styling rules to an element
timeout	JavaScript geolocation property that sets how long the device will wait for a position object
type	HTML <input> attribute that defines what type of data is to be collected in the input field
vibrate()	PhoneGap function that causes a compatible mobile device to vibrate for a set number of milliseconds
volume	property that specifies the audio volume of a compatible multimedia file
watchAcceleration()	PhoneGap function that polls the accelerometer every set number of milliseconds
watchHeading()	PhoneGap function that polls the compass every set number of milliseconds
width	sets the width of an element in CSS
window.onload()	JavaScript event that fires when a page loads and HTML elements are drawn in the browser
XMLHttpRequest()	JavaScript object that controls interaction with remote server(s)

Join The Development Club

https://learntoprogram.tv/course/ultimate-monthly-bundle/?coupon=BOOK19

This comprehensive membership includes:

☑ Access to EVERY course in LearnToProgram's growing library--including our exciting lineup of new courses planned for the coming year. This alone is over a $3,000 value.

☑ Free certification exams. As you complete your courses, earn LearnToProgram's certifications by passing optional exams. All certification fees are waived for club members.

☑ The LearnToProgram guarantee!

$19
MEMBERSHIP

Use the coupon code:

BOOK19

and save $20 off your first month!

THE LEARNTOPROGRAM GUARANTEE

Our Guarantee:
If you watch the course videos and complete the lab exercises, **you will learn to program**. Guaranteed. If you don't, we will personally pay your membership fees for the next 90 days.

The Development Club

More Information at: *https://LearnToProgram.tv*

32509449R00196

Made in the USA
San Bernardino, CA
07 April 2016